A NEW, OBJECTIVE, PRO-OBJECTIVITY NORMATIVE THEORY

An Objective Basis for Morality, Society, Politics, Law, Education, Etc.— And for Liberty and Peace

Frederick Farrand

University Press of America,® Inc.
Lanham · Boulder · New York · Toronto · Plymouth, UK

University Press of America,® Inc.
4501 Forbes Boulevard
Suite 200
Lanham, Maryland 20706
UPA Acquisitions Department (301) 459-3366

Estover Road
Plymouth PL6 7PY
United Kingdom

Printed in the United States of America
British Library Cataloging in Publication Information Available

Library of Congress Control Number: 2010933278
ISBN: 978-0-7618-5286-5 (paperback : alk. paper)
eISBN: 978-0-7618-5287-2

™ The paper used in this publication meets the minimum requirements of American National Standard for Information Sciences—Permanence of Paper for Printed Library Materials, ANSI Z39.48-1992

To my very dear partner Mary, my very dear children Joanne, Chris, Lee and Sue, and our lovely dogs, who overall significantly helped make this book possible. And to my grandchildren, the very lovely little Mia, Griffin and Olivia, who also helped via the joy and love they gave me.

And to all who attempt to be as rational or objective as possible, including via critically seeking evidence for views as opposed to simply believing a view or believing on the basis of merely alleged evidence, and including suspending belief where there is insufficient or no evidence.

Contents

Preface

This book's primary intended readership is moral and/or social and/or political philosophy undergraduates at second year level and beyond. The book would also be useful for beginning philosophy students, if combined with complementary introductory input. The book's theory is general, written so as to be equally useful for students of any of those disciplines. Relatedly, the intended readership also includes the general, well-educated reader, and undergraduates studying the philosophy of education, philosophy of law or jurisprudence, bioethics, environmental ethics, business ethics and so on. (Explanatory endnotes are mostly aimed at those general, well-educated readers and beginning philosophy students.)

The book also has sufficient at least implicit depth to interest professional philosophers and postgraduate philosophy students.

The book should also interest students and teachers of other, related disciplines not explicitly focusing on or mentioning philosophy, e.g., politics, sociology, economics, law and education, e.g., much of the book is interpretable as a school curriculum outline. Much is also interpretable as a new, normatively-objective psychology. The book's theory is applicable to those disciplines' unavoidable at least implicit normative foundations, and to each discipline's at least implicit claim to be objective or knowledge.

Frederick Farrand, Adelaide, South Australia, May 2010

Acknowledgements

Various ideas helpful for the book's main arguments came at least indirectly from Kant, A.P. Griffiths, W. Whewell, J.S. Mill, Hume and Bertrand Russell. Among my teachers, Martin Simons (The University of Adelaide, South Australia) was the most helpful, and somewhat directly helpful. George Couvalis and Lynda Burns (Flinders University, South Australia) were indirectly helpful. Some others at Flinders, and John Chandler of The University of Adelaide, were indirectly some help. Various strangers I emailed were also kind enough to make helpful criticisms and comments, especially Harvey Siegel, Laurence Houlgate and John Ozolins. I also wish to thank the University Press of America.

Conventions

Single quote marks round a term are used only to specify the term being focused on. Double quotes are used for quotations, speech, idioms and certain titles. Endnotes are used, positioned as indicated in the Contents.

INTRODUCTION—Including Some Assumptions And Some Preliminary Definitions

Abstract Summary And Rationale

This book mainly concerns normative theories and practices based on them.[1] The book's theory is general, applicable to all areas, to all 'ought' or 'should' end-related issues in morality, society, politics, education, law, economics, psychology, medicine and so on. It attempts to correctly, i.e., objectively, answer that most-important general question, asked by Socrates: How should one live?

The book also somewhat concerns meta-ethics,[2] relating its normative theory to meta-ethical issues and vice versa.

The book is primarily a positive monograph or work on a single topic, mainly explaining and defending a new, practical theory (and its applications) rather than, e.g., also or only trying to discuss and criticise other normative theories at length. The latter task has been done very well by others: there seemed no good reason to do it again—at length. However, the book undertakes that task to a not-at-length but significant degree: the book's positive arguments imply criticisms of all alternative theories. In explaining and defending its theory, the book thereby first develops a basis for those criticisms, then applies it.

The book is primarily a positive monograph largely as a result of my teaching and/or researching other normative theories for over 40 years, and finding them too problematic—via such criticisms and the many good criticisms of each theory here by various other normative theories, (a mutually-destructive process,) by meta-ethicists and rational skeptics here. After millennia of competing normative theories, with no clear winner, no theory anywhere near being so well supported by evidence as to be rationally unquestionable or acceptable to at least nearly all experts in the field, it seemed time to put all those theories aside and start again (along with explaining why those theories were put aside). As often happened also in science, a new theory, a new perspective, seemed needed. (This explanation of the book's somewhat unique approach is parallel to cases of thinkers who, having rationally critically at least representatively examined major religious theories concerning nature, the human condition, disease and so on, concluded they all lacked evidence—and so began looking elsewhere for a rational, evidenced, objective theory here. If this book's let's-look-elsewhere, rational exploratory approach is in general wrong, then so was, e.g., Darwin's.) (If sticking with traditional or mainstream approaches has failed to take us anywhere positive and demonstrably correct (objective), why stick with them?)

The book's main task is to try to rationally solve all fundamental normative issues as far as possible—arguing that, though there are problems, a great deal is possible. The book defends what it at least provisionally claims is, as far as possible, an objective normative theory, namely one uniquely sufficiently evidenced[3] and as evidence-based as is humanly possible for a normative theory, one able to be knowledge for us. Skepticism, denials and fallibilism regarding positive claims concerning evidence, rationality and knowledge or objectivity are often reasonable, which the theory accepts and discusses. However, some skepticism and denials here are unreasonable:- Consider practical scientific objectivity or knowledge, as exemplified in computer, communications, agricultural, transport, medical, building, electrical, plumbing, refrigeration, cooking and other technology. All skeptics and deniers of objectivity or knowledge use or rely on some such technology, e.g., regarding their housing, phones, toileting, lighting, clothes, beds, travelling, water and food. So in-practice they at least implicitly and provisionally accept that practical science involves what this book considers evidence, rationality and knowledge or objectivity. (E.g., alive deniers of all rationality and knowledge have not in-practice denied it would be rational to at least provisionally accept it is knowledge or true that (knowingly) jumping in front of (objects they know are) oncoming fast trucks is probably fatal.)

In ways the book's theory shows are impossible for other normative theories, its claimed objectivity involves being coherent with practical scientific objectivity's/knowledge's general nature. The book makes the on-first-view perhaps incredible claim that its theory's evidence is in important ways uniquely close to the general types of evidence involved in practical scientific objectivity, and as close to those general types as is possible for a normative theory.

Though the new theory argues that all other normative theories fundamentally lack evidence, it agrees with many of the general prescriptive conclusions of certain other theories, e.g., 'Be unselfish' (though it adds specific qualifications to such general conclusions). In that way, the new theory accepts that those older theories are often significantly on the right track, but it gives those (qualified) fundamentally vulnerable prescriptive conclusions what it argues is an evidenced basis, a rationally irrefutable foundation, or sound premises.[4]

The theory claims to have one objective primary and hence ultimate end (and identical standard), and plural a-objective or a-objectivity secondary ends inherently irrelevant to achieving that ultimate end, and hence unable to conflict with that ultimate end. (Analogously:- Suppose the primary artistic end is: Draw circles. To achieve this end it can be irrelevant whether circles are drawn via secondary-end preferences for this rather than that colour, drawing-implement etc.) Having just one ultimate end avoids a need to prioritise among conflicting ultimate ends.[5] There can be inconsistency among those secondary ends as such, but it is argued later that this is not rationally-problematic, and that, among persons committed to the book's theory, there would in-practice be resolution of any (merely theoretical, only potentially practical) conflict here.

The theory prescribes that great liberty is permissible regarding its secondary ends: here, e.g., regarding various cultural, sexual, artistic and other life-style options, do whatever you like. It also prescribes numerous liberties needed to achieve its primary end, e.g., the right and duty for all to be free from racism and sexism, and the right and duty to freely rationally critically investigate any view, especially regarding whether evidence exists for the view.

The theory's general guidelines include advocating applying that rationally critical, investigatory approach to the theory itself. E.g., they warn that some below-suggested practical specifics may be at least somewhat mistaken hypotheses, requiring further research. However, the book argues that vagueness and mistakes here are often manageable, resolvable or minimisable, suggesting that increasingly we can approach an overall very clear, practicable, basically-objective normative theory. The book suggests that this theory has some unavoidable problems, but not what it argues are the immense and fundamental, unmanageable problems of all alternative theories.

The book has two Parts. The much larger Part II mainly representatively discusses the theory's specific moral, social, political, educational, legal, economic, medical, psychological, environmental etc practical applications. Part I mainly explains and defends the theory and its attempted resolving of the is-ought issue.[6] To discover an objective normative theory, Part I unavoidably begins with a somewhat abstract investigation—but Part I soon increasingly also concerns substantive, real-life moral, social, political etc applications.

Appendixes further explain certain issues mentioned in this Introduction or in the book's main body.

Other Introductory Discussions (in-part expanding on the above)

(1) The book argues that, for reasons including coherence with or a pro- relation to objectivity, the objective normative end is 'Be pro-objectivity', stressing that this inextricably involves knowledge. (Our objectivity is the faculty-system[7] which directly seeks, acquires and contains knowledge.) Importantly, that end only *involves* objectivity or knowledge, just *some* knowledge, and is *not* that knowledge nor objectivity as such. The end is being *pro*-objectivity, involving the *practising* of pro-objectivity knowledge, in moral, social, political etc areas. (Analogously, being pro-jazz is not the same as being jazz.)

The book mostly concerns two issues regarding the previous paragraph:-

(i) Is 'Be pro-objectivity' a normatively empty or useless notion: is it *applicable* to morality, society, politics etc? (If that end is normatively empty, does the book's theory need to sneak in other, substantive but unevidenced, rationally-problematic normative notions?) What does 'Be pro-objectivity' specifically say we should do in those moral etc areas? And can we reasonably be expected to act on (apply) it? (ii) Is 'Be pro-objectivity' really an ultimate, objective normative end and standard, and, if so, the only one?

Firstly here, to be pro-objectivity one must know what objectivity and knowledge are, and that they are possible to at least an important, meaningful degree. (Some critics of pro-objectivity theory dismiss it by claiming there is no objectivity or knowledge, only subjectivity. So issues here need discussing.) There are various views, controversies and problems here. The Introduction's first part briefly discussed some issues here, Appendix A discusses them representatively, and the book's main body further explains or clearly implies what the book's definitions and views are here. Some preliminary remarks here and concerning related issues relevant to the book's theory and its applicability:-

One important aspect of objectivity[8] is that, when used to describe a statement, the terms 'objective' and 'true' fundamentally mean the same. The difference is that adequate definitions of 'objective' explicitly mention a contrast with 'subjective' (but definitions of 'true' often only imply that contrast). It is important for an objective normative theory to in-part define our objectivity as events existing *via our subjectivity* (e.g., in that objectivity exists in us as subjects, as mental events we can subjectively (consciously) experience, and is activated by our emotions (motivations)). Yet there is still an important contrast. Objective statements are true independently of various subjective events in that, e.g., subjectively, Harry might believe and/or desire that his investments will be profitable, but that is irrelevant regarding whether it is objective or true that they will be. However, our objectivity is dependent on certain subjective events in that, e.g., we value and hence choose to objectively investigate some matters but not others. E.g., many scientists value and hence seek medical cures, rather than counting the world's pebbles. This book is in an important sense the result of me subjectively valuing investigating whether objective values exist. (For such and related reasons, pro-objectivity theory requires and *prescribes* many subjective events. Pro-objectivity theory is not anti-subjectivity as such.)

The subjective and objective concerning statement X overlap importantly when one *knows* X. A simplified definition of 'knows X' involves X being true and one believing X because one is aware of evidence sufficient to confirm X is true. Objective statements are those all persons with sufficient rationality and appropriate other (e.g., sometimes, visual) abilities can know. Knowledge and objectivity are inextricable.

We often have that which is for us knowledge (and hence objective), and this can include the (meta-)knowledge that knowledge's problems are overall sufficiently manageable[9] for knowledge to be extremely useful in practice:- E.g., consider the above-mentioned scientific objectivity/knowledge as in computer, communications, agricultural, transport etc technology. This is increasingly spectacularly useful, though, e.g., computers sometimes don't work—but they are repairable or replaceable with better, working ones. Any problems internal to such technology and related knowledge are normally manageable. Such success and manageability clearly show that objectivity/knowledge is possible. (And, as should become clear(er) later, they help suggest that this book's pro-objectivity notions have sufficiently firm meaning, and indirectly suggest that those notions' practical applicability is manageable (though so far those suggestions are somewhat vague and weak).)

Similarly, further:- Much (often-simple) scientific objectivity/knowledge is survival-necessary for us. Death will result from acting on any doubt or denial that one can know that, to survive, one must avoid cliff-falls, decapitation, starvation, poison etc. Doubters and deniers of objectivity/knowledge who intentionally (knowingly) survive do so via in-effect admitting they and others possess much such objectivity or knowledge.[10] (And they are aware (know) of and (knowingly) communicate their doubts or denials, e.g., via computers, hence in-effect admitting they and others have much other knowledge.[11]) Because humans can obviously often successfully survive, and because our survival must be partly via knowledge, knowledge is obviously possible. (Relatedly, as expanded on later, that obvious practical success of survival-necessary objectivity or knowledge further helps give this book's basic practical pro-objectivity theory sufficiently firm meaning, and immunity from irrational skeptical attack here.)

Virtually universally-used simple survival-necessary knowledge involves much other, sophisticated knowledge, knowledge usable for non-survival purposes. (E.g., simple knowledge that cliff-falls can kill is, for experts, contexted within or involves much general, complex physiology, bio-chemistry and hence chemistry generally, and gravitational, human-body etc physics, and hence maths.) So, because that simple knowledge's necessity and related success shows it is an often-actualised possibility, and because it is contexted in much other knowledge, much other knowledge must also be possible.

Concluding comments here:- (i) That which is objectivity/knowledge for us is widely possible, so pro-objectivity theory has no unmanageable general problems here. (ii) This book's theory will be shown to be rationally-unquestionably linked coherently with and involve humanly-necessary and much other objectivity/knowledge—in a unique, overall way no other normative theory can match. (E.g., other theories are not overall pro-objectivity: they prescribe some other end(s).) (iii) The above vaguely suggests that 'Be pro-objectivity' is manageably applicable, a vagueness which this Introduction's Discussion (2b) significantly begins the clarification of—via beginning to show that 'Be pro-objectivity' is applicable to morality, society, politics, education etc.

(2) Discussion (1) above claimed that 'Be pro-objectivity' is the objective normative end, applicable to all moral etc areas.

(2a) It may on first view appear completely mistaken and absurd to claim there is an objective normative end and theory.[12] However, after this Introduction, evidence is presented which is argued to be sufficient to confirm that claim as basically true, and the theory overall as at least approximately and asymptotically objective or true, namely uniquely close to knowledge/objectivity and able to increasingly become as close as is possible for a normative theory. The book argues that the theory is *basically* objective, that its *fundamental* nature or foundation is rationally unquestionable. (The book's main, fundamentally important task is to get the basics right (objective).) But, regarding the theory *overall*:-

Beyond the foundation's or the basic general guidelines, either provisional acceptability, probable knowledge or error might be the case regarding some hypothesised 'Be pro-objectivity' specifics below. In some areas we don't have all the needed instrumental knowledge, (e.g., regarding which education(s) would overall be most pro-objectivity,) temporarily leaving us here significantly ignorant (and, regarding education and various areas, probably always at least slightly ignorant). Still, the book's arguments suggest that the most important pro-objectivity specifics involve no major overall uncertainty, and that overall the beyond-basics uncertainty or vagueness is manageable. Via accumulating more knowledge here, the theory is a self-improvable, work-in-progress but sufficiently-practicable-now theory.

(2b) Regarding those specifics, if 'Be pro-objectivity' cannot be shown to be applicable to practical, real-life moral, social, political etc issues, there is no practical point in investigating whether it is an objective end. Appendix B discusses the applicability issue, and applications soon increasingly become the book's main content, so this Introduction only makes some brief points here:-

Firstly, concerning whether 'Be pro-objectivity' is too empty or abstract, Kant's fundamental general 'universalisability' standard is far moreso—though widely and plausibly accepted as morally etc applicable. (Various problems here are discussed below later.)

Secondly, an end involving knowledge or objectivity can seem too problematic to be unambiguously and hence manageably applicable. Critics of the theory here made criticisms such as:- 'Which knowledge, and why? Should one know, e.g., how to play every board game?'; 'Surely knowledge or objectivity could never be humanity's primary aim. It is not sufficiently motivating', 'Surely various ends other than knowledge or objectivity are worth pursuing, e.g., happiness, or fairness', and 'Surely knowledge or objectivity is either useless or merely instrumental rather than an end'.

Apart from the first, such criticisms involve major misconceptions. Again, the theory's basis and ultimate end only *involve* knowledge or objectivity, just *some* knowledge, and the end is *not* that knowledge nor objectivity as such. The end will (soon) be argued to be the *practising* of normative knowledge, i.e., being *pro*-objectivity. (Analogously, being pro-jazz is not the same as being jazz.) And it will (soon) be explained that the only knowledge which pro-objectivity theory involves is pro-objectivity knowledge, i.e., either the practicable instrumental knowledge needed for that practising, or the theoretical fundamental knowledge objectively warranting practising only that instrumental knowledge.

Thirdly, relatedly, as a later detailed examination of that practicable knowledge shows representatively, 'Be pro-objectivity' is indeed applicable to all moral, social, political etc normative issues. That examination also shows the end involves much besides objectivity or knowledge. E.g:-

'Be pro-objectivity' implies that doing anything irrelevant to itself is permissible. Thereby that primary end is indirectly widely applicable, via permitting the above-mentioned great liberty and hence diversity in cultural, sexual, artistic, lifestyle and many other areas, regarding secondary ends. (Possibly apparent problems here are discussed later.) Regarding direct applicability, the theory's basis implies, e.g., that, to be maximally pro-objectivity, one crucial need is a society similar to (but not the same as) that advocated by J. S. Mill in *On Liberty*.[13] A narrow-minded, illiberal society is at least highly anti-objectivity. It does not promote the open-minded, free seeking for evidence both for society's established views and for alternative views, and the (self-)critical and often skeptical rationality, the liberal openness to new ideas, needed for citizens to be maximally pro-objectivity and hence collectively increase their pro-objectivity knowledge. Similarly, racist or sexist societies avoid giving many the educational etc opportunities and the economic, health-care, dietary etc resources people need (along with other factors) so they can become maximally pro-objectivity and relatedly objective (knowledgeable). That is, 'Be(ing) pro-objectivity' excludes many society-types, being best achievable via just one, very liberal general type, showing that 'Be pro-objectivity' is applicable to society. This means that pro-objectivity theory has at least very wide direct applicability, because a society affects a great deal of each citizen's life. E.g., pro-objectivity theory prescribes a unique type of democratic society, where all citizens can participate directly in politics.

Pro-objectivity theory will be shown to be applicable regarding gender issues, sex, the environment, material (energy, mineral etc) resources, population issues, medicine and animal-welfare, and to prescribe non-sexism, non-racism, types of happiness, rights, duties, justice, autonomy, equality, freedom, liberalism, education, sympathy, sociability, peace, direct-democracy, altruism, flourishing, fairness and much more—as specific applications of its general, ultimate end. The theory considers emotions and various other subjective experiences important, and crucial in some cases. Because our objectivity and any pro-objectivity occurs via certain subjective motivational and other events, and in opposition to others, the pro-objectivity end involves, i.e., applies to, subjectivity. And via that end's indirect applicability to its a-objectivity, secondary ends, it applies to many inherently subjective areas via that end prescribing freedom to do whatever gives you the most inherently subjective pleasure in each of the many a-objectivity areas.

The theory's applicability is already widely evident in that being pro-objectivity is a matter of degree, covering a range from, say, 'minimal (insignificant)' to 'significant' to 'maximal'[14]—and many people throughout history were and many more now are at least significantly pro-objectivity, in many areas. (The Enlightenment exemplifies this. And in that 'philosopher' means lover of knowledge and hence objectivity, anyone accurately describable as a philosopher is also at least implicitly and highly pro-objectivity.) Regarding the cognitive aspect of pro-objectivity, significant pro-objectivity begins, e.g., when one goes beyond simply believing whatever one's mainstream society or in-group believes, e.g., a religion or certain normative theory, say a 'Be sexist' or 'Be racist' theory, and one begins to ask if there is evidence for it, i.e., whether it can be knowledge (and hence really is true or objective). Here one goes beyond a merely instrumental view and use of knowledge, involving unquestioningly using knowledge to achieve that mainstream-unquestioned theory's end, e.g., by knowing how to avoid giving fair opportunities to a certain gender or race. Instead, one begins to rationally question that theory/end and that instrumental view and usage. Many such people further practise(d) such pro-objectivity, e.g., by helping to change their society's political, educational etc beliefs and institutions, e.g., to ensure fair opportunities and rational criticism in education.

In sum, the theory is obviously morally, politically, socially etc practicable or applicable, and, e.g., because so many reasonable persons have at least implicitly acted on it, it is reasonable to expect we can act on it, i.e., apply it.

The theory relatedly shows this further via (qualifiedly) prescribing many practices, e.g., happiness, fair justice and unselfish caring, practices already often practised by many now and in the past, practices prescribed by certain other, widely-held theories universally accepted as morally etc applicable. (Relatedly, where some clearly normatively applicable perspective, e.g., a certain feminist theory, is significantly pro-objectivity, or makes pro-objectivity theory more practicable or relevant regarding the human condition, a fully detailed version of pro-objectivity theory would include that normatively applicable perspective—but to explicitly discuss all such inclusions would make this book far too long.)

Concluding the Introduction:-

This book remains neutral concerning various controversial, arguably insoluble objectivity-related or knowledge-related (epistemic) issues. This neutrality and related assumptions are needed to achieve the book's practical aims. With this, like practical science, the book moves on, in a sense past those issues—here "painting with broad strokes" or focusing on the overall viable, productive "forest" regarding objectivity/knowledge, rather than on various problematic "trees" therein. Regardless of those underlying theoretical epistemic controversies, practical science moves on highly-successfully—showing in-practice that objectivity or knowledge is a sufficiently firm notion to be involved in a practical, normative theory's basis. The book suggests that, though that notion is from an (unrealistic) ideal viewpoint not perfect, the way pro-objectivity theory crucially involves it is the best way, indeed the only way, to solve fundamental normative problems as far as is realistically humanly possible. That involvement will be argued to uniquely give us (what is at least close to and about as close as possible to) an objective normative theory.

Arguably, only thence and via that theory's above-suggested applicability can we as far as possible correctly, i.e., objectively, deal with that humanly most-important general question, asked by Socrates: How should one live? With this, arguably, only via at least something like this book's examination of normative objectivity can we properly do what Socrates wished we'd do when he said that an unexamined life is not worth living.

So, moving on, first to argue there is an objective normative theory and end.

ENDNOTES TO THE INTRODUCTION

1 A normative theory concerns some end(s) it claims people should unconditionally aim at, namely whether they'd like to or not. One such (here primary) end can be or include

the instituting and/or maintenance of freedom for people to aim at whichever among certain other (secondary) ends they like.

2 A meta-ethical theory is a theory about ethical or normative theories. E.g., a meta-ethical theory asks whether there is evidence for any normative theory, namely whether any is or can be objective.

3 There are some unavoidable problems here, and can be other problems, mentioned below. E.g., it is often uncertain how much evidence is sufficient to confirm that a belief or hypothesis is true. Once, virtually everyone wrongly believed they had sufficient evidence to prove the sun goes around Earth.

4 When the new theory implies a prescriptive conclusion which, if too-abbreviated and unqualified, is the same as another normative theory's prescriptive conclusion, e.g., 'Be unselfish', as with all its conclusions the new theory arrives at this conclusion via premises radically different from those used by the other theory. This is like different arguments leading to the same, true scientific conclusion, with only one such argument being overall objective—the others being unobjective via having false premises or lacking evidence. E.g., consider the objective conclusion: 'Earth's shape is (approximately) spherical'. An ancient argument here concludes that Earth is spherical, via premises something like: 'The gods, being loving, perfect and beauty-admiring, gave Earth, home of their most-loved creation, humans, the only perfectly beautiful shape. The only perfectly beautiful shape is spherical'. Modern science (and some other ancients) used objective premises and arguments, namely involving sufficient evidence to confirm that Earth is (approximately) spherical. Note that unobjective premises only sometimes, merely by chance, lead to objective conclusions: unobjective premises typically lead to false conclusions. E.g., that gods-based argument also implies that the gods made us spherical.

5 E.g:- Suppose a theory claims that equality and freedom are its ultimate ends/standards, and hence equally ultimate ends/standards. These, like any ends/standards given equal top priority, can conflict. E.g., freedom includes freedom to become unequal. E.g., under capitalism there is freedom for persons to acquire highly unequal amounts of wealth. In practice, the standard used to prioritise between freedom and equality here is 'freedom (of the actually/potentially rich)'.

6 This concerns the claim that, whatever (objectively) 'is' the case, this has nothing to do with the issue of what normatively 'ought' to be the case. David Hume discusses this. E.g., Hume [2000] Monograph 3, Part 1, Section 1, paragraph 27. (The References And Bibliography below give(s) full citations.)

7 Our objectivity is not a simple, one-aspect faculty. It is a system of many interrelated aspects or functions, e.g., memory, reasoning and, often, perception. More on this later.

8 Other important aspects include:- It relates as far as humanly possible to mind-independent objects, and is hence as far as possible independent of numerous variable specific aspects among persons (subjects) studying such objects. Relatedly it involves impartiality among objective persons, e.g., in that all persons here studying the same aspect of an object would reliably come to the same conclusions regarding the object. However, this is at least somewhat of an ideal. E.g., real scientists being objective may focus on different aspects of an object, or measure them in different ways. Still, their thus-objective conclusions would cohere, not rationally-problematically conflict. (If conclusions conflict, not all of them can be objective/knowledge for us.) And, e.g., real, practical objects can be produced by scientific objectivity, e.g., cars, and all objective informed persons here can equivalently agree, sufficiently for humanly-important practical purposes, on what the object is and does. Pro-objectivity theory relates to such

practical (and other) objectivity.

9 (This endnote can safely be ignored by philosophy beginners.) This manageability can include reasonably using construction to mitigate some problem(s), e.g., as in scientific deductive arguments which ignore induction's problems. Appendix A is relevant here.

10 E.g:- Suppose someone, via confining their head in a plastic bag, in-practice doubts or denies evidence confirming it is objective or knowledge that, to survive, they need oxygen. Rational people here can see such doubters or deniers rationally unquestionably suffocate, die, putrefy and decompose, further confirming that knowledge. It is for us survival-necessary to regard what is reliably well-evidenced in such areas as knowledge, as true or objective.

11 E.g., consider someone writing or saying, "I doubt that any knowledge (or objectivity) exists." To do that meaningfully, such persons have much knowledge. They must know they exist, are conscious and have that doubt, know what those words mean and how to say or write the words, which shows they know sound and speech exist, or that paper, pens or computers or similar exist and normally work and are made via others' knowledge. And so on. Otherwise, they could say or write nothing, or only something accidentally (unknowingly) and for them and probably us meaningless. So, in theoretically doubting knowledge, in practice they admit knowledge (or objectivity) exists.

12 Because an 'error (un-objectivity) theory' rationally-unquestionably applies to innumerable claims of normative objectivity, it may seem applicable to this book's new theory. See, e.g., Mackie (1977)

13 Mill (1859)

14 Unless mentioned or contexted otherwise, when this book discusses normative pro-objectivity, 'pro-objectivity' refers to the maximal degree, i.e., where 'Be pro-objectivity' is always one's highest priority, i.e., ultimate end. This maximality is discussed further later, and qualified.

PART I: MOSTLY THEORY

PART I, SECTION 1: ARGUING FOR AN OBJECTIVE THEORY; PRO-OBJECTIVITY

Preliminary Comments (explained further soon where needed)

(1) To discover and defend an objective normative end and related theory or normative knowledge, Part I unavoidably begins with somewhat abstract discussions. But these are brief. The book soon concerns morally etc substantive matters and suggested practical applications.

(2) The inherently cognitive, *internal* general end (aim or purpose) of our objectivity is *knowledge*. Every specific use of objectivity, namely to acquire or supply some specific knowledge,[1] comes under and hence exemplifies that general end-aim, and helps constitute its achievement. With this, objectivity's internal motivation (to achieve that end) is inherently pro-objectivity and relatedly pro-knowledge, and vice versa, and knowledge is objectivity's content. A special, cognitively crucial content is objectivity's methods, involving certain assumptions which as far as we can know are reasonable.[2] These methods are a type of knowledge-how, e.g., knowledge of how to observe, count etc so as to acquire empirical knowledge. In sum, *knowledge* is objectivity's internal end—and, along with that pro-objectivity or pro-knowledge motivation, *knowledge* is objectivity's content or nature. (Relatedly, being pro-objectivity crucially involves being pro-knowledge.)

(3) Knowledge essentially involves coherence.[3] Knowledge necessarily lacks incoherence, e.g., in that what for us is empirical knowledge cannot be incoherent with what as far as we can tell is reality,[4] and in that incoherence means a lack of the comprehensibility we need for knowledge.[5] Incoherence means conflict, namely contradiction. If knowledge could contradict knowledge, one piece of knowledge would confirm that another piece of knowledge was false, namely not knowledge—and vice versa, meaning incomprehensibility. This incomprehensibility would be because:- Knowledge is *true*, and if a piece of knowledge is contradicted by a statement, this means the statement contra-

dicts a truth—and only a false statement can contradict the truth. So that statement must be false. But if the statement is knowledge, it too is true, so cannot be false. And it cannot be contradicted by the true or by knowledge.

In sum, such incomprehensibility is impossible. If something is incomprehensible or incoherent, it cannot be knowledge for us. Knowledge (or truth) cannot be both knowledge (or truth) and not knowledge (or not truth). No piece of knowledge can be incoherent with any other piece. (Such arguments can be reworded to apply to objectivity.) (Appendixes 1, 4 and the next, main part of this Section further explain coherence.)

(3a) Regarding this book's normative purposes, the following (often implicit) subtle distinction will be made between objectivity and knowledge: objectivity will be viewed moreso (but not only) as the *highly open but directable method* for acquiring knowledge, and knowledge will be viewed moreso (but not only) as objectivity's *specific cognitive contents acquired thereby* (and often also via choices, made externally to objectivity, directing objectivity towards certain contents[6]). This means, e.g., that to simplify discussion below it is objectivity's *knowledge* aspect the book tends to focus on as the aspect of objectivity which *pro*-objectivity needs to be specifically coherent with, and vice versa. (Hence, e.g., soon 'pro-objectivity knowledge' is given prominence.) (Those definitions and differences of emphasis could be slightly otherwise, but either way the theory's prescriptions would in-effect be the same. So the fact that those definitions, emphases and hence focus could be slightly otherwise does not ultimately matter regarding the book's practical normative aims.)

(4) If there are any, how many objective normative ends could there be? The description of any such end(s) would inherently be (normative) knowledge. This includes any specific content(s) of the abbreviated end-principle here, 'Be pro-X'.[7] And normative knowledge of the existence of the objective end(s) must, as with all knowledge, be inherently non-incoherent: knowledge/objectivity cannot include knowledge of plural objective ultimate ends, because plural ultimate ends will conflict. There cannot be conflicting specific 'Be pro-X' truths or pieces of (abbreviated) knowledge. Even if such knowledge could exist, it would be too rationally-problematic—and mean normative knowledge and hence an overall normative theory here which is impracticable, incoherent and hence useless in that here we could *not have normative knowledge* of which ultimate end to aim at. An ultimate end has an associated ultimate standard, and here there could be no objectively more-ultimate-than-ultimate standard via which to prioritise among those here incoherently both ultimate and not ultimate standards and hence ends. So such (and any) incoherent knowledge could not exist: there could only be *one* objective normative theory and associated primary or ultimate end/standard. This end would inherently objectively be the highest priority.

(5) If there is an objective normative end and related theory, how could they be discovered? Where should we start investigating? Many have attempted to discover them, starting and ending, typically problematically-circularly, in various places. This book's preliminary start crucially involves the following proposition (among related others mentioned soon), a proposition (among others here)

which is rationally unquestionable. It is: from the viewpoint of any standard, the standard and viewpoint are correct.[8] E.g., from a selfish viewpoint, selfishness is normatively correct. As 'correct' means 'truly, i.e., objectively, correct', here selfishness is viewed as the only correct/objective moral end. This relatedly applies to *pro*-selfishness or the end, 'Be pro-selfishness', as that selfish viewpoint is inherently pro-selfishness. The general point here has important implications:-

Thence, and related to (4) above, from *objectivity's* viewpoint, or judging via the standard, 'objectivity', a *pro-objectivity* standard and viewpoint are *the only* correct or objective standard and viewpoint. So this applies regarding normativity. With this, as a viewpoint involves a theory, from objectivity's or an objective viewpoint pro-objectivity theory is the only correct or objective normative theory, and 'Be pro-objectivity' is the only objective normative standard and hence end. It is of course *only* from *objectivity's* viewpoint that it can be *known* whether something is an objective normative end. (From other viewpoints, e.g., a selfish viewpoint, there can only be mere belief, without objectivity or truth.) Knowledge means truth. Therefore, 'Be pro-objectivity' truly is the only objective or correct normative end. This is the only coherent conclusion here, and not just because being pro-objectivity is coherent with objectivity. It is also coherent in that it is the only comprehensible and relatedly rational conclusion here. This conclusion is soon further shown to be coherent and confirmed, via objectivity presenting (inherently objective[9]) evidence additional to this paragraph's evidence. Next here:-

(6) A related argument, also involving coherence, involves another rationally unquestionable proposition, namely: an objective normative theory, one able to be knowledge, must have a basis and hence end/standard which favour and somehow involve (at least their own) objectivity or status as knowledge.

As the investigation mentioned in (5) above concerns a *normative,* moral etc theory, this part of the investigation's starting point, a part focusing greatly on objectivity or knowledge, could seem inappropriate. It could seem appropriate only for a theory applicable to cognition, learning or similar. However, this Section tries to begin showing that, if this part is sufficiently carefully investigated in relation to the issue of objective moral etc normativity, it will be seen to be appropriate, and the theory's basis and end/standard will be seen to involve much besides objectivity/knowledge. They will be seen to be applicable to life-as-a-whole. Next, a preliminary start to the investigation via that proposition:-

(6a) An *objective, normative* theory and hence its basis must involve objectivity in that normative theories inherently prescribe or are pro- some end(s), and being pro- an objective end means the theory here and hence its basis are *pro-* the theory's end's *objectivity*, i.e., its correctness. Otherwise the theory would not be in favour of the theory's end's correctness, of itself being objective, and of its own existence. This situation and the theory would be incoherent, self-contradictory. The theory would either be indifferent regarding its prescribed end, and hence not necessarily bother to prescribe or be pro- it, in-effect regarding its correct, inherent end as not correct, not inherent; or the theory would reject its own prescribed, correct end, and hence not prescribe the end it inherently prescribes. It would be anti- what it inherently is pro-. Either way, it would unobjectively regard the objectively correct as not correct. So the theory would not be that objective theory. It would not really exist (as itself).

In sum:- It is impossible and incoherent for an objective normative theory inherently pro- its objective end to not be *pro-* the theory's and the end's objectivity—and hence inherently *pro-objectivity* here. Objectivity, or knowledge, is inherently never incoherent. So an objective theory, one able to be normative knowledge, must have a basis and end positively involving or pro- at least their own objectivity and hence status as knowledge. There must be coherence here—a positive, pro- relationship.

Further here, (and as concluded by other arguments below,) the theory and hence its end/basis would not just favour their own objectivity. They'd also favour objectivity in a *general* way (where choices here are) coherent with the theory, because otherwise here there'd also be incoherence—which is ruled out by an objective and hence rational theory. (As explained further soon:- Those choices concern the acquiring and use of knowledge. E.g., knowledge of what causes avoidable cognition-impairing and hence anti-objectivity brain cancers can be either used to cause them, or used in a pro-objectivity way, namely to avoid them. It is *choices concerning knowledge,* or the *use* of objectivity, which can be either coherent or incoherent with pro-objectivity (theory), *not* the knowledge or objectivity here as such. Knowledge/objectivity as such inherently cannot be incoherent with pro-objectivity.)

So, because the theory is pro- its own objectivity, coherent with this it must also be pro-objectivity in *all other areas* causally-coherent with, and hence here within, the theory. An example is medical knowledge causally-coherent with pro-objectivity theory via being used in pro-objectivity ways, e.g., to avoid brain cancers which destroy one's ability to be pro-objectivity and relatedly objective (and which are hence anti-objectivity). Because the theory is inherently pro-achieving its end, it is pro- the therewith-causally-coherent, namely the means needed to achieve its end—and to know what the means are, and know how to implement them to achieve its end, the theory must be pro- (acquiring and using) the relevant medical, sociological, educational etc knowledge. To know which knowledge areas are relevant involves knowing which areas are irrelevant.[10] This covers all knowledge areas. The logical, coherent, rationally unquestionable conclusion here is that this means an objective normative theory must be coherently and hence *consistently pro-objectivity*, namely concerning all areas of life.[11] That is, as shown further soon, it must be a universally applicable, pro-objectivity theory, with the ultimate end, 'Be pro-objectivity'.

Concluding (2)-(6a):- Those arguments centrally involve pro-objectivity having a pro- relation to objectivity, and vice versa, and hence a *unique coherence* between pro-objectivity and objectivity. That is, relatedly, again, an objective normative end must be coherent with, pro- or positively-related to objectivity. 'Be pro-objectivity' obviously achieves that, in a unique way no other end can match. (Other ends are primarily pro- something *other* than objectivity, e.g., selfishness.) Similarly, the only end-prescription as close as possible to objectivity, or as closely normatively related as possible to objectivity, is 'Be pro-objectivity'. And, if a normative principle can be rationally claimed to be knowledge, the principle must be coherent with, pro- or positively-related to knowledge in a general way (where choices here are coherent with that principle). 'Be pro-objectivity' obviously achieves that, because objectivity is the faculty-system which acquires and contains knowledge. (And 'Be pro-objectivity' is inherently not incoherent with any knowledge, only with certain (inherently normative) choices concerning knowledge.)

Part I, Section 1.1: Coherence; More On Evidence For The Theory

This subsection, partly via expanding somewhat on those Preliminary Comments, begins the move from the recently-mentioned investigation's abstract, general starting point(s), to the investigation of *specifically* how an objective normative end could be normatively uniquely coherent with objectivity, i.e., be pro- or positively-related to objectivity—and, hence, its internal end and nature, knowledge, where (choices here are) coherent with that normative end. To do that, first the notion 'coherence' will be briefly further and simply (but here arguably sufficiently) investigated in relation to objectivity/knowledge. Then that investigation will be related to the notion: '(further) suggested evidence for pro-objectivity theory's end's objectivity'. Suggested evidence here is discussed. Later the universal normative applicability of 'Be pro-objectivity' is further investigated, with representative examples of its direct applicability. (After that, the theory's permitted a-objectivity, plural secondary ends are discussed, as examples of the indirect applicability of 'Be pro-objectivity'.) First then, a brief, *simplified* further discussion of coherence and objectivity or knowledge, soon related to normativity. (Appendixes 1 and 4 explain coherence yet further.):-

That which for us is knowledge and hence evidence crucially involves *coherence.* If knowledge has some foundation(s), the rest of knowledge must in an important sense be coherent with that foundation-knowledge, and vice versa. This is because a foundation cannot imply anything incoherent with or separate from itself, and, relatedly, in that a foundation is a premise and a premise at least implicitly *contains* its implications, there is a necessary coherence here.[12] If knowledge has no foundation(s), then it still must be coherent, in a way not (crucially?) involving such premise-containment etc.

Relatedly, as explained in this Section's Preliminary Comment (3), no piece of knowledge can be incoherent with or contradict any other piece, which helps confirm further that knowledge necessarily involves coherence.

Coherence regarding knowledge means that pieces of knowledge in an area, e.g., arithmetic, are connected (by and) for us meaningfully, or comprehensibly, so as to work together as a unity, a *system.*[13] This is much more than just consistency.[14] There is mutual *support* or pro- relations among such coherent, *linked* pieces of knowledge. In pure maths or arithmetic, '1=1', '1+1=1+1', '1+1+1=1+1+1' and so on are coherent or mutually-supportive in that, e.g., they all basically state and hence support 'X=X', or 'X is X (and not not-X)', a unifying notion here. Hence they support or are pro- each other, and 'X=X' supports or is pro- them. Relatedly, in an important sense, '1+1=1+1' is constituted by two of '1=1', and '1+1+1=1+1+1' is constituted by three of '1=1' or by '1+1=1+1' and '1=1'. Relatedly, the rest of arithmetic coheres therewith. E.g., '1+2=3' is '1+1+1=1+1+1', and '2+3=5 is constituted by '1+1=1+1' plus '1+1+1=1+1+1'; and '1+2=3' coheres with '3-2=1'; and '3x1=3 or '3 of 1 is 3 of 1' is a restatement of '1+1+1=1+1+1', which coheres with '3÷1=3'; and vice versa. And so on. No such piece of knowledge coheres with or is supported by '1+2=7', because that is not knowledge. Similarly, 'A cow, being a mammalian mother, produces milk to feed her babies' and 'Babies born from cows need to be fed cow (or very similar) milk initially' cohere. They are incoherent with 'Cows are reptiles, which do not need milk'. (Non-incoherence between knowledge in different areas, e.g., between '1+2=3' and 'A cow . . . produces milk to feed her babies', is discussed later, when the need arises.)

Further regarding systematicity, coherence regarding knowledge involves what William Whewell called 'consiliation' or 'consilience'.[15] A brief example, discussed further later, is the knowledge that observations of water rising (e.g., as evaporation or high tides) are coherent with observations of water falling (e.g., as rain or low tides) and with observations of orbiting planets, moons, satellites etc, because all events observed here crucially involve gravity: via the notion, 'gravity', each piece of knowledge or observation here supports each other. Gravity is a consiliating, a systematising, unifying or linking notion here, explaining all those events coherently, helping to form a knowledge area.

In sum, *coherence,* and hence systematicity, consilience or unity involving mutual support within knowledge areas, is an essential aspect of a notion being objective/knowledge, and hence of *evidence.* So if 'Be pro-objectivity' is the objective normative end, in the normative-knowledge area there must be a normative version of that coherence, systematicity etc concerning *only 'Be pro-objectivity*', hence providing *evidence* for that end being objective (and for that end-principle being abbreviated knowledge). So a *unique* coherence, systematicity etc is needed, i.e., one no alternative theory can match:-

Coherence and systematicity here are somewhat evident via the following explanation of a unique mutual causal-coherence between objectivity and pro-objectivity: (a) a person's objectivity is not possible without pro-objectivity causal factors, often including the person's at least implicit choice[16] to be objective; and (b) to help cause persons' objectivity via pro-objectivity factors persons can implement is not possible without objectivity as in persons at least implicitly knowing how to cause the existence/maintenance and implementation of those factors.

More than that explanation (evidence) is available here. Previous arguments show specifically that 'Be pro-objectivity' *is uniquely* consilient with, coherent with, pro- or supportive of objectivity or objectivity's internal end, 'knowledge', where (choices concerning) the knowledge is (are) coherent with that normative end. There is the required *unique mutual* coherence here partly because, as will become clearer, knowledge coheres normatively with or supports an objective normative end if the knowledge consists of both (i) knowledge of the means to achieve that end (and is used to achieve it), and (ii) knowledge explaining that the objective normative end is 'Be pro-objectivity', and relatedly that, because only that end is objective or correct, it should be achieved as the highest priority.

As also within every non-normative-knowledge area (e.g., arithmetic), there is a system here. Combining (i) and (ii) above forms a system, namely the normative-knowledge area, with fundamental (ii)-type knowledge being the consiliating or unifying, systematising principle. The systematicity involves that unique mutual causal-coherence between pro-objectivity and objectivity.

Clearly there is the mutual support here involved in coherence. More importantly here:- As explained further soon, via 'Be pro-objectivity' being one's highest-priority, ultimate end, i.e., by one being maximally pro-objectivity, and *only* thereby, the required *mutual coherence is maximised.* This implies that the *maximum available evidence* here applies only when 'Be pro-objectivity' is in-practice viewed (treated) as the objective normative end, namely an end uniquely objectively deserving to be one's highest-priority, ultimate end. This implies that the maximum available evidence here suggests it is normatively *correct* that one should view 'Be pro-objectivity' as the objective normative end.

Such unique-systematicity implications are pieces of knowledge supportive of previous arguments such as that, according to objectivity's (inherently overall) viewpoint and the related standard, 'objectivity', 'Be pro-objectivity' is the objective normative end. And those previous arguments are also knowledge within the normative-knowledge area, knowledge supportive of and systematically interrelated with those former pieces of knowledge—further showing the unique mutual coherence, systematicity etc here.

Summarising and concluding comments here:-

As previous arguments also show, 'Be pro-objectivity' is *uniquely* normatively coherent with objectivity. No other normative end-notion involves that coherence, because no other is entirely, exclusively or primarily pro-objectivity. (They are instead, e.g., pro-selfishness.) Where objectivity is rationally-undeniably possible, e.g., in practical science, *evidence* crucially involves coherence (and hence systematicity etc). Evidence is that which confirms whether a theory is objective/knowledge.

Because *evidence's essential nature involves coherence*, if there is unique mutual coherence between a normative theory and objectivity, or where there is unique mutual coherence between a normative theory and objectivity's internal end, this provides at least some evidence for the theory's objectivity. Coherence here suggests the theory is at least somewhat evidence-based or supported by the general nature of evidence. E.g., the recently-mentioned unique causal-coherence between objectivity and pro-objectivity is evidence that 'Be pro-objectivity' is the objective normative end in that the causally-necessary for objectivity, i.e., the pro-objectivity, is necessarily coherent with or supportive of objectivity, and vice versa.

There is other evidence for the book's theory. Arguably, the *combination* or consiliation of all evidence above and below confirms the theory. Further here:-

By 'evidence for the theory' I mean evidence of the *same, general* types as in overall highly-successful practical science. Expanding here on a comment in the Introduction implies that the general nature of evidence used in practical science is a sufficiently firm, successful notion to confirm a practical, normative theory by—if such evidence and hence confirmation is possible for a normative theory. The book argues that it is sufficiently possible.

Those claims may seem absurd. However, arguments below further indicate that, for this normative theory, the evidence-situation here is close, sufficiently close and as close as possible to the situation in practical science. (The related additional is-ought and other evaluative issues are discussed soon.) Along with coherence as a general notion, scientific objectivity concerning a specific issue involves evidence specifically constituting the coherence here. The specific evidence includes relevant sound arguments, which I've tried to present regarding the theory, above and below. Scientific evidence/objectivity also involves related relevant observation. I later argue there is related observable or empirical evidence for the theory, including for its structural form.

If there is evidence for just one normative theory, what would this mean regarding believing or practising an alternative theory? If a theory is not evidenced and hence objective, what is it? '1+2=7' is not an objective, evidenced theory. What do we think of such theories? What would someone be doing by believing or practising such a theory?, say by lending you $1, then $2, then insisting that therefore you owe them $7. This issue needs applying to normative theories.

Coherence (and hence systematicity etc), sound argument, observable evidence and that form are notions interrelated within pro-objectivity theory's basis. As shown further below, via those notions this basis implies and hence also involves the objective normative end, 'Be pro-objectivity':-

Part I, Section 1.2: Some Further Arguments (Evidence) Regarding An Objective Normative End

(Appendix 2 discusses the unavoidable circularity here (and elsewhere).)

Introductory comments:-

Firstly, some critics of pro-objectivity theory, somewhat followers of David Hume, argue that objectivity (reason) is the slave of the emotions (passions), (which I qualifiedly accept,) and that hence objectivity can only ever be used for emotion-chosen ends, not to discover any objective normative end—and, anyway, therefore, so their related arguments claim, there cannot be an objective normative end because there are ultimately only subjective and intersubjective ends, i.e., what I'll call 'primarily-emotional ends' (e.g., the achieving of, and pleasure due to achieving, objects (aims) naturally desired due to their evolutionary advantage, e.g., successful child-care and sex). Appendix 6 further discusses this criticism, arguing that unavoidable, non-cognitive, emotional influences on cognition (and on all intended practices) need not stop objective cognition seeking and discovering an objective normative end (nor our intended practices achieving it). That is, *pro-objectivity emotion* can motivate that search. Here there is emotion coherently *combined* (causally-linked) with objective cognition and hence with any objective normative end discovered via that coherence. This discovery would mean a further, special emotion-thought combination, discussed later, one of pro-objectivity motivation and pro-objectivity knowledge, able to overrule any pressure to achieve a primarily-emotional end.

Secondly, some other critics of pro-objectivity theory argue that objectivity would inherently and coherently regard its internal cognitive end, 'knowledge', as also the objective normative end, implying that, objectively, 'Be pro-objectivity' is not an objective normative end. So this criticism needs dealing with. Along with continuing the previous subsection's positive arguments concerning 'Be pro-objectivity' being the objective normative end, the present subsection begins expanding on previous preliminary negative arguments suggesting objectivity would not regard knowledge as the objective normative end. The expansion further confirms that knowledge is not an objective *normative* end, because knowledge is only objectivity's *internal, cognitive, general* end. Normativity does not only concern the internal-to-objectivity. Normativity also and greatly concerns that which is *external* to objective cognition, namely the *non*-cognitive, especially our emotions, feelings and publicly observable actions, and thence morality, politics, society and so on, plus non-objective cognition, especially non-pro-objectivity normative theories. So a *normative* end cannot only concern or be knowledge. That external-to-objectivity focus (applicability) has been briefly discussed above, will be again soon, and becomes the book's most-discussed topic. But for now, another issue here:-

Knowledge is also too general a notion to be an objective normative end. Among and within each of billions of persons, objectivity has been, is and can be directed to seek knowledge instrumental for countless chosen purposes or ends. This knowledge, plus knowledge unchosen by the knowers here but instilled into them by others, e.g., teachers, plus knowledge acquired incidentally and via our often highly-open curiosity instinct, plus other, limitless, potential knowledge, e.g., regarding pebble numbers, hydrogen *etc* atom numbers, *etc,* on every planet etc, mean knowledge is objectivity's *extremely general* end. As with Kant's 'universalisability' end, it is far too general, too open-ended.

This means knowledge is too ambiguous to be an objective normative end, an end which must be sufficiently practicable including via being sufficiently unambiguous. The normative is inherently the practicable: (realistic and in that sense objective) normativity concerns that which we should and *can* practise. If objectivity/knowledge as such was one's intended normative end, there'd be no sufficiently clear, unambiguous prioritisation regarding which knowledge to acquire or have among the infinite pieces of actual and potential knowledge. As there'd be no highest priority *specific type* of knowledge-as-an-end, here there'd be unresolvable conflicts among and within persons regarding whether to acquire or have this rather than that knowledge.[17] If knowledge as such was the objective normative end, we'd not *know*, e.g., *whether or not* we should count Earth's pebbles, everyone's toe-nail cuttings, the hairs on each mammal, and so on. That is, here we'd *lack normative knowledge*, and because knowledge is objective we'd here lack an objective normative end. The incoherence in that situation shows that knowledge as such cannot be an objective *normative* end. As points above imply, relatedly regarding objectivity as such. (Issues here relate to the recent suggestion that it is choices concerning the acquiring and use of knowledge which are the normative issue, not knowledge as such.)

In sum:- For an objective, hence coherent and hence unambiguous normative end, we need a single ultimate end, i.e., one highest-priority end—one which can be general, but not too general, one which is sufficiently specific to be sufficiently unambiguously practicable.[18] Then, if that end conflicts with something else, that ultimate end unambiguously has highest-priority—and the conflict is resolved. Here there is a clear way to discriminate, prioritise or choose among conflicting possible ends. There is no incoherence here. With this, objectivity or knowledge is a too-general end here, and hence too ambiguous.

Objectivity can know that its internal end is too general, too open-ended, giving no unambiguous normative guide—and, as arguments below suggest, that, apart from being objectivity's internal end, an end usable externally-to-objectivity instrumentally, knowledge can and should only be instrumental, a means to help discover, describe, defend (justify) and achieve an objective normative end, i.e., *involved* in our having and achieving an objective normative end-aim, as opposed to *being* one. Relatedly, as Appendix B suggests, objectivity can know that its internal end is so non-specific (general) that, if knowledge was one's normative end, one could spend so much time, energy etc in acquiring certain (e.g., pebble-number) knowledge, that this would be incoherent with one being as overall objective or knowledgeable as possible for as long as possible. (One could soon die due to lacking certain survival-necessary knowledge.) Here one would be using objectivity to acquire knowledge the acquiring of which is in-effect anti-knowledge and relatedly anti-objectivity.[19] Such incoherence also shows that (acquiring) knowledge as such cannot be an objective(ly-warranted) normative end, because objectivity means coherence.

Concluding these introductory comments:- Knowledge is internal to (the brain parts involved in) our objectivity. Can objectivity's cognition (further) confirm there is a sufficiently unambiguous, objective normative end implementable externally to our objectivity, an end coherent with and involving but not identical with objectivity's internal, cognitive end, knowledge, where, as objectivity requires, (choices concerning) this knowledge is (are) reciprocally coherent with that normative end? This coherence etc would mean that the objective normative end is 'Be pro-objectivity', and, regarding (choices concerning) knowledge, that this end would only mean acquiring and using knowledge concerning (describing and defending) itself, or useful regarding achieving itself.

Next, expanding on those introductory comments:-

(Often below, when discussing normative objectivity in relation to that external-to-objective-cognition moral, social, political etc focus, the term 'harmony' or 'harmonious' is used instead of 'coherence' or 'coherent', to emphasise the positiveness, the supportive or 'pro-' relation involved. And 'harmony' is a more moral, social and political normativity-related term than 'coherence'.)

That just-mentioned coherence of that normative end with that knowledge would mean a positive relation to objectivity's internal end here. As the previous subsection suggests, that coherence, along with the related unique mutual coherence between pro-objectivity and objectivity shown by previous arguments, would be some evidence for the objectivity of that normative end. Relatedly, one way to discover an objective normative end, or further confirm that 'Be pro-objectivity' is one, is via objectivity investigating which general type(s) of ends are overall incoherent with itself, namely those with a negative relationship to itself, and see if there is a contrasting end—one with a unique positive, supportive or pro-, harmonious relationship to itself. This involves seeing which ends conflict with objectivity, and so could not be objectively-warranted, and seeing which end(s) is (or are) left. This involves objectivity's overall view:-

To acquire knowledge, at a reflective and hence high level of thought objectivity has an *overall* view, namely a view overseeing and coherently interrelating all the factors involved regarding the issue being investigated. (E.g., to know if Earth orbits the sun requires a high-level, reflective viewpoint coherently interrelating much more than just the low-level visual etc perceptions suggesting the sun orbits a stationary Earth.[20]) That overall view also considers at least all the factors-related *evidence sufficient* to constitute knowledge. (E.g., to know Earth orbits the sun, and does so yearly, astronomers need not measure and write down the direction and distance between Earth and the sun, and so on, every 5 seconds over every year. Weekly over 2 years is probably sufficient.)

(As the term 'overall' is important here and elsewhere in this book, a distinction concerning its uses should be mentioned:- 'Overall' can refer to the relevant totality or fullness, or at least a 'sufficient totality or fullness'. (Analogously, a glass can be not completely full but full enough for a certain purpose or end, e.g., to quench your thirst.) Regarding the book's purposes, one totality is as in objectivity's overall view concerning issue X involving *all* the evidence sufficient to have knowledge regarding X. But, when the book discusses overall pro-objectivity or overall anti-objectivity, 'overall' does not necessarily refer to totality. It can mean 'on-average', a degree, as in 'Dinner was overall, i.e., on-average, delicious'. Regarding each mention of overall in the book, the meaning is representatively explained, or the context makes it clear whether overall refers to a totality or to such a degree.)

Importantly, via its overall (sufficiently full) view, objectivity can distinguish between and discriminate normatively regarding two pro-objectivity achievement-types (explained further soon):-

One is type-A: '(purely) *cognitive* pro-objectivity achievement' (or an equivalent term, e.g., 'Be(ing) pro-objectivity cognitively'), involving objectivity achieving only (some specific instance of) its purely cognitive end, knowledge. Objectivity here could be (but rarely has been) used to help acquire knowledge of what the objective normative end is. In one's psychological development type-A develops first; type-B only follows via that normative-knowledge acquisition plus the implemented choice to achieve that normative end.

Pro-objectivity achievement type-B is a much wider notion. It means interrelated non-cognitive (e.g., physical and emotional) and cognitive pro-objectivity achievements[21] involving the above-mentioned special emotion-thought combination of pro-objectivity motivation and pro-objectivity knowledge. All knowledge here *concerns* and is *used* to help achieve the pro-objectivity *normative end*, from a significant to a maximal degree. The maximal degree, explained further soon, is 'overall-objectively-warranted' where 'overall' refers to achieving that normative end long-term in the total number of ways possible for the individual(s) in the situation in question. The significant to almost-maximal degrees are overall-objectively-warranted but here 'overall' refers to achieving that normative end in not as many ways as are possible for the individual in the situation in question. Here one is *on-average* pro-objectivity at least medium-term. (This is of course an approximate notion.)

(That distinction between type-A and type-B is often only implicit below. When implicit, the context indicates which of type-A and type-B applies.)

Only objectivity's overall view can know (1) that objectivity cannot occur without the factors causally-necessary for achieving objectivity (and that there can also be causally-helpful[22] factors); (2) that regarding choosable causal factors,[23] their (as-far-as-possible etc) implementation to achieve that at least significant degree, *is* the achieving of the normative end, 'Be(ing) pro-objectivity'; and (3) that the causal factors crucially include implemented normative choices concerning the world *external* to (the brain parts involved in) objectivity.

Relatedly, via its overall viewpoint, as suggested above, objectivity can critically reflect regarding its internal, cognitive end, 'knowledge', and the normative objective end (because the normative end-principle is normative knowledge). Via that reflection, objectivity can know that *external*-to-objectivity choices concerning *acquiring* (and hence seeking and storing) various types of knowledge, and *using* knowledge in certain ways, can conflict with knowledge/objectivity, i.e., with *itself*—and relatedly with that normative end (as opposed to the knowledge *as such* conflicting with either that cognitive end or normative end-principle knowledge, which is impossible because knowledge cannot conflict with knowledge[24]). So, acquiring and using knowledge can mean conflict or a negative, anti- relationship with *objectivity's* nature and internal purpose, namely to achieve that cognitive end, and hence relatedly with *pro*-objectivity. This conflict is not internal, not due to incoherence within objectivity itself. It occurs via those choices *external* to objectivity—via *normative* choices of practices with end-aims incoherent with objectivity's (internal) end-aim and hence with normative knowledge. Specific examples:-

Practices incoherent with achieving objectivity's internal end or with objectivity's existence or nature are hence anti-objectivity, including using objectivity or knowledge to do so. E.g., Nazis did so via ending much objectivity or knowledge via using their physics and chemical etc objectivity/knowledge to murder many actually or potentially significantly pro-objectivity persons.[25] (This too-narrow oversimplification is expanded on soon, including by discussing Nazi cruelty's emotional effects.) From objectivity's *overall* view, such practices, though they can require much knowledge and hence fit type-A pro-objectivity, are in-effect overall (on-average) *anti-objectivity*. Regarding knowledge used instrumentally for such murderous ends, such practices only fit type-A. Regarding their ends, they conflict with type-B. So they conflict with the normative end-principle knowledge, 'Be pro-objectivity'.

Similarly, e.g., counting all Earth's pebbles would mean acquiring knowledge useless for maintaining or increasing knowledge overall because the time, energy etc could instead be used, e.g., learning how to avoid anti-objectivity dangers, e.g., Nazism, poison and starvation. Such counting would be overall anti-*objectivity*, and the knowledge-acquisition here would be incoherent with objectivity's internal end, knowledge. One and hence one's objectivity and knowledge would soon die if such counting is all one used one's objectivity for. E.g., one would not know how to avoid life's many dangers, or how to get food. Dying from starvation, poison, Nazi murder or whatever would obviously affect one's future ability to be(come) increasingly pro-objectivity and knowledgeable.

In sum, as with that Nazi knowledge-use, such useless counting or knowledge-acquisition conflicts overall with *objectivity/knowledge* and, due to pro-objectivity's pro-, causal relationship to objectivity, it also conflicts with pro-objectivity, and with the objective normative end-principle, 'Be pro-objectivity'.

Three conclusions here, knowable only via an objective, overall viewpoint:- (1) As a purely *instrumental* or *means*(-to-an-end) notion, i.e., as type-A pro-objectivity, pro-objectivity is highly ambiguous and can mean normative incoherence with objectivity, including incoherence with what objective *normative* theory says ought not to be done. This ambiguity and incoherence is avoidable only via having 'Be pro-objectivity' as the ultimate normative *end*—via type-B pro-objectivity. Only thence is normative coherence with objectivity or knowledge achieved, namely via acquiring and practising (using) only pro-objectivity knowledge, not just any knowledge. (Pro-objectivity knowledge is knowledge used to describe, defend (justify) and increase or maintain pro-objectivity. The next subsection discusses this further.) (2) Relatedly, knowledge is not an objective *normative* end. Regarding knowledge, the normative end, 'Be(ing) *pro*-objectivity', only means acquiring and using knowledge concerning or useful regarding achieving that normative end. (3) Anti-objectivity ends, ends inherently external to objectivity, are the general type incoherent with objectivity's internal end and nature. Those ends include ends the achieving of which involves knowledge[26] either overall useless regarding,[27] or used to overall limit or destroy, humanity's overall capacity to be pro-objectivity, as in the ends, respectively, 'Acquire pebble-count knowledge' and 'Be pro-Nazism'.

Arguments here and to follow shortly are evidence for soon further-discussed central claims of this book. Those conclusions and issues leading up to them include points involved in that evidence. The claims are:- Overall causal and other coherence with objectivity crucially involves the external-to-objectivity and hence moral, social, political, educational etc issues and related values, i.e., the normative. Universally-applicable, objective, pro-objectivity values, i.e., anti-anti-objectivity values, are inextricably involved with (our ability, motivation and opportunity to achieve (cause)) objectivity or knowledge. (This relates to the is-ought issue.) The above also implies that an objective end-principle must be special, unique knowledge and in that important sense *uniquely internal* to objectivity.

Again, achieving anti-objectivity ends occurs via practices, motivation and thoughts or emotion-thought combinations (choices) involving the ends being *external* to objectivity, and this achievement includes using knowledge in ways incoherent with objectivity's internal end, knowledge. Some critics of pro-objectivity theory argue that knowledge inherently cannot be used so as to be incoherent with knowledge. To further counter that criticism, an analogy explaining the crucial 'external versus internal' issue here:- The general internal end-purpose of our legs (including their associated nerves and so on) involves movement and standing. Specific purposes or ends *external* to but involvable in *directing* that internal end-purpose involve factors external to legs-as-such. E.g., one could desire to get home for dinner, here meaning one needs to walk home. We can choose to direct our legs to act on desires/ends involving moving or standing to achieve specific things coherent with continuing to move and stand, as in walking home for dinner. But we can act on a desire/end incoherent therewith. E.g., we can choose to direct our legs to jump off a building so as to break or destroy our legs, conflicting with their movement/standing internal end.

In such cases, in an important sense the incoherence involves a practical (not just theoretical) type of self-contradiction. E.g., in the latter legs example, legs are used in a practice which contradicts their own practicability and hence internal-end, and in the Nazi example knowledge is used in practices which contradict or stop it being practicable for many persons to have knowledge. Concerning acquiring knowledge, similarly regarding the pebble-count example.

'Acquire pebble-count knowledge', 'Be pro-Nazi' and all other anti-objectivity normative end-aims obviously crucially involve practices external to (the brain parts involved in) objectivity as such. Objectivity as such inherently cannot have internal, incoherent-with(in)-itself, anti-objectivity end-aims. But one's objectivity can reflect on and assess those end-aims, like it can assess whether a statement presently only alleged to be knowledge, and so presently external to one's knowledge, is objective, or pro-objectivity. Objectivity's assessing of such statements includes checking for any self-contradiction or self-incoherence, and for coherence with one's other relevant knowledge or with objectivity. E.g., a child may learn that her guess, the statement '1+2=4', is wrong because it is incoherent internally, stating '1+1+1 is 1+1+1+1', namely that, self-contradictorily, '1+1+1 is not 1+1+1', and, relatedly, that '1+1+1 is 1+1+1+1' is wrong via being incoherent with the arithmetic knowledge system, especially the basic, rationally unquestionable, definitively objective, universally presuppositional 'X is X', here interpreted as '1+1+1' is '1+1+1', i.e., '1+2=3'.

Objectivity's assessment of normative end-aims involves using the normative version of such statement-assessment, involving checking for *practical* incoherence with objectivity (as in finding Nazism and pebble-counting conflict overall with objectivity/knowledge). Thence, objectivity can know that, except for a-objectivity ends,[28] *all* end-principles and associated aims, theories, choices, practices, motivations etc *external* to objectivity are objectively wrong. With this, objectivity can know that the (externally applicable) *pro-objectivity* end-principle and choice (prescribing) thereof, alone being knowledge here, are, with the associated direct, Type-B-related pro-objectivity motivation, *uniquely internal* to objectivity—uniquely among normativity-related notions and factors. The internal-to-objectivity inherently cannot be incoherent with objectivity.

Anti-objectivity's externality and wrongness is shown further by considering a representative external-to-objectivity, non-a-objectivity end-principle, 'Be sexist'. A preliminary, simplified example here, of pro-objectivity theory's practical applications (Other reasons why sexism is wrong are discussed later, including in Appendix 5—which also further explains the following.):-

Sexists believe one gender is inferior or not correct, i.e., truly or objectively inferior or not correct. An extreme, silly but logical conclusion or extension of this is for sexists to believe that this gender is *always* inherently inferior or not correct, in all areas, i.e., including regarding objectivity. If sexists do not believe that the allegedly inferior gender is inherently inferior or not correct regarding being objective, this book implies that sexists cannot rationally believe this gender is inherently normatively-objectively inferior or not correct in any area, period. This implies that sexism of that and any type is objectively wrong. As the next paragraph shows, sexism is wrong whichever belief sexists have here, and there are only those two beliefs concerning a gender's capacity to be objective.

Under that silly but logical-conclusion scenario, suppose, when a gender 1 person states, 'To survive, avoid cliff-falls', hypothetical sexist Sam correctly believes this to be knowledge; but when a gender 2 person[29] states that knowledge, Sam believes it is false. Such potentially fatal nonsense shows that sexism, via taking it to that logical conclusion, is obviously *objectively* wrong, here because it is *objective* that, to survive, we need to avoid life-threatening cliff-falls. Hence it is objective that because sexism, taken to a logical conclusion, can contradict that cliff-falls knowledge, or any objectivity or knowledge, sexism is objectively mistaken, i.e., wrong. Relatedly, because being fully or consistently sexist must mean such *un*-objectivity, sexism and the choice to be sexist are obviously *anti*-objectivity and, like all other anti-objectivity values/choices, *external* to objectivity. Unobjectivity cannot be internal to or part of objectivity.

(The fact that regarding survival-necessary and much other knowledge, real sexists tend to not practise sexism, hence being inconsistently (illogically) and not fully sexist, shows they in-practice accept the required minimal pro-objectivity here. Coherence requires full acceptance. That fact concerning real sexists also shows they implicitly have that recently-mentioned view implying that the allegedly inferior gender is not inherently objectively inferior, period.)

In sum, sexist practices, taken to a logical conclusion, mean theoretical plus *practical incoherence with objectivity*. Sexism is incoherent, anti-objectivity and, because, like all anti-objectivity ends it is objectively wrong and hence *un*-

objective, it is external to objectivity; and 'Be non-sexist' is a pro-objectivity prescription. Relatedly, non-sexism was shown to be a value/choice *internal* to objectivity via being necessary for objectivity: non-sexism is a specific pro-objectivity value (under 'Be pro-objectivity'), because gender is *a-objectivity* (irrelevant) regarding whether a person is objective (and it is pro-objectivity to treat the a-objectivity as a-objectivity). That is, (as real sexists in-practice accept,) persons of either gender can be objective, so gender is irrelevant regarding their objectivity and is hence a-objectivity (and treating it as relevant conflicts with objectivity and is hence anti-objectivity). ('Racist' and 'racism' can be meaningfully substituted, respectively, for 'sexist' and 'sexism' in that argument. Various other substitutions are appropriate, e.g., 'socio-economic classism' and 'nationalism'.) (Again, regarding the is-ought issue, various values or prescriptions, pro-objectivity ones, are inherent in or *internal* to being *objective.* You *cannot* be objective or have knowledge concerning what 'is', without practising whatever pro-objectivity values or 'oughts' are relevant in the situation.[30])

So, at least in survival-necessary areas, those using objectivity or knowledge are necessarily at least implicitly and at least potentially[31] rejecting ends such as 'Be sexist', i.e., anti-objectivity ends. Here they treat the a-objectivity as a-objectivity. Otherwise they'd be dead.[32] Their objectivity at least implicitly assesses that sexist end as anti-objectivity, and they hence (survival-necessarily) reject it here. (This happens often. E.g., at least most people get at least some survival-necessary knowledge communicated to them by someone they know is of another gender (or race etc), e.g., a parent, sibling, teacher, doctor, author or media person.) If one is normatively coherent with objectivity in some area(s), e.g., via having non-sexist values concerning believing 'To survive, avoid cliff-falls', then, to be consistent with that coherence, one needs to accept such values and all other pro-objectivity values in one's life overall (fully, in all areas). Otherwise one's values are incoherent and cannot all be correct (objective). The only rational solution here is to have 'Be pro-objectivity' as one's ultimate end, the end one's objectivity at least implicitly assesses as correct in survival-necessary (and often many other) areas. With this, (as with real sexists surviving via not rejecting knowledge stated by someone of the allegedly inferior gender,) here one's objectivity at least implicitly and potentially assesses all alternative normative ends as incorrect, i.e., one's objectivity correctly rejects all other actually and potentially competing normative ends[33] except 'Be pro-objectivity'.

In sum:- Objectivity's internal end-purpose is exclusively pro-knowledge[34] and relatedly pro-objectivity. So it can discriminate regarding, assess and self-coherently reject normative ends other than 'Be pro-objectivity', namely all non-a-objectivity *external*-to-objectivity ends, because, as shown further below, they are all unobjective and anti-objectivity. (Objectivity can also discriminate against all other anti-objectivity things, e.g., cancer). Related (self-)coherence means knowing that 'Be pro-objectivity' is the objective normative end. Or, after rejecting anti-objectivity ends, objectivity sees that the only candidate left over which could be (and is) an objective normative end, is 'Be pro-objectivity'.[35]

Further evidence here:- To knowingly achieve any end, including an anti-objectivity end, one must *first* be (cognitively) pro-objectivity as in the limited type-A pro-objectivity above—in order to (1) have the survival-necessary knowledge one needs if one is to be alive, (2) know what the end is, and (3) acquire and implement the necessary means-end knowledge. So, being pro-objectivity is *necessarily fundamental* for *all* persons and theories. However, as discussed further in Appendixes 3 and 4, here they are only pro-objectivity to the *minimal,* unavoidable, fundamentally-necessary degree. They are only minimally and unavoidably coherent with objectivity. Full coherence with that (their) necessary fundamental pro-objectivity and survival-necessary knowledge[36] means being pro-objectivity *overall*, namely here (as far as possible) maximally in the type-B, normative way. This means being overall-objectively-warranted. (Relatedly, as discussed in Appendix 4, which relies in-part on part of Appendix 3:- A normative theory lacking overall (full) coherence with its and its theorist's necessary fundamental pro-objectivity and the theorist's survival-necessary knowledge, and hence with objectivity, is highly rationally-problematic—partly because, due to that incoherence, the theory is overall-objectively-unwarranted. In the previous sentence, 'theorist' can be meaningfully replaced by 'believer'.)

Concluding here:-

The normative choice to be pro-objectivity is *uniquely necessarily causally linked* to objectivity, and is hence *necessarily* and *uniquely coherent* with objectivity. Relatedly, the only *normative* end-choice *fully coherent* with objectivity is 'Be pro-objectivity', and the only normative theory for which there is such *evidence,* i.e., concerning coherence and objectivity, is pro-objectivity theory. (Other evidence here is explained or further explained below.)

Regarding choices, there are inextricable links among that normative end-choice, pro-objectivity motivation, objectivity's method-aspect and related assessment-aspect and, where (choices concerning knowledge are) coherent with that end-choice, objectivity's internal, cognitive end, knowledge. (This too shows there is an unavoidable is-ought relationship here, or shows how values (preferred choices) are linked with facts, namely the objective or (at least potential) knowledge. This suggested solution to the is-ought or fact-value problem is discussed further soon, and discussed yet further in Appendix 5.)

Normativity involves choices. The only normative end-choice exclusively and fully coherent with or positively, supportively related to objectivity's existence and reason for existence, and relatedly internal to objectivity, is 'Be pro-objectivity'. With this, as objectivity's internal motivation is necessarily pro-objectivity, the only normative end-choice coherent with that necessity must also be pro-objectivity, and hence also internal to objectivity: so the end-principle here, 'Be pro-objectivity', must be normative knowledge, pro-objectivity knowledge. That end-choice, being uniquely internal to objectivity and hence objectively right, chooses the only possible candidate for an objective normative end. Any end-choice external to objectivity cannot be an objective normative end.

Part I, Section 1.3: What, Normatively, Does 'Be Pro-Objectivity' More Specifically Involve? Some Applicability Issues

Developing some previous points:-

'Be pro-objectivity' would be too problematic a normative end if it prescribes only narrow, cerebral practices, (i.e., type-A pro-objectivity, including acquiring knowledge as such or just knowing,) or is so general as to be too general and hence too ambiguous, or if we could not understand what it specifically prescribes, or if it is not practicable for at least nearly all humans. What, regarding such applicability issues, does 'Be pro-objectivity' more specifically mean?:-

Again, being pro-objectivity involves many practices and associated factors outside cerebral brain-parts. Prescriptions here are practicable constituents or specific aspects of the general, 'Be pro-objectivity'. They are applications of and implied by 'Be pro-objectivity' (and not (allegedly) objective ultimate ends additional to 'Be pro-objectivity'). As shown further soon, these specific aspects or implications mean that 'Be pro-objectivity' is not too general. It also means that 'Be pro-objectivity' is widely normatively applicable, not too narrow, not prescribing only cognitive, cerebral practices:-

Normatively, 'Be pro-objectivity' means *practising pro-objectivity knowledge*. Specific, practised 'Be pro-objectivity' prescriptions are *actual* pro-objectivity knowledge—as distinct from *potential* pro-objectivity knowledge. (Below, the term 'pro-objectivity knowledge' is often used to cover either of potential and actual pro-objectivity knowledge—to save space and in that, depending on the person(s) or situation(s) in question, either could apply. The context makes it clear which is being referred to.):-

Knowledge as such is cognitive. But *pro-objectivity knowledge* is not just any type of knowledge as such. Actual pro-objectivity knowledge is *overall* pro-objectivity, namely not just cognitive and it is normative and hence either directly or ultimately *practical*: from an overall, objective normative viewpoint, *actual* pro-objectivity knowledge is only knowledge which is *practised*, i.e., *used,* to increase/maintain pro-objectivity overall. This means that theoretical knowledge describing and defending the objective normative end is only *potential* pro-objectivity knowledge—until, combined with pro-objectivity motivation, and with thereby *practised* instrumental, also-otherwise-just-*potential* pro-objectivity knowledge, the combination is used to help achieve that end. This emotion-thought combination involves that theoretical knowledge as the basis of or fundamental reason for that practising.[37]

So *actual* pro-objectivity knowledge involves far more than the cognitive. Inherently cerebral objectivity can only contain *potentially* pro-objectivity knowledge regarding the normatively-important world outside cerebral brain-parts. When knowledge here is only known, not used, it is a type-A achievement, not yet overall-objectively-warranted. Potentially pro-objectivity knowledge is just the cognitive *aspect* of the *overall*, objective normative end.

With this, potentially pro-objectivity knowledge, the knowledge as such here, is only *involved in* achieving the objective normative end, as opposed to *being* that end. One cannot be overall (normatively) pro-objectivity by just having such (or any) knowledge. One must put the relevant pro-objectivity instrumental knowledge into normative *practice* if one is to really (objectively) be *pro*-objectivity in the overall, type-B way.

The book will increasing show that, if sufficiently investigated, that (theoretically-informed) instrumental potential pro-objectivity knowledge is sufficiently unambiguous.[38] It specifies the general type of knowledge involved, specific types of which we can recognise or acquire, and practise via. That is, e.g., (partly via being theoretically-informed) it is at least manageable to understand and effectively use much such specific implicit knowledge we already have, and to acquire and use much more, increasing that manageability and effectiveness. This involves objectivity's assessment- and related method-aspects. The latter is (often implicit) knowledge of how to acquire (increase) knowledge. If used to acquire knowledge used in pro-objectivity ways, that methodological knowledge too is (actual) pro-objectivity knowledge. Similarly, also importantly, potential pro-objectivity knowledge includes educational-method knowledge usable to help students acquire potential pro-objectivity knowledge.[39]

Instrumental potential pro-objectivity knowledge is the practicable content of specific objective normative prescriptions, and vice versa. These will be shown to be applicable to all areas, involving (often approximate) knowledge of, e.g., which diets, upbringing, health-care, education, environment(s), material resource use, population-size, sexual practices, society, laws, politics, morality, economics, emotions and so on are situationally most pro-objectivity. Regarding that applicability, pro-objectivity knowledge or theory clearly also needs to be applicable by at least nearly all persons. This is very important:-

Pro-objectivity knowledge resides in brains needing many non-cognitive factors in order for it to be possible for the brains to acquire pro-objectivity knowledge, e.g., mentally-enhancing physical health. Objectivity's realistic, overall view here knows that those factors often require largely non-cognitive, non-intellectual practices, e.g., garbage disposal needed for that health, and that for some persons it is not *possible* to manage anything more cognitively difficult than such practices.[40] But as far as individually possible such persons can maximally achieve the pro-objectivity normative end and hence be overall-objectively-warranted as far as is possible for them. Individuals lacking (potentially) pro-objectivity knowledge in some area(s) can be maximally pro-objectivity here via being directed here via others' knowledge. So pro-objectivity knowledge or theory is applicable by those either with or without pro-objectivity knowledge, i.e., by potentially and ideally all:-

Objectivity's overall view considers all able to make at least in-effect pro-objectivity choices. The realistic, humanly-possible, 'practicable as-far-as-*possible* for this individual/being now' version of 'Be pro-objectivity' allows individuals here with the least abilities, e.g., children, and persons only capable of garbage disposal, (and countless non-human beings,) to achieve that end.

So, again, there is a need to qualify 'maximal pro-objectivity'. It is a relative term, relative to the pro-objectivity capacities of the individual. So, e.g., an individual with unavoidably little pro-objectivity knowledge can be maximally pro-objectivity relative to the individual's abilities, though this individual's pro-objectivity achievements would not be overall high regarding and relative to the very high, achievable-absolute degree of pro-objectivity knowledge some persons can have, and which is needed for all collectively to be individually maximally pro-objectivity. That distinction is like the distinction many teachers make when they give two students an A for effort, but for achievement one gets C and the other A. (When 'maximal', or 'significantly', 'highly' and so on, is used in this book to describe a degree of being pro-objectivity, the context makes it clear whether this or that degree of absolute achievement is involved.)

Concluding here:-

An *overall practicable* end is achievable individually-maximally over all capable of choice, even if they lack appropriate knowledge. E.g., teachers with pro-objectivity knowledge would thereby direct children lacking it to act in pro-objectivity ways, as far as possible getting children to understand the direction's warrant. (Achieving the overall, collective or societal pro-objectivity end requires a very high quantity and quality of knowledge among at least some.)

The individually practicable end here, regarding human intentionality and practicability overall, is 'Be pro-objectivity' with 'as-far-as-possible etc' as an at least implicit, important qualification. Each should do whatever is possible for himself or herself here, not aim at or be expected to achieve an unachievable ideal. Objectivity can know that a normative theory is useless and hence unrealistic or unobjective (unwarranted) if it prescribes an end impossible to achieve except perhaps for an elite minority. Objectivity, inherently realistic and relatedly rational, cannot be irrational, e.g., via demanding impossibilities.

Relatedly:- 'To respect' means 'to regard as warranted'. It is overall-objectively-warranted to maximally respect that end and that which best achieves it as far as possible etc. This crucially involves individuals. Thence, all persons doing their best to be at least in-effect maximally pro-objectivity are objectively equally deserving of maximum respect, including self-respect. (This should help motivate persons to be pro-objectivity.) Those with little knowledge or cognitive ability, including non-human animals, can often be in-effect helpfully pro-objectivity and doing their best here—if directed respectfully by people with pro-objectivity knowledge.[41] Pro-objectivity knowledge includes knowing that such respect is warranted.

(After Part I, Section 1.4 come Part I's Sections 2-3 which expand on those and suggest many, far more specific practical implications of 'Be pro-objectivity'. Part II does that at length.)

Part I, Section 1.4: Important Conclusions So Far; More Evidence

(1) Because the principle, 'Be pro-objectivity', is uniquely normatively-

coherent with objectivity, and relatedly is the objective normative end, and because that principle is (abbreviated) knowledge and hence internal to objectivity, it is the only *intrinsically* valuable[42] normative principle from an objective viewpoint. It can only exist in persons' brains/minds: here *persons* (practising it as pro-objectivity knowledge) are uniquely objectively intrinsically-valuable.

(2) It is objective to regard *all* at least potentially pro-objectivity persons as at least objectively highly-valuable due to them alone being able to knowingly achieve that end, and hence of at least potential objective intrinsic value—or objectively highly-valuable just due to their capacity to be directed to achieve that end. This is very important for a theory needing to be practicable, including motivating, for persons. (Similarly regarding many non-human beings.)

(3) Objectively-warrantedly, and according to common normative intuition, truth is inherently that which ought to be believed. And we *can not* believe without believing we believe the truth. 'I believe statement X' means 'I believe X is *true*'. Because (a realistic, practicable) 'ought' implies 'can', truth can not be that which ought not to be believed. Relatedly, coherent with this, because knowledge involves true belief, pro-objectivity knowledge or theory is inherently that which we ought to believe. With this, it is uniquely objective(ly intrinsically-valuable) to believe this theory. (Regarding this paragraph, and elsewhere, it is important to remember that 'true' means 'objective'.)

A simplified summary here:- Because pro-objectivity theory is true, we can and ought to believe it. (This should mean disbelieving alternative theories.)

(4) (Part I, Section 2 and Part II expand on the specific examples here.) (The following is not arguing that objectivity is the objective normative end.)

Related to arguments above, there is *observable evidence*, via quantitative practical science, that, all else (pro-objectivity-relevant[43]) equal, certain choosable factors best help achieve objectivity, e.g., only some types of diet, education and society, e.g., lead-free diets and the educational and societal practice, 'Promote critical, evidence-seeking, rationality'. So, compared to alternatives, those factors/types are (more) pro-objectivity. A theory prescribing implementing such factors optimal regarding maximising objectivity is a pro-objectivity theory. It prescribes pro-objectivity practices.

If only prescription-set P best and maximally achieves Q, then, from Q's viewpoint, or according to the standard, 'Q', practising P is warranted or correct. According to Q's viewpoint/standard, Q is the highest priority and so should be achieved to the overall highest or maximum degree. Rationally, this includes over the long-term. As Appendix B and Part II further show, because practising pro-objectivity prescriptions, those best promoting such factors, maximally helps achieve *objectivity long-term*, therefore, from *objectivity's* viewpoint, or according to the standard, 'objectivity', only *pro-objectivity* prescriptions and hence pro-objectivity theory are warranted or correct. (From objectivity's viewpoint, or if objectivity uses the term 'correct', 'correct' means 'objective(ly warranted)' or, regarding normativity, 'overall-objectively-warranted'.)

'Achieves (objectivity)' means 'causes (objectivity)'. The causally-connected-to-objectivity here, namely the causally-necessary here, is obviously closely connected positively to objectivity, i.e., causally pro- one's objectivity. The choosable causally-connected here is implemented pro-objectivity prescriptions and hence that implemented pro-objectivity theory. So objectivity would inherently at least implicitly regard that theory positively, as correct. That is important—but there is also something very important here regarding evidence:-

The observable evidence discussed in this conclusion (4)'s previous paragraphs is *observable evidence for pro-objectivity theory's objectivity*. That is, those causal-connections regarding *objectivity,* the causal factors here being practised via pro-objectivity theory, are *empirical evidence* for the overall-objective-warrant of pro-objectivity theory and its ultimate end.

Causal connections regarding any other end, e.g., happiness-maximisation, are not evidence for the other end and related theory being *objective.*[44] No other theory can have observable evidence that practising it will maximally cause (achieve) objectivity overall (collectively) long-term, including achieving the therein pro-objectivity knowledge crucial for maximally achieving objectivity. This is because practising another theory achieves another end, a *non*-pro-objectivity end. The other end would be given higher priority than and would hence conflict with the pro-objectivity aim of maximally achieving objectivity as and via actual pro-objectivity knowledge. So no other normative theory is overall-objectively-warranted. None has such (or any) evidence.[45]

In sum, only pro-objectivity theory is directly and coherently (systematically, consiliently etc) involved with and supported by empirical evidence.

Theoretical connections, e.g., as explained by various arguments above demonstrating theoretical coherence between 'Be pro-objectivity' and objectivity, are (systemisation-helpful, consilience-producing) related theoretical evidence for the overall-objective-warrant of 'Be pro-objectivity'.

(5) Further theoretical evidence:- Fundamentally crucial regarding normative theories, and as far as possible solving the above-mentioned is-ought and other issues concerning values:-

Combining this subsection's (1)-(4), their previous supporting arguments, and various other arguments above, further supported by Appendixes 2-5, implies that the only coherent, evidenced and hence objective definition of 'correct', 'valuable', 'right', 'good' and so on is '*objective*' or '*overall-objectively-warranted*'. (If '(normatively) correct' and so on do not mean 'objective', or 'overall-objectively-warranted', what would they mean? They'd mean 'not objective(ly-warranted)', implying incoherently, e.g., that 'X is correct' does not truly or objectively mean that X is correct.) To define 'correct' and so on another way, is to define via an unobjective, in-effect anti-objectivity standard. E.g., defining happiness-maximisation as (normatively) correct while claiming that 'correct' here does not mean objective, obviously defines via a standard other than 'objective' or 'overall-objectively-warranted'. So such claims or definitions are not made via an objective viewpoint. So they are unobjective: such definitions of 'correct' (and so on) and such claims are incorrect from an evidence-based, objective, overall-objectively-warranted viewpoint.

The same applies to any theory claiming that any such other standard is correct. Equating 'correct', 'valuable' etc with 'objective' or 'overall-objectively-warranted' is the only way to avoid a wrong (unobjective) standard or theory. Such equating or defining is the case in rational, evidence-based science. E.g:- To state that 'Gravity causes tides' is correct, is to objectively state that 'Gravity causes tides' is objective. And if scientists say evidence is valuable, they (correctly) imply that evidence is objectively-warranted, partly via its coherence with and crucial importance within (the rest of) objectivity. (Regarding normativity, the only rational, evidence-based or objective (correct) substitution for 'evidence' in the previous sentence is something like: '(inherently evidenced) pro-objectivity'.)

In sum, such equating or defining is needed by a normative theory aiming to be as evidence-based as is possible for a normative theory. Further:-

Normative theories at least implicitly claim, 'X is the correct end' or similar. The 'is' here implies truth or objectivity. 'Is' means 'is truly'. To verify that claim and suggestion regarding any specific theory, sufficient evidence is needed. This would give the theory's 'X is the correct end' (or similar) objectivity. Yet the 'is' in 'X is the correct end' at least implicitly defines that claim as true and *already verified.* If verified, the verifier has sufficient evidence. This would mean the verifier *knows* it, i.e., that the claim is knowledge and hence objective. Or, at the very least, a theory-believer here could believe that that claim is true and *verifiable.* If it is verifiable, it is sufficiently evidenced, though that evidence is simply not yet accessed. Again, the theory or theory-believer at least implicitly defines the theory as true, as objective.

Hence, either way, all normative theories unavoidably, hence necessarily, at least implicitly define their fundamental and other crucial notions, as in 'X is the correct end', as being objective, as sufficiently evidenced.

In other words:- The only *necessary*, sufficiently *evidenced* and hence rational, coherent definition of 'correct', 'valuable', 'right', 'good' and so on is 'objective' or 'overall-objectively-warranted'. Only a theory providing (inherently rationally-unquestionable) evidence for itself can objectively state that its end is correct, valuable and so on. Only one normative theory can show it is objective, i.e., correct etc. To show that pro-objectivity theory is wrong would be to show it is objectively wrong, namely unobjective. If pro-objectivity theory is objective, it cannot rationally be shown or argued to be wrong.

So, pro-objectivity theory is the only correct or objective normative theory.

The above shows, as A.P. Griffiths suggests,[46] that practices needed *for* being normatively objective, namely pro-objectivity practices, are uniquely necessarily immune *from* objective or rational criticism. The objective, being inherently non-incoherent, cannot (self-)coherently criticise or reject the pro-objectivity, or objective, pro-objectivity theory. (Analogously, a ball cannot hit itself.) Relatedly, objectivity cannot (self-)coherently criticise or reject its own presuppositions or its own cognitive and motivational pro-objectivity, or hence its normatively-applicable premise, 'Be pro-objectivity'.

Similarly:- To reject or doubt an objective normative theory or part-thereof for reason X is to at least implicitly claim that X is the correct standard or perspective. This claims that X is more objective than the objective. To prove this, one must prove there's a standard or perspective more correct than correct, as in there being a more correct pure-mathematical answer to '1+1=?' than '2', i.e., '1+1'. One may like and (hence?) find plausible some X, e.g., intuition, happiness-maximisation or comforting delusions, but such subjectivity is irrelevant regarding evidence concerning which standard or perspective really is objective. (Besides, likes or emotions can often be overruled, minimised, turned off—or redirected to other objects.[47] It is correct or (objectively) better to like correct rather than incorrect objects. Appendix 6 is relevant here.)

Relatedly regarding asking, "Why, namely according to which standard or perspective, should one be objective (or normatively correct or similar)?". This also implicitly raises the is-ought and evaluative issue, specifically here: 'Objectively, ought we to do what is objectively what we ought to do?' or 'Are normatively-objective practices normatively-objective practices?', i.e., 'Is it correct to be correct?', which correctly assumes correctness is the correct standard or perspective, and is like the pointless, irrational, 'Is this what it is?' or 'Is Z Z?'.

In sum, because the is-ought issue concerns whether an 'ought' or values can be *objectively* or rationally obtained from an 'is', there is no problem here only when the 'is' is pro-objectivity *knowledge,* or knowledge of objective values: pro-objectivity theory and its end-ought, 'Be pro-objectivity', is knowledge, objectively arrived at via the evidence (objectivity) supporting it. Here the 'ought' is incorporated *in* and by the 'is'. Only here is there no gap between an 'is' and an 'ought', or no objectively or rationally problematic gap. (Appendix 5 discusses these issues further.) With this, (as also implied by Appendix 2's discussion of unavoidable, holistic circularity,) there can be no naturalistic *fallacy* here.[48] 'Fallacy' means rationally-problematic, unobjective.

(6) The above suggests pro-objectivity theory has the maximum quantity and quality of (crucial) evidence a normative theory could have. What more or other evidence *could there be here*? (This comment temporarily ignores Part I, Section 3's discussion of more evidence, namely for pro-objectivity theory's structural form, because that evidence is not crucial here.)

Rationality's inherently realistic viewpoint involves not insisting that permanently unavailable evidence is presented, or not delusorily (irrationally) believing there must be more. Rationality involves considering all the available evidence regarding an issue. So it is rational to at least provisionally accept 'Be pro-objectivity' as the objective normative end. Hence it is irrational, namely mistaken, to regard any other end as objective—as correct.

Relatedly:- What (inherently objective) evidence is there or could there be to prove that the only normative theory as coherent with and as causally-related or necessarily connected to objectivity as possible is unobjective? Evidence proving that would be incoherent with the evidence supplied by that coherence etc, which is impossible because evidence does not involve incoherence. That question needs considering in relation to this book's evidence that alternative theories are unobjective.

ENDNOTES TO PART I, SECTION 1

1 As discussed soon, the knowledge tends to concern how to achieve an end external to objectivity, e.g., 'Get rich'. But that is beside the internal-to-objectivity issue here. A close analogy:- A calculator's only (inherently-internal) purpose is to objectively calculate numbers. Within itself, i.e., internally, it does nothing else. It does not aim to achieve any other end, e.g., calculate numbers so as to use them to achieve its owner's end-aim, 'Get rich'. Such aims are external to the calculator, but direct its specific uses.

2 Appendix 2 discusses the unavoidable circularity here (and relatedly elsewhere). The basic assumptions, e.g., 'X is X' or '1 object is 1 object (not 2 etc)', seem innate: that which is objectivity/knowledge for us is at least basically natural, an evolved capacity.

3 Later, when needed, I qualify the term 'coherence', arguing, via simple examples, for 'orthogonally-systematic coherence'.

4 Observations-of-reality issues here are discussed via simple examples later, and Appendix 2 suggests how to rationally view the unavoidable circularity here. Such issues, other issues and controversies here are also discussed in often complex detail by various epistemologists such as those referred to in Appendix A.

5 E.g:- Suppose gravity began unpredictably doing to us that which is incoherent with what we now know gravity does to us. E.g., suppose we unpredictably sometimes floated away from Earth instead of being attracted toward Earth. Because this incoherence would mean incomprehensibility, here we could have no knowledge, namely of an inherently predictable, universally-applicable law concerning gravity regarding Earth. We could not know what to expect next regarding gravity's effect on us. (Our observations of what we perceive as reality here and elsewhere are of course crucial regarding knowledge's mental coherence, presently being discussed in the book's main body.)

6 End-aims external but connectable to objectivity can direct objectivity to seek knowledge instrumental regarding achieving those ends. E.g., persons with the end-aim, 'Get rich', are motivated to direct their objectivity to acquire knowledge of how to get rich.

7 An end-*principle* is not an end. It is a statement describing the end. Statements can be knowledge.

8 This even applies when the viewpoint is, 'I am incorrect'. This implicitly states: 'It is correct that I am incorrect'. Fundamentally, correctness (objectivity) is unavoidably, necessarily assumed. This important issue is discussed later, including in Appendix 3.

9 'Evidence for X' is evidence for X being true, i.e., objective. So evidence is also objective. (Appendix 2 discusses the unavoidable circularity here.)

10 As just explained in the book's main body, to have knowledge of what is causally pro-objectivity is to know what is anti-objectivity (and vice versa). That is, those relevant areas cover, respectively, the positively causal or relevant and the negatively causal or relevant. All remaining areas cover the causally neutral or irrelevant here. This need to distinguish among areas concerns *all* areas because, (as Appendix B argues further,) regarding any one thing, e.g., pro-objectivity, logically every other thing is related to that thing either positively (coherently), neutrally (irrelevantly) or negatively (incoherently). So pro-objectivity theory concerns all things and hence all areas, i.e., it is *applicable* to *all* moral, political etc areas. (Regarding each thing with that positive (pro-objectivity) relation to itself, it applies via prescribing 'Do this thing'. Regarding each thing with that negative (anti-objectivity) relation to itself, it applies via prescribing 'Do not do this thing'. Regarding each thing with that neutral (a-objectivity) relation to itself, it applies via prescribing 'You are free to either do or not do this thing; please yourself'.)

11 The previous endnote explains this. And, as shown further later, this includes a-objectivity areas in that it is pro-objectivity to treat the a-objectivity as a-objectivity.

12 E.g:- If '1=1' or 'X is X' is a foundation, it implies '1+1=1+1' or '1+1=2' or '2 is 2', and so on, which cohere with or support '1=1' or 'X is X'. But '1=1' or 'X is X' cannot imply '1+1=3' or '1+1=1+1+1' or '1+1 is not 1+1' and so on, or cohere therewith.

13 E.g., '1=1', '1+1=1+1', '1+1+1=1+1+1' and so on are coherent, forming a system.

14 Consistency among statements only means they do not contradict each other. '1+2=3' and 'Cows are mammals' are consistent—but they are importantly separate regarding knowledge (though at a fundamental level they are linked (coherent) via, e.g., 'cows' involving plurality and hence arithmetic). Appendix 1 discusses consistency further.

15 Whewell (1858-60). Consilience is "extremely important" regarding knowledge, as pointed out by Simon Blackburn (*Oxford Dictionary of Philosophy* (1996) Oxford University Press p 78)). Relatedly, something like W.V. Quine's 'web of belief' is involved. Quine & Ullian (1978)

16 Unchosen objectivity seems possible, e.g., via one's (inherently pro-objectivity) curiosity instinct subconsciously motivating one to notice (know) one's environment.

17 Kant's universalisability end has a similar unresolvable problem due to being too general. E.g., the following universalisable prescriptions (ends) can conflict: 'Save innocent lives by whatever means seem likely to work, including deceiving intending murderers of innocents' and 'Never deceive anyone'.

18 E.g., 'Never (intentionally) deceive anyone' is a general end in that it covers innumerable actual and possible specific 'Tempted to deceive' situations; but it is also sufficiently specific for anyone with that as their ultimate end to always know what to do in any such specific situation.

19 Knowledge so acquired is of course not incoherent with other knowledge—an entirely cognitive issue. As shown further soon, it is the seeking or acquiring of that knowledge which is incoherent with being overall pro-objectivity—a normative, overall issue.

20 When on Earth, we naturally perceive Earth as basically stationary. Thence, we naturally perceive the sun as orbiting Earth. The natural is not necessarily the best, or correct: both such perceptions are in-themselves illusions, namely unobjective—which only objectivity can know, via its overall, high-level viewpoint reflecting on and unifying or (as Whewell says) 'consiliating' all the evidence here needed for knowledge. (However, again, in another, important sense, our objectivity is also natural.)

21 Non-cognitive intended achievements here occur partly via cognition, namely the knowledge directing the required practices.

22 Regarding an achievement which would have happened anyway via a here-sufficient combination of here-necessary factors, 'helpful' factors make the achievement better in some way, e.g., easier and/or faster. However, the helpful-there are necessary for that improvement. Regarding factors optimal for maximising pro-objectivity as soon as possible, pro-objectivity's ideal normative aim here, all those causal factors are necessary.

23 Other factors here are or were unchoosable, e.g., Earth's existence as a suitable place on which to evolve and accommodate those potentially pro-objectivity beings, humans.

24 This was explained near the beginning of Part I, Section 1.1.

25 E.g., many were rationally critical of Nazi racism: they at least implicitly had and used the pro-objectivity knowledge that, e.g., as explained shortly, racism is anti-objectivity.

26 Other ends here do not require knowledge, but have that limiting or destructive effect. E.g., certain bacteria inherently and ignorantly aim at an end which can mean the death of pro-objectivity persons.

27 Knowledge useless or irrelevant regarding achieving objectivity is in-itself hence normatively a-objectivity, and hence not incoherent with pro-objectivity. The general situa-

tion here is discussed later. And the knowledge as such, as opposed to what it can be used to achieve, is inherently not incoherent with the rest of knowledge/objectivity.

28 A-objectivity ends, discussed later, are external to objectivity but are inherently not anti-objectivity. So they cannot be objectively wrong. They are irrelevant to objectivity, i.e., a-objectivity. They are objectively neither right nor wrong.

29 I'm not implying there are only male and female genders. E.g., intersex persons are a third gender. Note too that here 'Sam' can be the name of a person of any gender.

30 E.g., the situation concerning sexist Sam did not involve (perceived) racial differences; so, though values concerning sexism were relevant, values concerning racism were not.

31 'Potentially' here refers to all possible or 'if' events, namely those which conceivably could occur but have not yet occurred and may never occur. E.g:- Here, if someone of a gender or race person P considers inferior were to state, "To survive, avoid cliff-falls" while P approaches a high cliff, then because P intends to survive, which here must be via that objectivity/knowledge, here-non-silly P would not disbelieve that statement. That is, here P would not be sexist or racist *if* such a situation occurred.

32 This is because the range of a-objectivity things here includes far more than sexism, racism and so on. In *every* possible survival-threatening situation there is *something* a-objectivity which consistently anti-objectivity persons would not treat as a-objectivity. E.g:- Suppose the only available objectively nutritious food to avoid starvation is berries on the west side of a plant, and it is a-objectivity (here-irrelevant) whether berries are on this or that side. Anti-objectivity (silly) persons here would (for some silly reason) believe that west-side berries are not objectively nutritious, perhaps poisonous, not eat them, and die. So *no* correct survival-necessary choice could ever be made by consistently anti-objectivity persons. They'd all die very soon.

33 Again, this does not include a-objectivity ends. In that normativity concerns choices which are either correct or incorrect, a-objectivity ends are not normative ends.

34 Again, this does not mean objectivity is inherently pro- seeking or acquiring simply any and all knowledge, and not able to critically reflect on whether seeking or acquiring some knowledge can be anti-objectivity.

35 A-objectivity ends are also left over. But, as explained in recent endnotes, and explained further later, none of them could be an objective end because they are irrelevant to and hence outside of objectivity. They are also not *normative* ends in that a *normative* theory prescribes only the end(s) the theory considers unconditional or ultimate; and pro-objectivity normative theory considers a-objectivity ends as just options, not ultimate oughts.

36 Coherence with survival-necessary knowledge requires disbelieving the unevidenced, and hence disbelieving non-pro-objectivity normative theories. Otherwise one is irrational and overall incoherent, namely mistaken. Appendix 4 discusses this.

37 The (directly) instrumental knowledge discussed here is the just-mentioned 'directly practical' knowledge. The theoretical knowledge discussed here is the just-mentioned 'ultimately practical' knowledge, and its general nature means it is 'indirectly instrumental' as explained in Appendix 6. 'Directly instrumental' knowledge is specific. These distinctions are mostly unimportant, and the book's main body mostly ignores them, e.g., normally using 'instrumental' instead of 'directly instrumental'.

38 The knowledge as such involved in (directly) instrumental potential pro-objectivity knowledge is ambiguous in that, again, it could be used in either pro-objectivity or anti-objectivity ways. E.g., knowledge of poisons can be used to avoid poisoning pro-objectivity persons, or to kill them. Directly instrumental pro-objectivity knowledge is defined primarily not by the content of the knowledge as such, but via choices concern-

ing how the knowledge is used. This instrumental knowledge needs combining with the (indirectly instrumental) theoretical knowledge explaining why choices here should be pro-objectivity. Each combination here is a pro-objectivity prescription.

39 The absolute ideal here is all potential pro-objectivity knowledge known by each individual. An achievable, i.e., practicable ideal here is less than that maximum but much more than presently achieved, and probably only possible long-term, and collectively because, e.g., no individual seems able to ever know all the specific knowledge involved. Still, importantly, judging via my 30 plus years teaching across all age and ability ranges, most people seem able to know all the general or guideline knowledge and at least the gist of why the guidelines are objectively-warranted, plus many specifics.

40 This does not mean all doing work such as garbage disposal are intellectually disabled. I often do such work. Many others here are at least potentially very able cognitively.

41 With this, pro-objectivity theory has serious reservations concerning, e.g., euthanasia of intellectually-disabled people. E.g:- They can be directed to practise pro-objectivity prescriptions, help us learn how to prevent and cure such disabilities, and, as suggested soon, their deaths can produce anti-objectivity distress in relatives/others. Also, treatment interpretable by some as cruel or non-respectful can generalise, e.g., facilitating them believing that murdering highly able pro-objectivity persons is acceptable.

42 'X is intrinsically valuable' means 'X is valuable for its own sake, not for any further purpose it may serve'. 'X is extrinsically valuable' means 'X is instrumentally valuable, i.e., valuable for some further purpose'. The intrinsically valuable is an ultimate end. The extrinsically valuable is, from an end's viewpoint, valuable as a means to that end.

43 This 'pro-objectivity-relevant' qualification applies to all this book's (often implicit) 'all else equal' qualifications of a notion. 'All else' covers more than the pro-objectivity-relevant. Anything a-objectivity is not pro-objectivity-relevant.

44 E.g., suppose there is evidence that, compared to lying unconvincingly, lying convincingly is more likely to help egoists fool people so as to achieve the egoist's end, 'Be selfish'. Such evidence would only be evidence that lying convincingly is here the better means to that end. It is not evidence that the end, 'Be selfish', is objective or correct.

45 As the previous endnote implies, some small *bits* of other theories can have evidence, e.g., with a pro-pleasure theory, a bit such as 'sex can give great pleasure', but this is merely instrumental or means-to-an-end evidence or knowledge, not evidence that the end is objective. So the overall theory contexting such bits lacks evidence, e.g., here, the theory that pleasure should be one's ultimate end. Relatedly, as normative theories primarily concern ends, not means, if the only evidence a theory has concerns means, this is not evidence for this *normative* theory being objective. There is no evidence, and can be no evidence, that any normative theory except a *fundamentally* objective theory, one with an objective *end*, is objective in any meaningful sense, i.e., sufficiently evidenced. An analogy is a car with some working bits not related to its primary, basic nature, 'drivability', say a radio and cigarette lighter, but the car overall does not work—it is not drivable. It lacks sufficient fundamental coherence, namely among the basic, important engine, wheel etc parts regarding its primary nature. Objectively, it is overall not what rational persons would call a '(working or real, i.e., objective or true,) car'.

46 Griffiths (1957-8) pp. 103-124.

47 E.g., many who once liked smoking changed to liking non-smoking, preferring their hence now healthier lives. (Evidence or objectivity concerning smoking's unhealthiness was crucial in redirecting the emotions crucially involved here.) See Appendix 6.

48 The naturalistic fallacy is a version of the is-ought issue. Moore (1903), e.g., 62-69.

PART I, SECTION 2: MORE PRELIMINARY DISCUSSION OF PRACTICAL APPLICATIONS

(Part II discusses this preliminary Section's examples, and many other examples, in more depth than is done here.)

This Section shows much further that 'Be pro-objectivity' is universally normatively applicable. The Section gives examples of pro-objectivity prescriptions or areas which are far more specific and more explained than most given above. Again, specific pro-objectivity prescriptions are practicable constituents of the general, 'Be pro-objectivity'—not additional (allegedly) objective ends. Before the prescriptions, some associated issues regarding them:-

Recent discussion implies that practices viewed as right, good, correct or similar by a theory are not objectively right, good, correct or similar unless the theory is pro-objectivity. (This can be a matter of degree, as in the above-explained 'significant (but not maximal) pro-objectivity'.) Otherwise, at least fundamentally, such views are merely claims, mistaken claims—regardless of how convinced or passionate theory-holders are, or of the fact that some such claims are common or popular intuitions or beliefs.[1] E.g:-

Suppose caring for babies is regarded as good by theory T because T is explicitly based on common moral intuitions, and normal humans commonly intuit (believe) they should care for (at least their close-circle's) babies. The ultimate at least implicit basis here involves emotions, involving projection of sympathy and love or similar regarding children—emotions which evolved as common because the practice of caring for one's group's next generation's gene-bearers is commonly crucially evolutionarily-advantageous for the group or humanity. But, as implied above (and specifically explained below), moral or normative intuitions and evolutionary-advantage as such are not objective normative standards.

Still, this Section shows there is often significant overlap between pro-objectivity prescriptions and various other theories' prescriptions. (Here the other theories are to some degree correct.) The latter include many prescriptions at least implicitly based on common normative intuitions involving emotional/moral projections. This is because, for us, pro-objectivity practices are those which are pro-objectivity for us *evolved* humans—and, evidence suggests, various normative intuitions involving emotional/moral projections evolved, becoming normal among humans (in common environments). That is, some of the overlap is because, for any society/group to survive, it must regard certain general types of practices as morally or normatively correct, as what ought to be done. E.g:- Human babies need care for years, and unless a society cares for them instead of letting them all die, the society will not survive. So 'care for your group's babies (if reasonably possible, e.g., if resources permit)' normally tends to be thought morally correct, world-wide. It is an evolved, natural, common moral or normative intuition, and, relatedly, parents and others naturally tend to project positively-valued lovability, and associated 'he/she needs caring for', onto (especially their group's) children, and naturally experience positively-valued care-motivating sympathy towards them if they appear to need care.

So, regarding such and all survival-necessary areas there is a 'survival-necessary normative core', namely core values consisting of on-average survival-necessary normative values and involving related normative intuitions/projections—a core common to all survival-viable societies. This common core, with some qualifications, is *also* necessary for pro-objectivity, so there is overlap here between pro-objectivity theory and other theories at least implicitly also prescribing that core. Practices fulfilling thereto-related human natural needs here, e.g., inherently dependent babies' needs for food, safety etc, in short, '(basic) child-care', are practices needed for us to achieve, maintain and increase (the rest of) pro-objectivity. (E.g., most basically, dead children cannot be pro-objectivity or help produce the future generation needed to maintain/increase whatever pro-objectivity exists. Similarly regarding children who are physically and/or psychologically severely undernourished.)

More generally, as indicated in the Introduction, a non-pro-objectivity theory may have various isolated bits the same as bits of pro-objectivity theory, e.g., too-abbreviated, unqualified pro-objectivity prescriptions such as 'Care for children' and 'Be unselfish'. But it is important to remember that non-pro-objectivity theories lack fundamental and overall coherence. The premise(s) via which they arrive at such prescription-conclusions are not objective. As Part II Section 1.3 explains further, they can seem right only due to emotional/moral intuition/projection, as opposed to evidence. For that and/or some other reason(s) the theories contexting any such bit are not overall-objectively-warranted. As isolated prescriptions uncontexted or unqualified via pro-objectivity, they can be somewhat or potentially pro-objectivity, but are not overall pro-objectivity. E.g., consider a pro-unselfishness theory, ultimately at least implicitly beginning with the premise, 'Be unselfish', and thereby (problematically-circularly) concluding: 'Be unselfish'. This prescription can also be isolated as an unqualified bit within pro-objectivity theory. However, as discussed further soon, pro-objectivity theory qualifies it by the need to be unselfish only in pro-objectivity ways—among all at least potentially pro-objectivity beings. 'Be unselfish' as such, i.e., unqualified, includes requiring one to be unselfish in some overall-objectively-*un*warranted ways, say via sharing one's food, weapons, financial etc resources with irredeemably anti-objectivity Nazis, in-effect helping them to affect pro-objectivity persons in anti-objectivity ways.

A general major point here is that such unqualified bits or prescriptive conclusions need linking to objective *premises*, so that, along with premise-related qualifications, they can become normatively objective. An Introduction endnote is relevant here. It explained that, if pro-objectivity theory implies a prescriptive conclusion which, if too-abbreviated and unqualified, is the same as another theory's, e.g., 'Be unselfish', as with all its conclusions pro-objectivity theory arrives at that unqualified conclusion via premises radically different from those used by the other theory. This is only 'conclusion-overlap', and is like different arguments leading to the same, true scientific conclusion, with only one such argument being overall objective—the others being unobjective via having false premises or lacking evidence. E.g., consider the objective conclusion: 'Earth's shape is (approximately) spherical'. An ancient argument here concludes Earth is spherical via premises something like: 'The gods, being loving, perfect and beauty-admiring, gave Earth, home of their most-loved creation, humans, the only perfectly beautiful shape. The only perfectly beautiful shape is spherical'. Modern science (and some other ancients) used objective premises and arguments involving sufficient evidence to confirm Earth is (approximately) spherical. (Note that unobjective premises only sometimes, merely by chance, lead to objective conclusions: unobjective premises typically lead to false conclusions. E.g., that gods-based argument also implies that the gods made us spherical.)

In sum, though pro-objectivity theory overlaps and significantly agrees with many prescriptions from various other theories, it only totally agrees with them if they (change so as to) have evidenced premises and are qualified thereby.

Also, importantly, pro-objectivity theory totally rejects many prescriptions from some other theories, including some based on common, non-survival-necessary (indeed only sometimes survival-helpful, potentially survival-threatening) normative intuitions—e.g., the intuition or primarily-emotional normative projection involving in-group members viewing perceived out-groups as morally suspect, evil or a threat, preferably needing to be, e.g., kept at bay, perhaps attacked, dominated or eliminated. (Any previous evolutionary advantage here is arguably a disadvantage these days, with the possibility of groups/societies destroying each other by modern weapons.) Such intuitions, and associated dispositions and emotions can lead to nationalistic war, social-class domination, racist hatred, religious conflict, genocide, slavery and excessively violent imperial expansion. Pro-objectivity theory prescribes ignoring or overruling any such intuitions or emotions, and prescribes ending such practices.[2]

Prescriptions in this Section (and others) are sometimes just suggestions. At least some may need critical research. One aim of this book it to just suggest hypotheses here for future research. The theory is a work-in-progress, fallible regarding various specifics.[3] Some prescriptions below (and above) may only be probable or approximate knowledge. Some are perhaps only possible knowledge, which should hence perhaps only be accepted and practised provisionally, as trials in trial-and-error knowledge-acquisition. (Such qualifications and warnings are normally implicit below, but should be remembered.)

However, we already at least implicitly have much at least approximate knowledge in various pro-objectivity areas, knowledge interpretable as explicit pro-objectivity knowledge. (E.g., we know approximately which quantity and qualities of sleep are on-average long-term most likely best for various types of persons to think their clearest, concentrate best and learn at their best rate, and approximately which diets are helpful here. This existing (at least approximate) knowledge is (re-)interpretable as pro-objectivity knowledge regarding human motivation and ability to acquire other pro-objectivity knowledge.)

Any approximateness or uncertainty involved with pro-objectivity knowledge is often manageable. Overall, we could already manage to soon greatly increase pro-objectivity, judging by facts such as the increasing advances in (knowledge of how to achieve advances in) health-care, education, diet, productivity and technology, and the advances in intellectual and related freedoms achieved in the past few centuries in much of the world. Similarly, various societies/groups have already become at least significantly directly pro-objectivity overall, though they tend not to explicitly use that term. E.g:- Some influential groups in some powerful societies promote critical rationality. As mentioned in the Introduction, significant pro-objectivity begins, e.g., when one goes beyond simply believing a normative theory (is true) largely because one's society/group believes it, and instead begins to ask if there is evidence for it, i.e., whether it can be knowledge (and so really is true). Similarly regarding religion, the basis of many normative theories. Such types of significantly pro-objectivity critical rationality have definitely increased world-wide over recent centuries. And various societies have outlawed and greatly reduced racism and sexism, showing, as explained in Part I, Section 1.2, they are pro-objectivity societies here.

In sum, because such significant pro-objectivity, knowledge generally and knowledge (re-)interpretable as pro-objectivity knowledge have greatly increased, it seems likely we can increasingly reduce uncertainty and approach a maximum presently-achievable, major absolute degree of pro-objectivity over at least much of the world. (Education could do much here, reasonably quickly.)

The examples below, of prescriptions this book suggests are needed to achieve that, can be ordered systematically. The hierarchy here would be similar to (but not the same as) Maslow's hierarchy.[4] It could be interpreted to go from practices which are the minimum needed to be minimally pro-objectivity in some area, up to practices optimal for maximising pro-objectivity overall—involving a pro-objectivity-optimal balance among those practices.

As this is a preliminary Section, examples of prescriptions here only outline representative parts of a complex, coherent, balanced whole. Precisely what constitutes any such (on-average[5]) balance, often among competing factors,[6] is obviously somewhat uncertain—another issue needing research. Its complexity means some unavoidable approximateness and fallibility.

One important issue regarding that balance is that there can be too much emphasis on the cognitive or intellectual. Objectivity's overall view includes viewing the achievable absolute maximisation of pro-objectivity knowledge as a long-term achievement. This view recognises that there can be so much direct short and medium term focusing on that cognitive task, and so little attention given to short and medium term *non*-cognitive pro-objectivity needs, needs very important regarding that long-term cognitive maximisation, that the cognitive maximisation is not achieved or is more slowly achieved.

Suggested prescriptions below, because they are abbreviations, involve implicit qualifications. E.g:-

One concerns the need for the above-mentioned fallibilism, self-criticism etc due to above-exemplified and other uncertainties. Despite such uncertainties or vagueness, one can still be as objective as possible here—and this can often reduce or manage such uncertainties. A related qualification (and prescription) is that it is pointless (irrational) to be consumed by wariness of knowledge-seeking's fallibility. After all, it is only via objectivity/knowledge that we can know problems exist here—and that solutions are often available, or that some mitigation, construction, and/or an acceptance of approximateness, is reasonable.

A qualification following 'Do X' or similar is: 'only if X is pro-objectivity, which involves X fitting into that coherent, pro-objectivity-balanced whole, as part of a complex system of causal chains'. E.g., suppose X is 'be(ing) alive'. To be a pro-objectivity prescription, this needs qualifying because 'be(ing) alive' is not necessarily coherent with pro-objectivity. E.g., euthanasia of the otherwise slowly miserably dying can be pro-objectivity. And consider Nazis who as far as can be known were most likely to remain mass-murderers of actually or potentially significantly pro-objectivity persons, and could only be stopped by being killed. Their being alive was overall-objectively-unwarranted.

Relatedly, a 'situationality' qualification may be needed. Something pro-objectivity in one situation or case might not be elsewhere—as in it being overall anti-objectivity for those Nazis to have been alive, but pro-objectivity for their defeaters to have been alive. Similarly, say, eating nuts is pro-objectivity for Harry but is anti-objectivity for Sarah, via her nut allergy. A 'need for situational flexibility' qualifies the recently-mentioned balance. Similarly, a qualification often needed involves 'version or type(s) of'. E.g., as argued shortly, some types (quantities/qualities) of happiness can promote pro-objectivity; others do not.

Next, the suggested representative prescriptions. These have moral, social, political, legal, educational, economic, medical, environmental, psychological and other implications—involving human flourishing, duties, rights and virtues. (N.B: These prescriptions exemplify Section 1.4 (4)'s important point that certain practices provide empirical evidence for pro-objectivity theory.):-

A crucial prescription here is: 'Be pro-objectivity-directed universally altruistic', i.e., 'be universally unselfish in ways directed by and at pro-objectivity'. This involves supplying, as far as possible, in that flexible balance, all pro-objectivity needs of all at least potentially pro-objectivity beings. A type of universal unselfish caring, involving all actual and potential pro-objectivity beings and other factors,[7] and hence redeemable overall (on-average) anti-objectivity beings, is pro-objectivity. This excludes only beings who, as far as can be known, are irredeemably anti-objectivity,[8] like those Nazis. It most importantly includes children, who need to be given the start in life they need to become maximally pro-objectivity adults.

A basic social-psychological need here is the emotional security achievable only via knowing oneself is loved and cared for unselfishly. Such security involves normatively-objectively subjectively-needed trust and confidence. Lacks here, for children and adults, tend to mean one is, e.g., so anxious and/or depressed and anti-social, that one, and often those one affects, could not adequately acquire and practise pro-objectivity knowledge. Knowledge is crucially largely societally acquired and resourced, involves a society's language, and the sociability and society needed for optimal social acquisition of pro-objectivity knowledge requires such altruism-produced security. This involves pro-objectivity *societal coherence* (harmony), a coherence coherent with (the rest of) pro-objectivity, crucially needed for overall (total), balanced pro-objectivity.

Relatedly, that benevolence involves aiming for peace (non-incoherence or non-conflict) within and among persons. This pacifism also needs qualifying. E.g., intellectual passivity is anti-objectivity or anti-knowledge; and war is pro-objectivity if victory, e.g., over Nazis, seems likely to increase overall (world-wide, long-term) pro-objectivity, including pro-objectivity peace.

This altruism and peace would also involve pro-objectivity legally-protected fair or just balances among society's benefits and costs (in the overall (widest) senses of 'benefits' and 'costs'). Sympathy, motivating distribution of benefits to anyone presently unfairly treated here, e.g., regarding health-care, is another aspect of that pro-objectivity benevolence.

Within the (approximately, fallibly, flexible) balanced system of pro-objectivity factors, most important overall is a type of society (and its optimally-sustaining environment), its education system and largely thereby its rulers' pro-objectivity knowledge. A society involving such benevolent caring, ruled via explicitly pro-objectivity versions of various prescriptions J.S. Mill advocates in *On Liberty,* would be far more pro-objectivity than, e.g., societies stifling rational criticism. Relatedly, educational institutions developing imagination and rational critical abilities are more pro-objectivity than, e.g., narrow-minded, dogmatic religious schools, colleges etc. Teaching philosophy, which should involve developing imagination and rational critical abilities, can crucially help create and maintain that society. The word 'philosophy' literally means 'highly pro-knowledge', which implies being highly pro-objectivity. Philosophers by definition are the most directly pro-objectivity persons. (If people claiming to be philosophers are not at least highly pro-objectivity, they're not philosophers.) Teachers should primarily be philosophers, and only thence, namely via a highly theoretically-informed context, also teach other subjects.

Via such education, this (preferably world-)society can be ruled by direct democracy.[9] Direct democracy (practicable and affordable now via the internet) is prescribed by pro-objectivity because, e.g:- Knowledge-acquisition is a large-scale collective, fallible work-in-progress, meaning that absolutist, rationally-uncritical dogmatic rule by a tiny minority, which commonly occurs in political dictatorships,[10] is objectively-unwarranted. To rule, vote or decide regarding issue X, an important notion is '(X-relevant) pro-objectivity-directed informedness', i.e., people 'informed (knowledgeable) in ways directed by and at pro-objectivity'. All people with equal sufficient such (X-relevant) informedness objectively deserve equal decision-making rights regarding X. Across all issues, or overall, there'd be far less or no such informedness in a dictator's mind than, e.g., among Australia's and USA's well-educated present citizens. And in a highly pro-objectivity society, via appropriate education at least nearly all persons would have sufficient such informedness regarding some issues, hence entitling at least the vast majority to vote here, ruling out dictatorship.

In other words, decision-makers (here all voters) would need to demonstrate sufficient relevant potentially pro-objectivity knowledge[11]—meaning evidence-based politics, with objective(ly-deserved) voting etc rights. As argued later, in a-objectivity areas a different, degree-of-subjective-preference voting scheme seems appropriate. (Part II discusses both democracies at length.)

Relatedly, that society's altruism would prescribe treating each individual as an individual, not treating different individuals the same, under a normatively-objectively inappropriate blanket rule such as 'All (except the extremely insane, criminal etc) over 18 get a vote, only one vote, and typically only once every few years, in-effect regarding all the often-unforeseen issues over those years'.

Pro-objectivity individualism would also prescribe acting on the fact that pro-objectivity knowledge can only exist in and be practised via (crucially socially-educated) individual brains, and that different individuals have different needs, abilities etc here. E.g:-

Suppose, all else pro-objectivity-relevant equal, eating fish oil to improve brain functioning, plus having a loving soul-mate, meditation, a pet, fun with friends and exercising more so as to reduce somewhat mentally-disabling depression, would increase Jim's pro-objectivity achievements from their at present just significant level. 'Eat fish oil', 'Find a loving soul-mate', 'Meditate', 'Get a pet', 'Have fun with friends', 'Exercise more' and 'Overcome depression' are prescriptions pro-objectivity society would help Jim implement. However, another individual may have significantly different pro-objectivity needs, and, if so, would be helped accordingly. (These are examples of flexible, pro-objectivity situationality.)

Relatedly, pro-objectivity society would benevolently practise the pro-objectivity knowledge (prescription) that each individual's emotions are very important. Happiness is one emotion which can be especially important:- Reducing depression or any suffering increases happiness or lessens unhappiness. Happiness tends to be subjectively-evaluated as intrinsically-valuable, and can also and thereby be extrinsically-valuable (instrumentally useful) regarding pro-objectivity. Happiness (and various other emotions) can help maintain or improve other pro-objectivity factors, as with Jim. One crucial pro-objectivity need is the absence of misery so disabling that overall pro-objectivity achievement is minimised or impossible. As suggested by various researchers, beyond that disabling degree there is probably a pro-objectivity-optimal range of happiness,[12] up to the point where it will soon be that "bliss means ignorance", including ignorance of pro-objectivity—though such issues are complex[13] and hence somewhat uncertain. But it is certain that, if happiness-maximisation is one's ultimate end, this conflicts with being overall-objectively-warranted: pro-objectivity would not be one's highest priority. However, maximising pro-objectivity *fulfilment*, involving types of flourishing, a balanced mix of passion, contentment and other emotions, involving types of happiness, is an achievement associated and hence coherent with maximising pro-objectivity. So, much, qualified happiness is for humans an achievable ideal *aspect* of the end, 'Be(ing) pro-objectivity'.

Generally regarding emotion (and, importantly, with (a) below, similarly regarding various aesthetic experiences):-

(a) First, concerning indirectly pro-objectivity emotions, e.g., happiness:-

Very importantly, various emotional experiences and their objects[14] can be *both,* (i) from one's subjective viewpoint, intrinsically-valuable, and (ii) from (pro-)objectivity's overall, primarily cognitive viewpoint, objectively extrinsically-valuable, as with Jim's pro-objectivity improving generally via him loving and enjoying his new soul-mate. Such emotion-thought combinations are '(pro-objectivity) subjective-objective evaluation-combinations':-

Because of pro-objectivity effects as in (ii), subjective-objective evaluation-combinations mean the *end*, 'Be pro-objectivity', is achieved at all, or achieved more easily and/or quickly and/or to an improved absolute degree and/or in more areas. From pro-objectivity's overall view, because its normative end is intrinsically-valuable to it, therefore, (as also implied by Part I, Section 1.4 (1)-(2),) it is objectively *intrinsically-valuable* to have such *end-achieving combinations* of (i) and (ii). The *overall* situations here, crucially involving subjective-objective evaluation-combinations,[15] are objectively intrinsically-valuable.

The (i) here concerns at least potentially pro-objectivity deep human needs. Fulfilling one's own needs pro-objectivity-optimally here is crucial 'unselfish self-care', discussed further in Part II, Section 1.8.1.1. Fulfilling others' needs optimally here, contexted via subjective-objective evaluation-combinations, is crucial overall-objectively-warranted altruism.

Those crucialities mean that so-contexted emotions/objects subjectively evaluated as intrinsically-valuable are *objectively highly-valuable.* From a pro-objectivity viewpoint, they should be experienced or enjoyed, without reservation, *as* subjectively intrinsically-valuable and objectively highly-valuable, because this is crucial regarding achieving the objectively intrinsically-valuable end.[16] (Such experience/enjoyment is part of pro-objectivity human flourishing.)

With this, the *objects* of those pro-objectivity emotional experiences are *primary*, essential factors in the experiences—and *persons* are often the objects or crucial aspects of the objects.[17] As with Jim's soul-mate, one way in which persons are objectively uniquely highly-valuable is that only persons can fulfil many of the recently-mentioned and various other deep human needs, needs the fulfilling of which can increase pro-objectivity. And, again, it is objective to regard all at least potentially pro-objectivity persons as objectively uniquely highly-valuable due to them alone being capable of knowingly achieving the objective, intrinsically-valuable normative end, and hence of at least potential objective intrinsic value; or objectively highly important just due to their capacity to be directed to achieve that end. Regarding each other thus, involving the enjoyable mutual respect objectively deserved here, and involving other mutually-bonding emotional experiences or enjoyment, will help concerning the social harmony (coherence) crucially needed for humanity-overall maximal pro-objectivity, interrelated with other pro-objectivity coherence.

(b) Directly pro-objectivity emotions, e.g., as in our curiosity instinct, also involve experiences subjectively-evaluated as intrinsically-valuable. E.g., it can be enjoyably challenging to solve problems, to seek worthwhile (namely pro-objectivity) knowledge and deeply fulfilling to acquire it. In a pro-objectivity context, these emotions should be enjoyed or experienced as subjectively intrinsically-valuable and objectively directly, fundamentally valuable.

(c) Finally here, generalisable comments regarding Part I, Section 1.2's claim that, from the pro-objectivity overall viewpoint, Nazis and similar were/are wrong for reasons other than reducing actual and/or potential objectivity/knowledge as such, reasons overlapping normative intuitions common in many societies, e.g., concerning cruelty:-

The present Section implies that claim. E.g., Nazi violence, cruelty and malevolence terrorised, bereaved, starved and otherwise distressed millions, causing massive reductions of at least potentially pro-objectivity subjective-objective evaluation-combinations and therewith-involved needed, fulfilling experiences. Pro-violence, cruelty, malevolence and similar are anti-objectivity.[18] They conflict with what normal humans deeply need regarding experiencing the emotions/objects involvable in that natural interaction between the non-cognitive and cognitive via subjective-objective evaluation-combinations. Cruelly disaffecting the subjectively-evaluated as intrinsically-valuable and objectively at least highly-valuable here can make it *far less possible* for one to be pro-objectivity—e.g., say, via Nazis murdering pro-objectivity Johan's much-loved family (he escaped), his loss causing him to be long-term depressed to a pro-objectivity-disabling degree. For such and other reasons, Nazism, cruelty, pro-violence and similar are wrong. Limiting or destroying anyone's potential to become pro-objectivity, or delaying the development of that potential, is anti-objectivity. And, of course, (via being pro-violence, pro-cruelty etc,) Nazis do not have pro-objectivity as their highest-priority—and are wrong for that general reason too.

The previous paragraph can be adapted to apply to all other groupism,[19] e.g., sexism and economic-classism and, relatedly, to egoism or selfishness.)

Finally here, again, prescriptions suggested in this Section are often expanded on later, and many others are discussed later.

ENDNOTES TO PART I, SECTION 2

1 It was once widely believed that the sun orbits Earth, and that racism, slavery, monarchy and sexism are right. That is, popularity or the number of believers is not necessarily a guide regarding a belief's objectivity.

2 Pro-objectivity theory prescribes not allowing any irredeemably anti-objectivity group to disaffect pro-objectivity. But this is not an unobjective, ignorant prejudice based on generalised, primitive groupist intuition or primarily-emotional projection.

3 Fallibility here, in this book, is because in an important sense these hypothesised prescriptions come from just one person, me—though many other persons indirectly helped suggest many of them. The prescriptions come from decades of studying experts in sociology, education, history, psychology, economics, politics, anthropology, natural science and so on. But there are gaps in my and their knowledge here, and probably at least a few errors. People (including me) trying to be pro-objectivity might also unknowingly suggest some non-pro-objectivity hypotheses, e.g., due to them naturally liking a common normative intuition they are subjectively strongly influenced by, hoping it is also a pro-objectivity prescription. Much care and rational criticism is needed.

4 (It is important to note that 'similar' does not mean 'the same as'.) Maslow's hierarchy orders what Maslow considers human needs, from basic, survival-necessary needs such as food, up to certain alleged cultural, intellectual and similar needs. Maslow (1962). Beyond basic biological needs, pro-objectivity needs differ at least significantly from Maslow's alleged needs.

5 An overall view considers what is optimal on-average, long-term. Sometimes, large short-term deviations from that average could mean long-term optimality regarding maximising pro-objectivity. E.g., there could be a temporary need to work much longer and sleep much less during an emergency, the resolution of which is important regarding long-term maximal pro-objectivity.

6 E.g., the health needed for maximal pro-objectivity involves a balance between rest and activity.

7 'Other factors' here include such things as rivers. A pro-objectivity world would require rivers, trees, a certain climate-range, certain quantities and qualities of food and so on—and such factors may need us to put resources into them to help them become or remain pro-objectivity. E.g., massive climate change could destroy humanity, the potentially most pro-objectivity beings (as far as we know).

8 'Irredeemable anti-objectivity' refers to an at least *high* anti-objectivity degree. If there is reasonable doubt whether someone is irredeemably anti-objectivity, extra pro-objectivity education, counselling and/or other help should be given, to give them more opportunities, motivation and ability to become pro-objectivity. The number of undoubtedly irredeemably anti-objectivity people would be a tiny minority, consisting of much the same types modern (2010) societies typically remove from society anyway, to protect the vast majority, e.g., murderous psychopaths lacking the brain parts needed for sympathy—as with many fanatical Nazis.

9 'Direct democracy', also called 'participatory democracy', ideally involves all adults being the legislators. Here voters vote on *issues*. Each issue is in-effect decided by a referendum (practicable and affordable now via the internet). There are no politicians, except in that all voters are politicians: in direct democracy, voters are in-effect rulers and the ruled. Each voter can represent themselves in politics.

10 Some temporary dictatorships can be highly pro-objectivity. E.g., parents and teachers tend and need to be somewhat dictatorial with young children, and this can (and should) be primarily to ultimately help liberate children to later become autonomous, maximally pro-objectivity adults, not needing dictating to. This is very different from typical political dictatorships.

11 Existing (2010) societies often do something much like this anyway, regarding important decisions. (Politics is important.) E.g:- You'd prefer a neurologically-informed qualified surgeon to operate on your brain, or a mechanically-informed car mechanic to fix your car brakes, than have simply anyone do so, and than if everyone had an equal right to decide what to do. Society institutes laws, training, qualifications etc to protect such rational preferences, legally differentiating among individuals according to their degrees of proven relevant informedness. This is inconsistent with one-person one-vote.

12 See, e.g., Gaudry and Spielberger (1971). Much research discussed in such books is re-interpretable as potential pro-objectivity knowledge.

13 E.g.:- Some happiness is anti-objectivity, e.g., drug-induced bliss meaning long-term ignorance. Being *un*-happy can motivate seeking pro-objectivity knowledge, e.g., unhappiness regarding diseases can motivate searching for cures. Still, here, and generally, there's probably an important type of pro-objectivity happiness due to self-respect from knowing oneself is at least seeking useful knowledge, and potentially more pro-objectivity happiness for one if one discovers cures

14 This excludes anti-objectivity emotions and their objects (aims or ends), as in racist hatred. A-objectivity emotions and objects are discussed later.

15 Here, and elsewhere in this book, the subjective and objective are shown to be capable of harmoniously or coherently working together to achieve an objective, subjectively-desired end. Appendix directly 6 concerns this. Appendix 4 does somewhat.

16 Pro-objectivity benevolent facilitating of such enjoyment and fulfilment should increase the motivation of persons here to be pro-objectivity.

17 E.g., a pro-objectivity father's children are the objects of his subjective-objective evaluation-combination emotional experience of love for his children, and it is objectively a highly-valuable experience for him to subjectively regard his children as intrinsically valuable. (This would be a greatly facilitating aspect of giving the pro-objectivity care needed by children.)

18 Violence and similar needing to be used by pro-objectivity persons against unwarranted violent attack, e.g., by Nazis, would never be cruel or malevolent. 'Cruelty' means being intentionally more violent, pain-inflicting or hurtful than is (normatively-objectively) needed. Similarly regarding malevolence. Pro-objectivity persons would only do what is needed, as far as they can know. Universal (pro-objectivity) peace and benevolence would be their overall, long-term aim here.

19 'Groupism' is the social version of egoism or individual selfishness. Groupism involves an in-group trying to benefit itself unwarrantedly—at the expense of people believed to be an out-group.

PART I, SECTION 3: STRUCTURAL FORM; A-OBJECTIVITY; MORE ON PRO-OBJECTIVITY

'Be pro-objectivity' is an abbreviation implicitly involving objectivity's or knowledge's structural form. This form then is also normative objectivity's or pro-objectivity's structural form:-

As W. Whewell shows,[1] increasing objectivity/knowledge in an area involves increasing systematic hierarchical and breadth-wise unity, namely what he called 'consilience', a type of harmony or coherence:- Consider an area involving events which, centuries ago, were unclear, apparently inconsistent, separate events, e.g., the moon's and sun's positions relative to Earth's and each other, water alternately rising and falling as tides, falling as rain, rising as evaporation, floating as clouds, our being held on Earth unable to fly (unaided) or jump very high, and so on, plus, later, people (and sea-water, boats etc) going half-way round the then known-to-be-round Earth and not becoming upside down and falling off Earth. That area became comprehensible and in-part-thereby knowledge—via the notion, 'gravity' and other unifying, coherence-producing high-level overall notions. All such lower-level events were explained crucially via gravity. The notion, 'The law of gravity', unified all those events in the minds of those who thereby became knowers here. Those events thereby became comprehensible, becoming (approximate) knowledge. Knowers here knew why each event occurred, and how they were linked via gravity, all coming under the same, overall principle here, the law of gravity. (Objectivity involves an overall view.) Before that knowledge, people who'd seen or heard of any such apparently conflicting events only knew that each event *happened*, believing them to be separate, not knowing there was a common cause.

Yet the here-unifying notion, 'gravity', is in an important sense *irrelevant* regarding our comprehending other events. E.g., gravitational changes explain how astronauts' movability changes according to whether they're in space (floating weightlessly) or on Earth (e.g., heavy, unable to float weightlessly); but throughout such changes the words on astronauts' suits, e.g., 'USA', remain unchanged. A structural term for such irrelevance is '*orthogonal*', as shown by Diagram 1 below, using the Introduction's example of colours of drawings being independent of a drawing's shape. (Orthogonality is important regarding pro-objectivity theory because, as analogously explained in the Introduction, pro-objectivity theory's orthogonality permits plural, a-objectivity secondary ends, ends inherently non-incoherent with its primary end, meaning great liberty there.) Differences, changes or choices within one dimension, e.g., the horizontal, are irrelevant regarding what happens within the other, due to the dimensions' orthogonality. (E.g., circles changed from red to blue remain circles.) The dimensions' orthogonality, their *independence*, is illustrated by them being at right-angles to each other:-

Diagram 1: An Orthogonal Structure

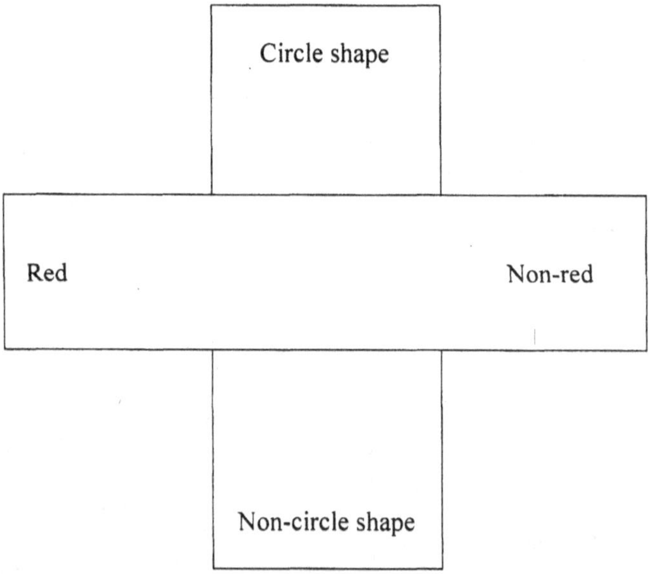

Further:- Changes in gravity are also orthogonal to circles' colour, and much else. This helps make our universe comprehensible. We'd find it incomprehensible if, e.g., with every colour change, *all else* changed, or even all in just one presently independent, unaffected area changed or was affected, e.g., if roundish shapes became rectangular-prisms and vice versa, changing roundish human body-parts, wheels etc into rectangular prisms, and making rectangular buildings, pages etc round, till the next colour change. Without such orthogonality we'd have *no knowledge* because reality would be incomprehensible—and because we'd soon not survive or exist. E.g., via some object's colour changing, humans could change to corpses, or to stones, or existence could change to non-existence. But such things do not happen, crucially because knowable reality, the objective, involves that orthogonal structure. We have *objectivity/knowledge*

partly and crucially *via that structure*. (So, as shown further soon, orthogonality is importantly involved in normative objectivity/knowledge.)

Similarly:- To have comprehensibility and in-part thereby knowledge, a mind must unify many perceptions and notions, present and remembered—avoiding cognitive and perceptual dissonance, namely disunity or incoherence. E.g:- Consider inverting spectacles. Putting these on the first time makes the wearer's visual world appear upside down. Initially the spectacles create disunity or incoherence, e.g., where one's feet feel the ground is conflicts with where one sees it and sees the sky, and with where one remembers they previously were visually. After wearing these spectacles for perhaps a few weeks, the brain restores unity—inverting the inversion, giving the spectacle-wearer coherence here. The sky is visually again above, the ground below. Yet there is more than systematic unity involved in such coherence. There is also systematic orthogonality. Where the ground appears to be is orthogonal (irrelevant) regarding whether one sees that the ground is grass-covered or concrete or whatever, or how it feels to one's touch. And so on. We'd have no comprehensibility or knowledge here if *all* nature was a systematic unity, meaning everything is connected, so that any change changes all else. Here, e.g., whenever we put on any type of spectacles, the nearby sky would change, from space containing air etc to, say, mud or concrete, and the ground would change, say, to sky, porridge or music; and we would change into something else.

In sum:- Knowledge's and hence objectivity's general form involves systematic *orthogonality*, not just unity. There is unity, e.g., within the 'gravitational' and 'rectangles-are-not-round' knowledge areas, but just as those two knowledge-areas are orthogonal to each other, so each other such unified area is orthogonal to certain other areas. Knowable reality has a systematic orthogonal form, involving *harmony or coherence within* each area here, but *irrelevance or independence among* certain areas. This qualifies previous discussions of coherence[2] or harmony: for pro-objectivity theory, and objectivity/knowledge overall, 'coherence' is short for 'orthogonally-systematic coherence'.

As this form is the general structural form among knowledge or of objectivity, it is the general objectively-warranted structural form. Relatedly, this form, applied normatively, to normative knowledge or normative objectivity, is the general structural form involved in overall-objectively-warranted practice. This is very important. E.g:- It means there is an objective duty to conform to that freedom-instituting form. Pro-objectivity persons would happily conform. Here society would be highly liberal. It relatedly means that the maximally pro-objectivity person is not single-mindedly only pro-objectivity via excluding a-objectivity ends: this person is primarily pro-objectivity *and*, secondarily, in an important sense free to do any of the many other, a-objectivity things. This is because the a-objectivity is *irrelevant* regarding our being pro-objectivity:-

Because, regarding objectivity generally, the irrelevance means objectively mutually-*independent* areas, the form's normative version means that in areas irrelevant to achieving the primary end there is no objective warrant for us not having *independence* (freedom) to do whatever we like. Thence, a structural version of 'Be pro-objectivity' is: 'As far as possible, according to appropriateness be either harmonious with or irrelevant regarding the normatively objective. That is, being pro-objectivity primarily means being pro-objectivity and, secondarily, freedom regarding the a-objectivity.' (As implied above and further argued soon, being pro-objectivity necessarily (orthogonally) involves the a-objectivity.) (The a-objectivity is the dimension or general area orthogonal to the pro-objectivity. As suggested further soon, within that general area are various specific areas, e.g., an area containing certain music preferences and an area containing certain sexual preferences.)

Part I, Section 3.1: Concluding Remarks Here

(1) Observations of orthogonality regarding *objectivity/knowledge* are *empirical evidence* for the structural form of an *objective normative theory.* This evidence then, when related to previous arguments/evidence for pro-objectivity theory, is evidence confirming that it is objective (right) that we should *practise* via that form, pro-objectivity's form. (Orthogonality regarding any non-pro-objectivity normative notion is of course not evidence that this orthogonality relates to an objective normative notion.)

(2) A coherent and, regarding orthogonality, non-incoherent normative theory can have only one ultimate or primary end. But ends orthogonal and hence irrelevant to that end cannot be incoherent with that end. One's ends here can be innumerable, changed among, and are inherently secondary:-

The primary or highest priority is: 'Be pro-objectivity'. This end is a duty: it objectively, unconditionally, *should* be achieved. However, secondary to that, you may if you like also achieve any other end(s) irrelevant to that achievement. Diagram 1 analogously showed that. (E.g., if one's primary end is 'Draw circles', one can also have innumerable thereto-orthogonal, secondary colour-preference ends (and drawing-implement, music-preference etc ends). Here monism or singularism is compatible (non-incoherent) with pluralism.

Pro-objectivity's orthogonality allows any a-objectivity end to be either one's permanent preference, or only sometimes preferred to an alternative, and allows one to have any mix of permanent and changing preferences here. As long as the primary end is achieved, it is irrelevant thereto which or how many thereto-orthogonal, secondary ends are achieved. These a-objectivity ends are permissible according to that objective end/standard. Their non-incoherence therewith and permissibility are only knowable via pro-objectivity knowledge. Hence they're also *logically* secondary to 'Be pro-objectivity', the primary end, the ultimate standard. Logicality is an aspect of objectivity.

(3) Not every a-objectivity thing is an end. Ends are choosable, i.e., options. A distinction is needed between options and persons' non-options. E.g:- In many situations persons' ages can be a-objectivity, and a person's age is unchoosable by the person and hence a non-optional aspect of the person. But a person's a-objectivity music-preference is obviously an option.

Pro-objectivity's orthogonal structure implies treating the a-objectivity as a-objectivity—and this applies to *non*-optional a-objectivity aspects of persons (and other things) and to optional a-objectivity, namely, respectively, to what persons at-the-time unchoosably *are* here, and to what persons prefer and are free to choose to *do* here. Regarding treating the a-objectivity as a-objectivity, that 'non-options versus options' distinction will increasingly be shown to be normatively important. E.g., in the following example acting on preferences regarding a-objectivity *options* is *not* anti-objectivity, but acting on preferences regarding *persons'* a-objectivity *non*-optional aspects *is* anti-objectivity:- Suppose Charles, needing to employ workers, prefers persons of age A1 where the choice between A1 and age A2 is a-objectivity, and he employs workers via that preference. This is anti-objectivity, unfair discrimination against A2 persons, likely to have anti-objectivity social, emotional, economic etc effects on them. This is very different from, e.g., Charles preferring an a-objectivity music-type different from his workers' preferences, and Charles and each worker only listening to their individual, often changing preferences via earphones, not having an anti-objectivity affect on anyone. Persons have consciousness and emotions, or affectable subjectivity. Music does not. Persons have *interrelated psychology*, and how one aspect of a person is treated can (dis)affect other, pro-objectivity-important aspects. Further here regarding aspects such as age, gender or race, treating an *aspect* as relevant regarding employment-desirability and so on is to treat the *whole person thus* regarding employment-desirability and so on. Persons cannot come to work without their age etc. (One can come without playing one's preferred music loudly to all. Here there is a choice.) Pro-objectivity, inherently fair, caring persons would not treat anyone's non-optional a-objectivity aspects either negatively or positively. Pro-objectivity persons would have no preference here, or at least (objectively observably) not act on any (inherently-subjective, here-private) preference. They'd, e.g., toss a coin to choose.

Part I, Section 3.2: Pro-Objectivity's Structural Form, Diagrammatically

The following notes further explain Diagram 2 (below), and hence the theory's practical implications. Readers should refer to the diagram before and during reading these notes:-

(1) From objectivity's overall viewpoint, it is of positive value, i.e., warranted, to be normatively pro-objectivity. The '+' on top of the diagram's vertical dimension indicates this. Pro-objectivity is the top, i.e., primary, positive, priority. Evaluations within or via this dimension's top (superior, correct) section are cognitive, emotionally-activated but not in-themselves primarily-emotional or emotionally-based. (Some such evaluations *concern* emotions (as opposed to being based on emotions). E.g., happiness can be of positive pro-objectivity value.) The cognitive, objective, highest level of thought's reflective viewpoint resides here, and oversees, judges or decides all else, at least in a meta-knowledge or general-guidelines way. So it is logically and cognitively primary, and the a-objectivity is secondary.

That viewpoint is aware, as far as possible (for the individual here), of uncertainties such as those mentioned above, and of their manageability. That viewpoint considers situationality. (Pro-objectivity knowledge includes knowing if X is pro-objectivity in one situation but anti- or a-objectivity in another.)

(2) Anti-objectivity things are of negative value, i.e., unwarranted. The minus sign on the lower (inferior and wrong) section of the vertical dimension indicates this.

(3) A-objectivity things are objectively neither warranted nor unwarranted.

(3a) So things within the horizontal dimension are objectively of neutral value—a meta-evaluation.[3] The '0' (zero) there represents the zero (neutral) effect things here have on pro-objectivity. The zero does not represent an absence of value or meaning. That meta-evaluation is *about* all things *within* this dimension. Within the dimension, the things include certain other evaluations. These evaluations are subjective, and can be of great positive value and meaning here. They include various aesthetic and emotional preferences.

Things here include (i) certain non-optional aspects of persons, e.g., gender as in gender being irrelevant regarding knowing that, to survive, you need to avoid cliff-falls; (ii) non-person a-objectivity options, say, certain types of music; (iii) differences among equally pro-objectivity options, say certain foods; and (iv) those a-objectivity subjective evaluations, which concern (ii) and (iii).

(3b) Evaluations here may vary unpredictably within and among persons, but this is irrelevant to the primary, vertical dimension.

If evaluations in some area are permissibly unpredictably variable, we cannot have (non-meta-)knowledge here. For that and other reasons, pro-objectivity theory says we cannot know which a-objectivity thing is right or wrong, as it is pro-objectivity meta-knowledge (and, equivalently, a pro-objectivity meta-evaluation,) that there is no right and wrong here. So here, as there is no (objective) warrant for doing otherwise, as far as pro-objectivity-possible we should be free to do what we like. But Frank's freedom to do X here, say, sing, ceases to be a-objectivity if X begins to affect others in anti-objectivity ways, e.g., if his singing disturbs others studying pro-objectivity knowledge. That is, regarding something which can be a-objectivity, pro-objectivity allows the 'maximum pro-objectivity-possible' freedom here; but there are limits to freedom here.

Due to their 'no right and wrong' nature, any inconsistency among a-objectivity choices is non-inconsistent with the coherence involved in objectivity/knowledge, in achieving the primary end, and within the vertical dimension's pro-objectivity section. There is hence no rationally-problematic inconsistency issue here. If inconsistency Y was inconsistent with the coherence involved in knowledge, in achieving the primary end, etc, then Y would *not* be a-objectivity. Y would be anti-objectivity. (More on those issues later.)

(3c) Because the pro-objectivity meta-view is that a-objectivity things are objectively equal, on a par, merely different, not objectively superior or inferior, the dimension is drawn level (horizontal). Relatedly, from that pro-objectivity viewpoint this dimension of life is open or fluid: nothing objectively belongs in any particular place, e.g., at a positive, (objectively) superior end of a dimension.

Subjectively, individuals would place or move a-objectivity options according to their preferences. E.g., regarding a-objectivity music, say yesterday Jane put jazz at the 'most-preferred' (subjectively-positive) end of her a-objectivity dimension; today she put Mozart there.[4] (If such evaluations are shown on the horizontal dimension, this subjectivity and permissible variability needs to be indicated, e.g., via 'SV+' representing Jane subjectively positively valuing this or that here, to distinguish these evaluations from objective evaluations.)

(3d) Comments in (3a)-(3c) and Section 2 implied that hostility among persons with conflicting a-objectivity preferences regarding options is anti-objectivity. Treating the a-objectivity as a-objectivity forbids hostility. Hostility among persons here who could maintain/increase their pro-objectivity means a lack of the social harmony optimal for that maintenance/increase. Hostility here also conflicts with pro-objectivity via wasting (personal energy, emotional etc) resources which could have been used for those pro-objectivity purposes. So hostility here is anti-objectivity, involving those persons becoming less pro-objectivity than they were before. Maximally pro-objectivity persons would peacefully resolve such preference-conflicts, e.g., via friendly coin-tossing, taking turns or voting. Harmonious, civilised liberality is needed, involving no normatively (morally, socially etc) significant practical conflict. Fulfilling such needs is another aspect of the pro-objectivity peaceful, benevolent social harmony mentioned in Section 2. Types of equality are also involved. E.g., as (3c) implies, all preferences concerning options here, and the options here, are objectively equal: pro-objectivity persons would not become hostile over the objectively equal. They'd act on their knowledge that there is no normatively-objective *reason* or *permissibility* for hostility here.

In other words:- Here, concerning in-themselves conflicting a-objectivity options there'd be only *purely theoretical* conflict, as in merely *on-paper* conflict, as in only between the *written* or merely thought-of 'Draw in red' and 'Draw in blue'. Pro-objectivity persons aware of any such conflict would not allow it to affect their normatively-relevant *actions*. There'd be an in-practice, in-effect, harmonious resolving of any such theoretical conflict. Analogously:- Suppose the primary end is 'Draw circles'. It is thereto irrelevant whether circle-drawers have mutually-inconsistent secondary ends here, e.g., 'Draw in red' and 'Draw in blue'. From the primary, ultimate viewpoint here, as long as circles are drawn, it does not matter which colour is used. And any colour-preference conflicts are resolvable among a certain type of persons, avoiding in-practice normatively-significant conflict.

Diagram 2: Pro-Objectivity's Orthogonal Structure

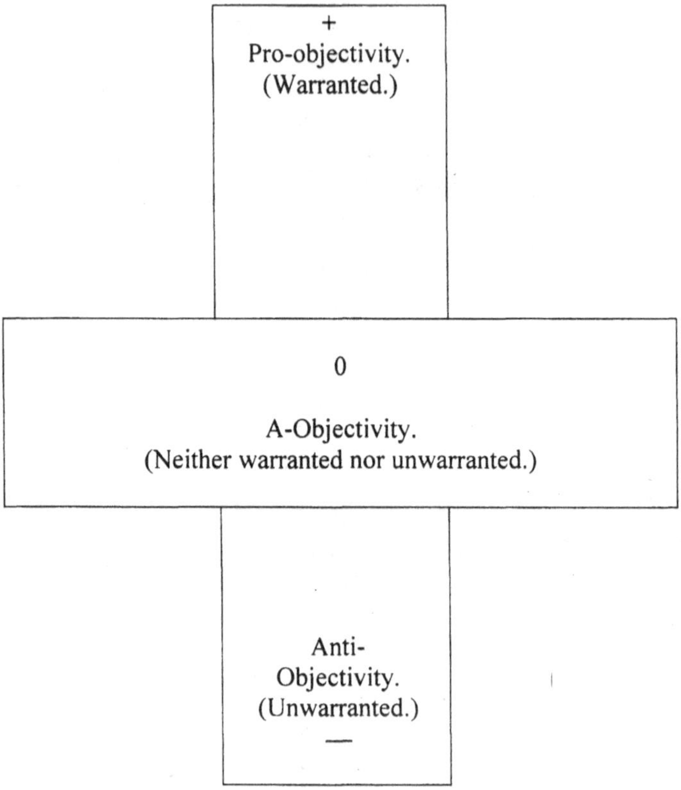

Part I, Section 3.2.1: Concluding here

(Such conclusions are explained further in Part II.)

1) This diagram shows that being pro-objectivity involves unity consistent (non-incoherent) with diversity, or convergence consistent with divergence. Pro-objectivity people converge (cohere or harmonise) regarding the one objective normative end, will diverge regarding their a-objectivity non-optional aspects, may and typically will diverge regarding a-objectivity cultural, sexual, artistic, life-style, sporting, musical, leisure, hobby, housing, clothing, garden, transport, entertainment, educational, intellectual, food, drink, family-type and other a-objectivity optional preferences. (As suggested above, and explained further in Part II, only *some* cultural, sexual, artistic etc preferences are a-objectivity, or are a-objectivity only in *some* situations.[5])

Though pro-objectivity orthogonality non-incoherently combines pro-objectivity monism or single-mindedness with a-objectivity pluralism or open-minded liberalism, this does mean there is no *pro*-objectivity pluralism, open-mindedness and liberalism. Within the vertical dimension's pro-objectivity section's meta-unity, meta-convergence, meta-monism or meta-single-mindedness, there are prescriptions advocating types of inherently open-minded criticism, individualism, imagination, creativity, pluralism and liberalism, namely interrelated social, intellectual, political etc freedoms. E.g., pro-objectivity society would single-mindedly promote free, open-minded, rational political criticism, encouraging divergent reasonable views where imaginative hypothesis-construction is needed, namely in the absence of needed knowledge. Here there is only one right (objective) general way to discover the correct hypothesis, and that involves promoting such freedom, openness, criticism (including self-criticism), imagination and divergence.

2) The *freedom* to do whatever one likes regarding a-objectivity options is distinguishable from the options as such, say certain music-types. The freedom would be instituted via pro-objectivity knowledge. Arguably, happiness and similar resulting from that freedom would have, relatedly, pro-objectivity effects—via persons here being pleased with pro-objectivity theory for instituting that freedom, making pro-objectivity further motivating. Similar pro-objectivity effects seem likely via persons being pleased with pro-objectivity theory and society not viewing any of their non-optional a-objectivity aspects as inferior, and with the associated freedom pro-objectivity society would institute here, namely freedom from objectively unfair age, sexual, racial etc discrimination. Similarly regarding the related (self-)respect persons would experience here.

CONCLUDING REMARKS REGARDING PART I

(1) Pro-objectivity theory covers every possible choice and other thing. It is universally (morally, socially, politically etc) applicable because each thing has either a positive, negative or neutral (orthogonal) relation to each other thing, i.e., including 'Be pro-objectivity'. (Appendix B discusses this further.)

Relatedly:- As 'Be pro-objectivity' is the only objective normative end, hence prescribing *universally* what objectively ought to be done (which includes instituting a-objectivity freedom of choice), hence covering *all* possible choices, there can be no *other* end of objectively equal or higher priority in *any* area. E.g:- Suppose aesthetics has what all concerned agree is an ultimate end, X; or consider an individual who considers X the aesthetic ultimate end. Aesthetics, like *all* other areas, is an area where if any actual or imagined end therein conflicts with that objective end, the objective end would be the objectively higher (and highest possible) priority. Partly analogously:- There's a story of a ruler who gave his highest-priority aesthetic end/standard, 'A unique red substance flowing across bright green grass, daily', higher priority than his highest-priority moral end/standard, 'No-one should kill (murder) innocent persons'. That substance was blood spurting from beheaded humans, and to achieve that aesthetic end, the ruler watched his soldiers obediently behead innocent persons on such grass daily, there being no more criminals available. In sum, for coherence, which the objective inherently involves, an objective normative standard must cover all possible choices, applying to all areas: there can be no other standard of objectively equal or higher priority able to conflict with or overrule it, anywhere.

(2) Pro-objectivity theory seems the only evidence-based normative theory: it has support importantly similar and related to the support evidence gives in science, including via coherence. Scientific evidence involves related sound arguments; regarding pro-objectivity theory such arguments are hopefully above. Scientific evidence involves related observation; the book shows there is observable evidence available for the theory and relatedly regarding which choices and other factors are pro-objectivity, and for the theory's structural form.

The theory's addressing of the is-ought and other evaluative issues, (discussed further in Appendix 5,) coherently relates to or *involves* such evidence. This is unique among normative theories.

There is overall no evidence or objective-warrant for alternative theories. No other normative theory can provide objective non-empirical arguments for itself, for its end and standard, and can combine those arguments with external, empirical evidence for the prescriptions implied thereby, and for itself generally, this coherence-involving combination showing that the prescriptions and theory are objective, and also provide external, empirical evidence for an objective-end-related structural form involved in those arguments' contents and prescriptions.

The evidence for pro-objectivity theory is at least indicative, and arguably sufficient. Such evidence seems the only *possible* evidence for a normative theory. What other evidence could there be? The theory claims only to be as evidence-based as humanly possible. It is irrational to ask the impossible. It is rational to at least provisionally accept the alternative for which there is the only available or possible evidence. At least, the theory overall seems evidenced sufficiently to be approximately and asymptotically true or correct.

(3) However, the book's fallibilism suggests my theorising may somewhat err. I welcome any (objectively) better theory. If someone can prove, i.e., objectively, that this book's theory needs fundamental alterations, those alterations will produce a more objective theory.

Regarding some specifics, some fallibility or erring is likely. Much more needs to be done regarding my suggestions here. That is, sufficient evidence is needed regarding the pro-objectivity or otherwise of some of the book's hypothesised prescriptions. Still, the first, most important, fundamental task, Part I's main task, is to provide a sound-as-possible *theoretical basis* for practice, and *general guidelines* for normative specifics—while stressing that much more needs to be done regarding such specifics and other reducible uncertainties. Again, one such general guideline is that it is pro-objectivity to be fallibilist and skeptical about uncertainties and merely probable knowledge and hypothesised or merely provisionally-acceptable specifics. Pro-objectivity is a long-term project. In various specific areas, probably the best we can hope for in the long-term is approximate or asymptotic knowledge. But that is better (more objective) than ignorance or mere belief.

(4) Above are the most important, fundamental arguments for the theory, or hopefully sufficient arguments to convince at least most readers. Appendixes

present thereon-expanded and other arguments for those not yet convinced, or for those wanting further explanation of certain points above.

Part II also further argues for the theory, often explicitly. But Part II primarily concerns practical applications of the theory. With this, Part II further discusses the issue that it is normatively pointless having an objective theory of what humans should practise if the theory is not practicable. Here 'practicable' means the theory is sufficiently unambiguous and its uncertainty is manageable and can be lessened, and that normal humans can have sufficient ability, motivation and opportunity to practise it. The above makes various suggestions indicating that the theory achieves such practicability. Part II expands greatly thereon.

During Part II's primary task of discussing practical applications, more comparisons are made with various alternative theories. This involves further, more specific discussions and criticisms of various alternative theories.

ENDNOTES TO PART I, SECTION 3

1 E.g., his "Inductive Table of Astronomy" in Whewell (1858-60) Ch VI, Book XI.

2 A Section 1.1 Preliminary Comment (3a) endnote indicated this qualification.

3 'Meta-' in such terms refers to a thought about some other thought(s), here an evaluation about some other evaluation(s). Here there is an objective evaluation concerning evaluations in a-objectivity areas, namely that they are subjective, and neither pro-objectivity nor anti-objectivity.

4 The distinction between options and persons' non-optional aspects applies here. Jazz as such is an option and non-sentient, not in-itself affectable in anti-objectivity ways by anyone's preferences or changing preferences regarding jazz.

5 E.g.:- There can be a-objectivity dance options, involving, e.g., non-sexism. But if dancing involved treating one gender as inferior, this would be sexist and hence anti-objectivity. And a sexual practice which is a-objectivity in 'consenting informed adults' situations would be anti-objectivity in an 'adult having sex with a child' situation.

PART II: MOSTLY PRACTICAL APPLICATIONS

Part II's Preliminary Remarks

(1) Part II's discussions of the theory's universal applicability are only representative, in order to avoid a long book. Other books are planned, covering more specifics, focusing on (somewhat) separable areas, e.g., education.

(2) The most important applications involve society, and, within society, education (defined in an overall way, e.g., to include socialisation, upbringing and self-education). Education is overall the most crucial choosable factor in that promoting knowledge is arguably the primary task of education, and 'Be pro-objectivity' means practising pro-objectivity knowledge, and education (defined broadly) at least implicitly puts many normative values into persons' minds. Other normative values common in human minds, namely those evolved, emotionally-based intuitions discussed at Part I, Section 2's beginning (and below), are hence not put there via education but, importantly, can be reflected on via education—and thereby promoted, (re)directed or overruled.

Though education would play that crucial part within pro-objectivity society, it is only a part. Other parts of the interactions constituting society affect education. E.g., (formal and/or informal) political institutions are the ultimate authority in society, and can greatly affect education. However, education affects those other parts. E.g., to have this or that political etc institution, in an important sense the idea that it should exist and the idea that it should affect education in this or that way, and so on, come first—and ideas come from and/or are assessable via education (in the broadest sense), including self-education.

As the Introduction suggests, a considerable proportion of humanity, especially in democratic societies with a prominent liberal, rational, critical tradition and education, is already significantly pro-objectivity. But those persons are typically only *implicitly* so. Becoming explicitly properly so would mean they have clear knowledge of the objective end and its warrant, and know they should achieve it maximally. To help them acquire that knowledge and become explicitly and maximally pro-objectivity is education's task.

(3) Realistically (objectively), it tends to not be the fault of persons presently only significantly pro-objectivity that they are not more pro-objectivity. The previous sentence, appropriately adapted, also applies to persons only potentially pro-objectivity. To achieve or more widely and/or easily achieve the objective normative end, persons here must first know clearly what it is and why it is warranted, and know sufficiently how to achieve it. Such knowledge is typically absent, due to lack of awareness rather than due to those persons' intentions. Many governments, educators and so on intentionally stifle free rational criticism and so on, limiting such persons' opportunities to gain that awareness. But those governments etc typically also lack that awareness.

In sum, people are not responsible, not normatively at fault, for not doing something they are not aware they could and should do, and most people lack that awareness. One aim of this book is to increase that awareness, hence create that responsibility and motivate action coherent therewith—especially by educators in schools, universities and similar.

(4) Regarding pro-objectivity theory's practicability, persons' *opportunities*, at least potential *abilities* and *motivations* are each crucial. These would be promoted or developed by pro-objectivity society, especially via education.

(4a) As it is the objective end, 'Be pro-objectivity' should be achieved to the maximum possible degree. Part I stressed that 'Be pro-objectivity' is short for 'Be pro-objectivity as far as possible for the individual(s) in the situation(s) in question, and so on'. This means that terms such as 'maximal pro-objectivity' are short for 'maximum possible pro-objectivity for the individual(s) in the situation(s) in question, and so on'. Here an individual's opportunities, abilities and motivation are relevant, and not a normative issue where the individual had no choice regarding them or where, as suggested in (3) above, due to lack of awareness it was not individually possible to pro-objectivity-optimise them. However, this can be possible and choosable.

(4b) Achieving the pro-objectivity end can be an ongoing achievement for an individual. Like ends such as 'collect stones', given the awareness discussed in (3) above, that end is at any time both presently and then cumulatively achievable for at least nearly all individuals. Suppose Juliet is now as maximally pro-objectivity as is possible for her, i.e., given her present state of knowledge and other resources. Her present individual end-achievement can thenceforth also become a means to achieve that end more widely. It can be a means to help her learn more (potentially) pro-objectivity knowledge, and then practise it. (An end which is for every individual reasonably achievable, or practicable, is also more motivating for many more individuals than is an end very difficult to achieve. This manageable achievability is exemplified further below.)

(5) Regarding each separable aspect of achieving that end, again, an (on-average) balance among them is needed, and hence a distinction is needed between 'optimal' and 'maximal'. Analogously:- Consider Frank, who starts putting maximum effort and time every day into singing. He soon exhausts and permanently damages his vocal chords. Frank will now achieve less here than the maximum possible in the long-term than if he'd put in a here optimal effort, one less than the maximum, as just part of a balance involving rest and other practices which would have optimally kept recreating his personal resources needed to achieve that long-term maximum singing. The objective or rational, overall view involves a longest-term view.

Relatedly:- When there is uncertainty regarding which choice is pro-objectivity-optimal, or right, the chooser can spend so many resources, e.g., time and mental energy, deciding what to do, that the overall situation, regardless of which choice is made, is thereby sub-optimal, i.e., not as pro-objectivity as it could be. Putting maximum or more-than-optimal effort into agonising over such choices wastes resources. What would have been a better balance without that agonising and waste, becomes a worse balance. If it is uncertain which choice is at least probably optimal, until sufficient evidence is available here the chooser should choose via any (non-anti-objectivity) emotional preference or via chance, e.g., coin-tosses, and quickly provisionally accept the thereby chosen. This can also more quickly provide some such evidence, namely via trial-and-error. This means the overall balance will be closer to optimality.

(6) Similarly, as stressed earlier:- We will at least often not precisely know the optimal pro-objectivity balance among factors, sometimes competing factors, or to what degree we should practise prescription P1 rather than P2, or implement pro-objectivity-means M1 rather than M2. E.g., we cannot precisely know what quantity/quality of sleep rather than awakeness is optimal regarding a certain person being maximally pro-objectivity in situation S1. And the quantities/qualities of P1/M1 and P2/M2 need to be considered in relation to various other pro-objectivity needs. E.g., obviously there is much more to being pro-objectivity than just being either asleep or awake. E.g., there could sometime be an illness-related need for parents to spend much more time than usual with their children, meaning the parents temporarily get much less sleep than is on-average the daily pro-objectivity-optimal. An overall view looks beyond the daily-optimal here, say to a weekly-optimal amount of good sleep.

Though there will be some uncertainty regarding what such (on-average) balances and degrees or quantities/qualities are, pro-objectivity theory, because it involves what we can know, only aims to prescribe that which seems optimal as far as it is possible to know . . . . And what we know can grow.

(6a) Balance issues are a type of borderline issue, as in the problematic 'Where is the correct borderline between sleep and awakeness in situation S1?'. Similarly: 'How much violence of type V is needed to optimally defend pro-objectivity in situation S2? Where is the borderline between too little and too much violence?'. Because we lack foresight (knowledge) regarding the precise effects of doing X rather than Y in some situation, and because if we do X this means we cannot know what effects Y would have at the time, we can never know precisely where such borderlines should be. We can only go on general knowledge regarding what seem similar practices in relevantly similar, past, situations. Again, pro-objectivity concerns the 'as far as is possible to know . . .'.

(7) For reasons such as those mentioned in (5)-(6a) and elsewhere above, it should be stressed again that skepticism about some of my specific prescriptive claims below may be warranted. The claims are in some cases merely what seem to me probably correct, based on evidence acquired via my studies in philosophy, psychology, history, sociology, science, anthropology, politics, education and so on, and via teaching across all age ranges and abilities over decades (while also studying). But that evidence, and/or my interpretation of it, may sometimes be insufficient. Or I may sometimes be totally wrong. All that seems certain to me is that at least *something like* the overall set of suggested applications in this book is at least highly pro-objectivity. More research is needed.

(8) Because objectivity has an *overall* view, an objective normativity concerns maximality, all things over all time, and a balance involving all pro-objectivity factors, as far as possible. One cannot be maximally pro-objectivity unless one aims to do whatever one can regarding that balance and all things over all time. This includes having a collective or societal aim here, concerning all humanity. So one should do what seems likely, as far as one can know, to

pro-objectivity-benefit all living and future potential persons overall, which involves considering all other beings and all other things. This is what 'Be pro-objectivity' fully and really (objectively) means.

So applications (prescriptions) below concern all actually and potentially at least significantly pro-objectivity beings and all other, non-living things. Children are extremely important beings here. Because, when very young, they lack crucial pro-objectivity education, here they are only potentially pro-objectivity. Obviously children need special consideration because they are the only beings who can become the needed future maximally pro-objectivity persons. Relatedly regarding their crucially important educational etc needs.

Concluding these Preliminary Remarks:-

There are implications here concerning pro-objectivity politics, inclusivity, environmental responsibility, treatment of animals, education, rights, duties, virtues and so on, and for pro-objectivity definitions of child-abuse and abuse generally, and hence of child-protection, all of which and more are discussed below.

PART II, SECTION 1: FURTHER ISSUES AND APPLICATIONS

Part II, Section 1.1: Pro-Objectivity Needs A Certain Type Of Society And Sociable Individuals

(Many points here are expanded on later.)

Pro-objectivity theory prescribes a type of sociability. Total, holistic individuality (unsociability), as in the 'state of nature' described by Hobbes, would be extremely anti-objectivity. However, as suggested above and argued further soon, in many areas pro-objectivity society would promote various types and often high degrees of (sociable or friendly) individualism:-

One piece of pro-objectivity meta-knowledge is that pro-objectivity knowledge is often so complex that no individual who soon after birth always lived in isolation from other humans could avoid major mistakes, and learn anywhere near enough to become even borderline significantly pro-objectivity. Optimal human learning can only be in large part an interpersonal process, involving society providing language and other educational etc resources, and involving co-operation and the above-mentioned altruism and hence harmoniously helping each other, e.g., by mutually-respectful instruction, learning and criticism. For such and other reasons total, unsociable or isolated individualism is ruled out.

Pro-objectivity society would encourage pro-objectivity types of individualism, and permit a-objectivity types. E.g., individualistic, creative imagination and independent rational criticism of widely-accepted views can facilitate insights needed for as-yet unknown pro-objectivity knowledge very different from those views. (This book was written largely via individualistic criticism of all other persons' normative views.) Relatedly, pro-objectivity society would encourage all to be strongly individualistic and hence independent here, hence not too socially-dependent as in conforming to social pressure to accept, believe or do X merely due to that social pressure, as in many teenagers smoking etc due to non-individualistically, weakly conforming to peer pressure they are too dependent on. (Social coherence via such pressure, weak or non-individualistic, non-independent-minded characters and hence conformity is anti-objectivity. E.g., Hitler's followers were highly socially-coherent here.) Instead of such conformity regarding X, each individual would be encouraged to independently investigate whether X is pro-objectivity on independent, evidenced grounds—ignoring any social pressure to do otherwise. Normatively objective (correct) individuals here would harmonise partly via their shared strong-charactered assertive and sociable individualism, and shared need to promote it among all.

This also implies that a certain type of harmonious, sociable democracy,[1] one constituted by such inherently independent-minded individuals, would be most pro-objectivity: totalitarian rule by some dictatorial egoistic individual(s) is unwarranted. Pro-objectivity relatedly needs a democratic society large and productive enough to provide, and where all have access to, schools, universities, libraries, hospitals and so on, such access helping to develop such educated-to-be-independent, sociable, democratic individuals, and fulfilling all their other, health-care etc pro-objectivity needs as far as possible.

The ideal pro-objectivity society would be world-wide, because maximal pro-objectivity implies overall or universal harmony. With anything less than a world-wide maximally pro-objectivity society, there could be conflict within and among societies, with anti-objectivity results—e.g., via war leading to the death of highly pro-objectivity persons and the wasting of resources which could be used in pro-objectivity education, health-care etc. Here different societies/groups would be like the conflicting individualism pro-objectivity rules out.

More on specific aspects of pro-objectivity society is below. These involve rights and duties only knowable and implementable societally:-

Part II, Section 1.2: One Fundamental, General Duty/Right; Thence-Derived Specific Duties And Rights; Related Virtues And Flourishing

'Duty' is defined here as that which one normatively-objectively *ought* to *do,* either to benefit some being or other thing in a pro-objectivity way, or to otherwise cohere with the pro-objectivity standard. 'Rights' are defined here as pro-objectivity *entitlements* all at least potentially pro-objectivity beings and other things *inherently have,* due to their at least potential pro-objectivity. For persons, rights involve and those entitlements are, pro-objectivity benefits society has a duty to give them. Under those definitions 'duty' and 'right' are contrasted, the contrast involving 'do' and, often, 'give', versus 'have' and 'be given to'. This could be viewed as implying that a right cannot be a duty. This is sometimes correct, but this book defines 'Be pro-objectivity' as both the fundamental general right and duty. And, regarding some situations, this implies that a specific practice is a duty and a right. E.g., in political discussions one has the right and duty to state any relevant pro-objectivity criticisms.

Anyway, regardless of the complexities etc concerning those notions, the objectively important overall issue is that every at least potentially pro-objectivity person has that fundamental, general right and duty *solely due to being at least potentially pro-objectivity*—and all should protect that right and fulfil that duty as far as possible, and all specific rights/duties derived therefrom.

Numerous specific rights and duties are derived therefrom, i.e., are thence implied regarding specific situations. So they are 'derived rights or duties', not stand-alone warranted notions. Hence none of them, e.g., the (abbreviated) duty 'Always be unselfish (in pro-objectivity ways)', is a fundamental standard. Their warrant is derived *from* the *fundamental*, hence stand-alone, 'Be pro-objectivity' standard's overall-objective-warrant.

That example, 'Always be unselfish etc', shows that not all specific or derived duties are rights: unselfish persons practise a 'do' and 'give' notion here, and not a 'be given to' notion. Similarly, one can have a specific pro-objectivity right which is not a duty. E.g:- Young children have the pro-objectivity right to be fed, educated and otherwise cared-for in pro-objectivity ways. Such things are given to them. It is unrealistic (unobjective) to expect very young children to understand and so take seriously the (here age-inappropriate) claim that they have an objective duty to eat that healthy food and be educated. They can only realistically be motivated to eat and be educated thus via other means, e.g., via adults making school enjoyable, positive, caring and interesting.

However, an overall view of duties and rights realises that, when young children are older, if they have at least normal capacities, that right will involve *reciprocal* or *associated* duties. Here children do have a duty to understand, take seriously and fulfil those duties as far as possible, e.g., duties to treat their parents/carers/teachers well, eat that healthy food and be educated. And they'll acquire a duty to use their thence-acquired health, education etc to benefit humanity in pro-objectivity ways when or if they become mature enough for that to be possible. (All pro-objectivity duties should be fulfilled 'as far as possible etc'.)

Concluding/summarising remarks here:-

Sometimes the terms 'duty' and 'right' cover the same practice, sometimes not, depending on the situation or practice. Whichever is the case here, over a normal life-span a maximally pro-objectivity normal person would practise the same general-guidelines or prescriptions overall (in total). What matters is what happens overall in practice. So those (and other) issues regarding terminology can be a-objectivity. Discussions below of rights and duties accept such flexible conclusions, e.g., sometimes using 'duty' where 'right' would be as meaningful, or vice versa. The terms 'rights' and 'duties' are often not explicitly mentioned below, but all pro-objectivity normative issues involve rights and/or duties.

As discussed below, to fulfil a pro-objectivity duty long-term is a pro-objectivity virtue. And to be granted and exercise all one's rights here, plus fulfilling all one's duties, i.e., being virtuous here, means normatively-objective flourishing. One has a right to be helped to develop, and a duty to develop, all one's pro-objectivity cognitive, emotional, physical etc capacities so as to achieve and maintain (one's at-the-time achievable) maximal pro-objectivity. Regarding Socrates's question, 'How should one live?', and his 'An unexamined life is not worth living.', this flourishing is objectively how one should live, and involves an objectively examined and worthwhile life.

Part II, Section 1.3: Concerning Knowledge, Free Speech And Associated Issues

Again, the absolute ideal or maximum regarding knowledge is each person knowing all pro-objectivity knowledge. This is impracticable. The practicable, human-relative ideal is whatever, in the situation in question, is the achievable democratically *collective* quality/quantity of knowledge optimal regarding each person being as pro-objectivity as possible long-term. With this, as Part I suggests, a balance is needed among cognitive and non-cognitive pro-objectivity achievements (duties). (The just-mentioned flourishing requires that balance.)

Relatedly, the absolute ideal requires unlimited pro-objectivity cognitive and non-cognitive (e.g., motivational, material, temporal and energy) resources. These are not available. Any at-the-time soon-achievable maximum or ideal is relative to existing resources. This involves doing the best you can with what is available in the situation. So, e.g., students with limited capacities for acquiring knowledge can be maximally pro-objectivity as far as is possible for them at the time. Again, it is not rational or objective to demand the impossible or unavailable. We can have *knowledge* that the best possible thing is being done. A practicable theory with a knowledge-involving basis can ask no more.

Similarly, we can only do the absolutely optimal pro-objectivity thing if we know what it is. Perfect, full knowledge may be unavailable in many areas. It is irrational to demand that we know now what we do not know. Knowledge is increasing, but there is much we do not yet know. We can be pro-objectivity by knowing we do not yet know some specific knowledge. Objective or rational criticism involves the available *evidence*. This can be evidence that, *in* some area, there is insufficient or no evidence and hence no knowledge. This is *meta*-evidence, i.e., evidence only *about* the area. (In certain areas, e.g., religious or other non-objectively-based normative theorising, we can only have meta-evidence or meta-knowledge that, as far as we know, there'll *never* be evidence or knowledge (fundamentally confirming a theory) *in* the area.)

Where more pro-objectivity knowledge is needed, we need to do more than be rationally skeptical, critical or suspend belief. Sometimes here it will be most normatively objective to do what *seems probably* optimal, given our limited knowledge, or as far as we can know at the time. Sometimes suspended belief plus provisional acceptance can be warranted, at least temporarily. Here we accept some hypothesis as possible knowledge in that we practise it till we know whether it is knowledge. It is pro-objectivity to *act on* possible or apparently probable knowledge where there is a pro-objectivity necessity to act. E.g:- We know we must have *some* types of food so we can be alive, think etc so as to be maximally pro-objectivity, but suppose we do not know which diet is even approximately optimal here. Here we'd need to provisionally eat whatever seems to work best as far as we know, till our knowledge advances. 'Best', of course, means optimal(ly). Doing our best, as far as we can know, is clearly the most normatively objective thing we can do. (Doing so long-term is a pro-objectivity virtue, and doing one's best is an aspect of pro-objectivity flourishing.)

Provisional acceptance can involve trial-and-error research. Yet any errors help us negatively specifically *know*, i.e., know what not to do next time. This leaves us less possibly correct alternatives to test. So, often, increasingly, we can still know something and hence be as objective as is practicable, eventually achieving something positive.

Regarding such issues, because it can be optimally pro-objectivity to be self-critical, skeptical, regard ourselves as fallible and welcome others' rational criticism, a qualified humility is a pro-objectivity duty/virtue. Humility here would be qualified/balanced by confidence that one has some significant pro-objectivity knowledge, which can increase via research involving the same careful rational self-criticism etc. Going from such confidence to intellectual arrogance would be to become anti-objectivity, having lost that humility.

Some related applications regarding knowledge and free speech and so on:-

There is no objective right to (intellectually arrogantly believe one should) be free to say whatever one likes, without evidence. There is an indirect pro-objectivity right to freely make any a-objectivity statement one likes.[2] Regarding direct pro-objectivity, the only rights/duties are as in the following (also see Appendix 4's (a)-(d)):- (i) A duty/right to freely make evidenced, pro-objectivity statements, namely pro-objectivity knowledge. (ii) If insufficient evidence is available, one has a duty to be self-critical etc. All have a duty to be aware they are fallible and may sometimes have merely apparent evidence.[3] Here suspending belief is dutiful. And so on, as mentioned above. (iii) If time etc permits, where one lacks important pro-objectivity knowledge there is a right and duty to learn from the more informed or, otherwise, ensure the issue is researched. (iv) If there is a pro-objectivity need to act immediately, the recently discussed provisional acceptance is a right and duty—if possible making it clear to all concerned that the accepted prescription is not (yet?) pro-objectivity knowledge. (v) A right and duty to politely helpfully question or positively criticise others who seem to be believing without sufficient evidence. (vi) A right and duty to creatively propose reasonable hypotheses, suspending belief concerning them until they are tested. Where there is no knowledge, free, creative imagination can provide possible knowledge via such hypothesising. (vii) A duty/right to help and encourage all appropriate persons regarding such rights/ duties.

So there is no objective right to free speech *as such,* or to have or state a belief, as such, including within "double-barrelled questions". An alleged right to free speech as such licenses persons freely making anti-objectivity statements and uninformed (unevidenced) statements merely alleged to be knowledge or true. As this is overall-objectively-unwarranted, such often-alleged rights are objectively wrong(s). Clearly, e.g., if you are not a raper of children, you would warrantedly think it wrong for others to have the (alleged) right to freely state or believe that you are. And any such others would here be anti-objectivity and could affect you in anti-objectivity ways, e.g., via upsetting or imprisoning you.

Similarly, and only apparently paradoxically, *objective* statements can occasionally be anti-objectivity e.g., via upsetting someone or as in telling intending murderers where their intended pro-objectivity, innocent victims are. Part II,

Section 2.2.1 explains this. The presently relevant point is: there is not necessarily an objective right to freely make objective statements; a statement's (type-B) pro-objectivity is the fundamental, normative issue, not its (type-A) objectivity.

That fundamental issue and certain recent points mean that claims such as 'You ought to respect my beliefs' and 'I have a right to my beliefs' are overall-objectively-unwarranted. A belief objectively deserves respect only to the degree it is likely to be pro-objectivity knowledge and is hence supported by evidence—and is hence not mere belief. The only beliefs one has a right to believe are pro-objectivity knowledge.

Three sentences previously, 'faith' can be substituted for 'beliefs'. As 'faith in X' means one has no evidence for X, faith is objectively always unwarranted. Relatedly, it is also pro-objectivity knowledge that X here can have innumerable conflicting (incoherent), normatively-problematic contents. E.g., many people have faith in this or that conflicting version of one of mutually-conflicting Hinduism, Islam, Christianity etc, and hence in their conflicting normativities. The situation is incoherent in other ways. E.g., if faith in X is evidence that X is true, then innumerable conflicting notions are true or knowledge. E.g., the Roman gods would still rule, as would the Inca gods, the Nordic gods, and so on, and their alleged normative commandments would all be correct. There'd be many, conflicting 'The One True God(dess or Set Of Gods and/or Goddesses)' and conflicting true normativities. But, as Part I shows, truth and knowledge are not like that. They are not incoherent. Some have faith that Easter Bunny exists and secretly (un-evidencedly) gives people chocolate. And so on, e.g., regarding fairies, goblins etc. This often refers only to children, but countless adults have other, *equally* unevidenced, irrational beliefs. (They can be so common among a society's adults that they are statistically normal here, and on an alleged normal-means-right basis they are regarded as right, with many believing that they hence have a right to their faith.) In sum, it is irrational and objectively wrong to respect faith, and belief as such. Similarly regarding respecting opinions, if 'opinion' means 'a belief for which the believer has no or insufficient evidence'.

Similarly regarding respecting people's wishes. A wish involves the belief that it would be good if X happens. Wishes are only worthy of pro-objectivity respect if they are pro-objectivity. E.g., dying pro-objectivity persons would wish their bodily organs to not be buried or burnt if the organs could prolong the lives of at least potentially pro-objectivity others. (A pro-objectivity society's laws would require such organ donation to be universal.)

Similarly regarding respecting what a person believes is meaningful for them. Similarly regarding trying to help someone feeling depressed and/or alienated, by finding something, perhaps anything, this someone will believe is meaningful. The notion, 'meaningful', involves thoughts, experiences, practices, emotions and feelings which are not necessarily pro-objectivity. E.g., finding bingo meaningful can be anti-objectivity, and Hitler's finding domination and extermination meaningful was extremely overall-objectively-unwarranted. (This paragraph applies to 'quality of life' claims, e.g., as in some bio-ethical theories.)

The previous few paragraphs raise the issue of unobjectivity in the form of merely alleged evidence, which some believe is the correct alternative to real evidence, evidence sought and used by our objectivity:-

Part II, Section 1.3.1: Unobjective, Alleged Evidence; Religion And Normativity

As discussed in Part I, our objectivity uses coherence, inherently reality-related observation (including concerning illusions[4]), sound reasoning and so on as evidence, namely the cognitive or cognitively-interpreted rational notions which, if sufficient, crucially help constitute knowledge, e.g., as in practical science and relatedly pro-objectivity theory. Relatedly, 'evidence for X' is evidence for X being *true*, i.e., objective. So evidence is also objective or true.

But many believe or unthinkingly presuppose there is or are some other type(s) of subjective or non-objective evidence or knowledge, or people here define 'objective' and related terms another way, to thereby define their beliefs as true. Here there is immense incoherence and a lack of those reality-related etc rational notions. E.g:- Many religious people believe that their religious faith is evidence that their alleged god(s) exist(s) and prescribe(s) the correct normativity. Many believe their emotions are evidence that related beliefs and the emotions' objects are objectively correct, as in racists believing race R is (objectively) inferior, and as in racist hatred's object, 'Treat race R badly'. Often, relatedly, many believe that their moral intuitions are evidence that the associated morality, e.g., for some, racism, is correct. But the intuitions, emotions, emotional-objects, alleged gods and normativities here conflict greatly, with arguments for them involving at least implicit problematic circularity, as discussed in Appendix 2. That problematicity crucially involves a lack of inherently objective evidence. The alleged evidence here then is unobjective. and merely alleged.

Relatedly, actual evidence includes evidence there can be only one objective normativity. The general situation here is that evidence is that which can only confirm that *one* specific entity or set of entities is the content of X etc in any true 'X is Y', 'X causes Z', 'X exists', 'X does not exist' etc. There cannot also be evidence that conflicting content is also true. E.g., evidence can confirm that, e.g., virus type V1 causes disease D1, that Obama is (in 2010) the USA's President, but not anything contrary thereto. If faith is evidence, an analogy here with religious faiths is that goblins cause D1 and Reagan is U.S.A's President. Relatedly, associated with faith that their alleged god(s) exist(s), all religions have at least implicit faith that opposing religions' gods do *not* exist. Regarding the latter faith, if faith is evidence, religions would be (incoherently) mutually destructive of each others' and hence all gods. There would be no god(s).

Similarly, if faith is sufficient evidence to confirm a truth, or provide knowledge, it could be that, e.g., a child's faith that Easter Bunny exists means Easter Bunny truly exists. Due to someone's faith, it could be that Hitler or a teacup is President of the USA. It would also be true that many inmates of psychiatric institutions are the one true god(dess), Ruler of Planet X, Christ, President of the USA, and so on. And if emotions are evidence, then, e.g., racist hatred proves racism is right, and compassion towards races unfairly discriminated against proves racism is wrong. And so on. Most obviously, if faith or feelings are evidence, then a scientifically-unobjective faith or gut-feeling of a group here that, e.g., poisonous liquid L is safe to drink, would mean L truly *is* safe. The objective situation is that the resulting deaths would be evidence that the group's beliefs should have cohered with evidence as in survival-necessary knowledge/science, i.e., been pro-objectivity, not religious or emotion-based.

In sum:- Various beliefs, or emotion-thought combinations as in intuitions, spine-tingling awe and faith-based experiences prompting religious beliefs, need to be ignored by rational people seeking actual evidence, as in or coherent with scientific evidence, as in the evidence for an objective normativity.

Part II, Section 1.3.2: Summarised And Wider Implications Of This Section So Far; Pointers To The Rest Of The Book

This Section's discussions above concerning knowledge, free speech and associated issues clearly have wider implications. E.g:-

As with religious and racist beliefs, persons with many other (e.g., sexist) beliefs (faiths/intuitions) also have no right to have such beliefs. These and all persons have an objective duty to ask whether there is evidence for their beliefs, and to rationally critically research them.

Relatedly, a certain type of education system and society are needed, to promote the ideas in this Section. E.g., an expanded version of the previous two subsections needs to be included in that education. (The whole book can be interpreted as a curriculum outline.) It is a pro-objectivity duty to provide that education etc, and all have rights to such education etc. Importantly, a certain type of evidence-based, fallibilist, self-critical democratic society is implied. E.g., religious-based rule, even via (some other type of) democratic government, is in-effect dictatorial, e.g., because here (alleged) gods are viewed by religious voters as having a superhuman, absolutely superior, unevidenced divine right to dictate what humans do. Careful but freely expressed, rational political criticism is needed, involving evidence, which means a pro-objectivity type of democracy.

Many such educational, political etc issues mentioned in Part II so far are expanded on below. This is often done in other contexts, as all aspects of maximal pro-objectivity constitute an interrelated, coherent whole—consisting of many conceptually separable aspects. Those and representative other practical normative implications of the theory are the main focus of the rest of the book.

The rest in part considers emotions in relation to society, e.g., racist hatred, and the benevolent compassion involved in pro-objectivity society. Part II so far has mostly concerned the cognitive aspects of pro-objectivity. Another highly important part of one's mind or psychology is its non-cognitive aspects, including the emotional. As Part I stressed, one piece of pro-objectivity knowledge is that pro-objectivity involves emotions. Pro-objectivity knowledge includes knowing that the cognitive and emotional parts of our brains are physically[5] interconnected, i.e., interrelated. E.g., most basically, our cognition and its knowledge would not exist unless they were motivated to exist; and we will not be pro-objectivity if we allow certain emotions to successfully influence us to believe the unobjective or do the anti-objectivity. These emotions include the motivational aspect of faith and other motivations for believing merely alleged evidence. For such reasons, emotions need further discussion:-

Part II, Section 1.4: Emotions And Pro-Objectivity

One piece of pro-objectivity knowledge is: 'To be pro-objectivity, humans need to experience certain emotions, or certain emotions in certain situations'. These emotions are no problem for and are prescribed by an objective and hence inherently *human* normative theory. These emotions are causally-coherent with objective normativity. However, other emotions, or certain other emotions in those situations, are or can be a major problem. E.g., again, racist hatred can be viewed as evidence that its possible object, 'Racist violence', is morally good. As a lead-up to issues here, a discussion regarding emotions generally:-

Emotional objects are either an end or a means to an end and hence involve an end. A positive object is an emotionally-(positively-)valued normative achievement, e.g., having desired sex, or, for racists, enjoyed racist acts. A negative object is an event the opposite of which one emotionally values (positively). E.g., concerning parental grief over the accidental death of a much-loved healthy child, the parents would strongly prefer the child to have lived.

Object X can be emotionally valued on various grounds, e.g., beliefs such as 'Normativity X is prescribed by the true goddess, Mergo'. Another content for X can be valued via knowledge that this X is pro-objectivity. Whether something is or remains of emotional value can crucially depend on belief, knowledge or evidence—associated with emotion. E.g., consider Ted, who values smoking, initially believing it to not be unhealthy, but who is increasingly confronted with evidence that smoking is unhealthy. Such evidence is initially unwelcomed (emotionally negatively evaluated) by Ted. But the evidence increases, until Ted ceases to emotionally (positively) value smoking. Ted stops smoking primarily because of (his rational acceptance of) that evidence in association with him emotionally valuing (evidence regarding) his health. He has always valued his health, his ultimate end-aim, and regarding smoking he (eventually) emotionally values the evidence, the truth, and hence non-smoking, as a means to that end. Similarly regarding Ted later emotionally valuing and obediently practising a normativity he once believed to be ordained by Mergo, but ceasing to do so via his increasing awareness that there is no evidence for Mergo's existence and that normative belief. But here there is no emotion like the health-valuing emotion associated with Ted eventually emotionally valuing evidence concerning smoking. Here Ted only has the direct pro-objectivity emotion valuing evidence about what is objectively right to believe, and pro-objectivity rightness-motivation regarding what is objectively right to do. Here he has the end, 'Be normatively objective'. Later he realises this evidence means he should have 'Be pro-objectivity' as his *ultimate* end. Then he views his previous ultimate end, 'Be healthy', as still subjectively valuable but also as a means to that objectively valuable end emotionally valued by his pro-objectivity emotion.

So there can be much openness and alterability concerning emotions and their objects, including among/within means-to-an-end-objects and end-objects.

Knowledge and hence evidence are objectivity's internal general end-object, as explained in Part I, Section 1. Relatedly, because evidence is inherently objective, it is of value to objectivity and relatedly to (at least Type-A-related) pro-objectivity emotion. However, evidence regarding X may not be valued by another emotion, say Ted's pre-pro-objectivity desire to maintain the object, 'psychological comfort and security', via believing Mergo exists and lovingly kindly cares for him, via being a parent-substitute or a special, supernatural parent. An alternative here, believing that oneself is or may be alone in that there is not, or possibly not, a being with super-human powers caring for oneself, meaning one has to manage life significantly on one's own, helped only by other mere humans, is too fearful for many. This common (often normal) psychology, a major problem for pro-objectivity, is that of the child feeling inadequate and hence wanting a parent or parent-substitute to manage issues for the child, e.g., to provide help, security, and comfort, and tell the child what she/he should do, i.e., prescribe the correct normativity. An objective, pro-objectivity psychology is very different, involving adults managing for and among themselves, as fully responsible persons, and independently acquiring evidence regarding correct normativity. (To achieve an end such as 'comfort', or 'group cohesion and survival', it can in a limited, instrumental, type-A sense be rational to use religion, namely as a means to that end. But utilitarian and selfish ends such as 'comfort' are not objective, and do not involve all the (type-B) rationality involved in seeking, understanding and achieving an objective end, as shown above.)

Ted initially disliked that evidence concerning Mergo, feeling conflict between (i) his objectivity, plus its pro-objectivity motivation, and (ii) that other emotion and its (selfish) object, '(child-like) psychological comfort and security (via faith)'. But eventually Ted becomes rational here and at least significantly pro-objectivity. He understands and rejects that childish, faith-involving psychology. He decides, as a now fully responsible adult, to manage his own life as best he can, involving giving that inherently objective evidence regarding Mergo priority over the emotionally valuable object associated with faith in Mergo. Here, evidence, knowledge and hence truth are valued more highly than (child-like) comfort, security and simple-minded, dependent normative obedience. Here the pro-objectivity emotion, associated with its inherently evidenced object, here knowledge concerning religion and psychology, overrules the other emotion and its unevidenced but (to-the-childish) emotionally attractive object.

But often the latter type of emotion and object win in such conflicts, typically via the object being subjectively-evaluated as intrinsically-valuable:-

Part II, Section 1.4.1: More On Emotions And Their Objects; The Subjectively-Evaluated As Intrinsically-Valuable

(Points here can be adapted and applied similarly to emotions/objects not subjectively-evaluated as intrinsically-valuable, but still subjectively valued.)

Part II, Section1.4.1.1: General Points Here

Normal persons view some emotional objects as intrinsically (and hence extremely positively) valuable. As far as a person's conscious experience is concerned, the objects are not valued for any other purpose beyond themselves.[6] E.g., many feel that objects such as an orgasm, hearing certain music, and one's children being safe and happy, are valuable for their own sake. E.g., many parents view their children's happiness as priceless, as something they'd not exchange for anything, e.g., for any amount of money. Because objects viewed as intrinsically-valuable are viewed as ultimate ends, and vice versa, the issue of *subjectively* evaluating objects as intrinsically-valuable is important regarding an *objectively* intrinsically-valuable end, an objective normative (ultimate) end.

Why some objects are commonly subjectively-evaluated as intrinsically-valuable is easily and directly explainable via evolutionary theory, as in the explanation concerning child-care at Part I, Section 2's beginning. Some other common emotional objects are indirectly explainable via evolution. E.g., the more a group is emotionally dedicated to one set of normative etc beliefs, the more likely the group will be cohesive and that thereby the group's children will be well cared for and hence survive to pass on the group's genes, all else equal. A group is very likely to be so dedicated and cohesive if it believes its beliefs are absolutely right, i.e., unquestionable. The intrinsically-valued is believed to be absolutely normatively right. A disposition, on-average adaptive during human evolutionary history, to regard one's group's or society's normative values and at least some of its other beliefs as intrinsically-valuable objects, is a general disposition (moral intuition) covering many specific, often-conflicting values/objects and other, often-related, religious etc beliefs. That disposition often combines with an evolved common disposition to religious belief via emotion, such as spine-tingling, dependent awe, useful to motivate belief in some super-being(s) and associated values/objects useful for the group cohesion crucial for passing on a group's genes. Here, and elsewhere, emotion is used by evolution to fool people into believing whatever achieves evolution's aims on-average. If values are believed to be a god's commands, they are believed to be absolutely right, absolutely intrinsically valuable. So a religious disposition is a useful evolutionary tool: it can further cement that group cohesion. Hence a combination of religious belief and associated normative beliefs is commonly an intrinsically-valued object (a problematic one for pro-objectivity).

With some other objects, explanation is often difficult, sometimes perhaps too difficult, e.g., regarding various intrinsically-valued experiences of music and sunsets, and, moreso, intrinsically-valued bottle-top collections and so on.

This book will not be concerned with such difficulty. Where objects here are normatively significant, that significance is a concern. E.g., it can be significant that some object here, or this or that evaluation of it, is pro-, anti- or a- objectivity in the situation in question.[7] So, on with that normative focus concerning objects. First, some general issues here:-

An object can be internal to the person. E.g., an emotional object can be another emotion or feeling, as in 'I'd like to like exercising', and 'feeling pleasure' is the object of the emotion, 'desire for pleasure'. Many emotional objects are (primarily) external to the person, as with one's children showing they're safe and happy. Other objects are combinations of internal and external (sub-)objects, as in having sex due to desiring both pleasure and to produce an heir(ess).

A normatively important issue here concerns certain achievements achieved via achieving objects subjectively-evaluated as intrinsically-valuable. An example is the pleasure normal parents can experience due to first achieving their object, 'my children are safe and happy'. Normatively importantly, normal parents here only fully, genuinely and reliably feel all the potentially available pleasure if *that object* is achieved *first.* And, regarding the pleasure, the only motivation to achieve it can be unconscious, innate motivation. Unless there is conscious intention, there is no normative issue. E.g., normal parents would tend to *not* be consciously selfishly motivated only or primarily to feel that pleasure, namely *without* having achieved their object, 'my children are safe and happy'. They'd not be motivated or content to feel the pleasure *instead* of that achievement. Parents often feel *dis*pleasure or anxiety till their child-care object is achieved. These are *punishing*-emotions, emotions which negatively further motivate *achieving that object*. The child-care then, is the conscious, intended object. It is the normative object. If, apart from normativity, the pleasure can reasonably be called an object, in relation to the child-care it is a secondary object, and the child-care is the primary object, e.g., in that it must be achieved *first* and parents (also unintentionally) get that *punishment* if they don't achieve it. The pleasure seems evolutionarily (genetically) installed, as a reward for achieving and a motivation to keep achieving the (here also evolutionarily-installed) primary object, child-care (so as to pass on genes). Correspondingly regarding that punishment.

The general, normatively important point here is that happiness or pleasure felt due to an achievement need not be the primary or ultimate, inherently selfish object of conscious intentions—conscious intentions or choices being normative issues. So if one chooses to have 'Be pro-objectivity' as one's ultimate end-object, and one feels pleasure due to achieving that end, that pleasure was *not* one's real end-object. (Some critics of pro-objectivity theory, psychological egoists, claim that selfish pleasure is unavoidably one's real ultimate end-object, a non-cognitively, unconsciously installed object, implying that 'Be pro-objectivity' cannot be a real, primarily-cognitively consciously chosen ultimate end, and relatedly that there can be no such, objective end, as there is really only the *subjectively* evaluated as intrinsically-valuable end-object, selfish pleasure.)

Two conclusions here:- (i) *Knowing* that evolution uses emotion/feelings to try to fool us into valuing and aiming at certain objects frees us from being so fooled. Thence we can autonomously or freely choose whether to aim at those objects, and ignore or overrule any desire for pleasure or other feeling as a reason for our objects/practices. (ii) Concerning child-care and many other intended objects, the subjectively (and hence consciously) evaluated as intrinsically-valuable object is the intended or chosen object, not the achievement-produced pleasure. It is important regarding a normative theory's practicability to understand that normativity involves choices and hence the choosable, not the unconscious and hence unchoosable—and that often the conscious, cognitively-*choosable* object is *not* pleasure or any feeling. And it is because of *intended achievements* that one feels at least most, perhaps all, of any achievement-produced pleasure.

With this, achievers of object X would tend to feel most happy due to achieving X and are most likely to be further motivated thereby to achieve X, if they know X is most worth achieving, i.e., if they know X is really the only *objectively intrinsically-valuable* end, an objective, choosable normative end—the objective ultimate end-object. So, compared with other theories' inherently non-objectively intrinsically-valued end-objects, the pro-objectivity end-object is most likely to also be *subjectively* evaluated as intrinsically-valuable, further motivating its achievement. And the pleasure/happiness due to its achievement would be a pro-objectivity feeling motivating one to keep achieving it—not the primary or only reason why one would intend to achieve that objective end.

Here, as suggested by discussions of autonomy soon, we can autonomously choose to and use emotion to help achieve that end, rather than simply be used by emotion to achieve primarily-emotional, evolution-installed ends.

So, the total emotion-thought combination here could perhaps always fairly easily overrule any evolved emotion-thought tendency to believe and practise religious, emotion-based and other non-pro-objectivity normative theories.

Part II, Section1.4.1.2: Pro-Objectivity And Anti-Objectivity Emotions Here; Evolution-Based Normative Theories; Emotional Perception

Objectively intrinsically-valuable practices involve subjectively or emotionally valued internal and/or external objects (coming under the overall object, 'Be pro-objectivity'). Internal objects here include one's potentially pro-objectivity knowledge and one's pro-objectivity feelings and motivations, as in 'I desire to be more motivated to learn potentially pro-objectivity knowledge'. An object-achievement here becomes an aspect of the objectively intrinsically-valuable only via association with other, external object-achievements, namely practising potentially pro-objectivity knowledge in the world outside one's mind.

The emotion actually motivating such object-achievements is pro-objectivity. But, as mentioned near the start of Part II, Section 1.4, a major problem is that other, anti-objectivity emotions and their objects subjectively-evaluated as intrinsically-valuable can conflict with the pro-objectivity—and sometimes win. (In other words, the more influence non-pro-objectivity emotion has, the less objective or rational one is overall, meaning one is more likely to believe a normative theory other than an objective theory.):-

An anti-objectivity emotion and its object viewed as intrinsically-valuable could be believed to alone be of true ultimate value. This would be an insoluble problem regarding motivating people here to be pro-objectivity, unless they can be shown and will accept sufficient evidence confirming that the belief is too problematic. It could be difficult to gain that acceptance and hence remove that belief, e.g., if the emotion and its object give believers great comfort and security on which they, childishly (foolishly), are highly dependent.

Another problem here is if people view both an anti-objectivity object and pro-objectivity as intrinsically-valuable and hence of ultimate value. If both are of true ultimate value, they are of equal value. Here, as Part I suggests, one of them could not correctly be given priority over the other when they conflict. We could not *know* which one to act on. Regarding that cognitive issue, does the fact that some emotional objects are *naturally* subjectively-evaluated as intrinsically-valuable mean pro-objectivity would lose in a conflict here because it is *objectively*-based—objectivity as such apparently being purely *cognitive*? And if there is conflict between the cognitive and the emotionally or non-cognitively natural, or between reason and passion, will the cognitive or reason naturally lose? Part II, Section 2.1 and Appendix 6 argue at length that our directly pro-objectivity emotion, which motivates and hence combines with objective cognition or reason, is also *natural*. So, to avoid unneeded repetition this subsection primarily focuses on related issues regarding that question:-

In Part I, the pro-objectivity standard/end was argued to be of primary, ultimate, objective intrinsic value. From an objective, cognitive viewpoint, we can know that is so as far as is possible. Part I and recent arguments also suggest we cannot know this regarding any emotion. We can only merely believe it, without evidence. So, as far as we can *know*, the pro-objectivity has top priority if there is a conflict between it and an emotion and its object (or anything else).

Importantly, as Part I, Section 2, Ted and Appendix 6 suggest, because reason or objectivity has its own directly motivating emotion or passion, that pro-objectivity knowledge would be helped here by *pro-objectivity emotion.* The conflict would not be just between cognition and an emotion, or between reason and passion. It would be between (i) the pro-objectivity emotion and its object, here the objective normative end, and (ii) another emotion and its object(s), which, via conflicting with the normatively objective, are objectively wrong.

Yet, at least often due to obvious evolutionary adaptiveness, it is natural for normal humans to believe that *various* emotional objects are of intrinsic value, and sometimes the relatedly *powerful* emotions here can overrule pro-objectivity emotion (and its object), meaning anti-objectivity wins in that conflict:-

At least partly via such evolutionary-adaptiveness and related power, many believe that emotional objects naturally evaluat*ed* as intrinsically-valuable are actually intrinsically valu*able*. That is, the subjectively-evaluated here is quite commonly thereby believed objectively valuable. Thence, many at least implicitly believe an associated normative theory, e.g., some version of Utilitarianism, which has a basis including that incoherent belief, namely, here, that maximising the evolution-installed hence-popular subjective feeling, 'happiness', should be humanity's ultimate end. (Again, popularity is not an indicator of objectivity.)

Relatedly, at least partly due to the fundamental role evolutionary-adaptiveness plays regarding what many naturally subjectively-evaluate as intrinsically-valuable or naturally find meaningful, many believe evolutionary-adaptiveness is the fundamental general normative end. Evolutionary-adaptiveness is often (questionably) viewed as having the specific end-object, 'Survival, as in *victory* of, the fittest', and emotions/feelings associated with victory here are viewed as desirable objects associated with that end-object, and relatedly as intrinsically-valuable. Happiness, or an elated sense of power, due to military conquest, political victory, economic success and so on, are objects here. Various factors here can go with groupism. In sum, relatedly many at least implicitly believe a theory claiming that a primarily-emotional, groupist version of evolutionary advantage should be their normative end-aim. Nazis did/do.

Yet, the evaluated-as-intrinsically-valuable is obviously not necessarily the knowably intrinsically-valuable. Relatedly, again, none of the standards, 'evolutionary-advantage', 'happiness' and so on is the objective normative standard. The objective normative standard is knowably intrinsically-valuable. If the merely evaluated-as-intrinsically-valuable was the objectively intrinsically-valuable, the rationally-unquestionably valuable, then innumerable conflicting valued emotional end-objects would be objectively intrinsically-valuable. E.g., Nazi militarism, racism etc (evolutionarily advantageous for Nazis if they'd won World War II), playing bingo, sex with non-human animals, *and* their *opposites*, would all be objectively valuable. Each emotion/object in evolutionary-adaptive opposing-pairs, as in 'fight or flight' and 'selfishness and unselfishness', would be objectively valuable. And so on. This incoherent situation is largely that found throughout history, meaning frequent conflict within persons, between nations, socio-economic classes, races, political parties and so on. (As Part I and Appendix 4 suggest, a coherent, evidenced, objective normative theory is the only reliable long-term way to achieve peace.)

As Part I implies, that incoherence further shows that evolutionary-adaptiveness and related powerfulness of emotions/feelings cannot be objective normative standards. Further:- Human evolution was unchosen by humans, and is in that sense outside inherently choice-involving normativity. Evolution has been an unintended, blind, significantly random process, and hence a predominantly-failures, undirected-by-knowledge/objectivity process, extremely slowly producing only that which is merely on-average adaptive, adaptive in merely contingently common, often conflicting types of situations (e.g., food-abundance and food-shortage, peace and war), including producing a related conflicting mix of emotions/feelings, as in those opposing-pairs, to merely on-average probably deal with that common mix of situations, merely to pass on genes. From an objective viewpoint, failures are errors, i.e., unobjective, and a process occurring entirely without knowledge/objectivity and hence producing predominantly errors and an incoherent mix is not an objectively-warranted, inherently rational process.[8] With this, our objectivity also evolved as in-part a very open capacity but in large part as merely instrumental regarding primarily-emotional ends. It does not naturally easily commonly direct us towards the pro-objectivity end, otherwise pro-objectivity theory would have been commonly believed for ages.

In sum, nature- or evolution-based normative theories cannot be objective.

Relatedly:- Evolution or nature has given us often-normatively-problematic 'emotional perception', parallel to visual perception projecting different colours onto different physical objects. Emotional perception projects different values onto different normative objects as in normal persons hating and relatedly disapproving of cruelty to children, but approving of kind child-care. Such evolved projections are the basis of some (hence basically simplistic) normative theories. (Here, simplistically regarding assessing ends, objectivity is merely instrumental regarding primarily-emotional, on-average evolutionary-adaptive objects.)

Emotional perception/projection has that similarity to physical, visual perception. (One normatively important difference is that emotional perception is fairly open: emotions are often redirectable and their objects are often alterable, choosable; but physical perceptions are entirely closed or 'encapsulated'.[9]) As with evolution and, relatedly, visual perception, emotional perception/projection can be error-prone (unobjective) from an overall, objective viewpoint. Relatedly, emotional perception is objectively-normatively ignorant because it is non-discriminatory concerning whether emotionally-projected-onto objects are pro-, a- or anti-objectivity. This issue relates to recent discussions concerning faith, merely alleged evidence, (non-pro-objectivity[10]) intuition and similar. These often involve normativity-related, intrinsically-valued emotional objects. Indeed, e.g., what many call moral intuition, involving subjectively intrinsically-valued normative objects, seems likely to be at least often at least significantly based on emotional perception. The two may at least often be identical.

Regarding emotional perception, what are issues here for pro-objectivity?:-

Humans often emotionally-perceive and hence simplistically believe that the object of the emotion is objectively intrinsically-valuable. Various normative theories are at least implicitly ultimately based on such belief, e.g., the belief that pleasure/happiness (or victory, dominance, religiosity, wealth or whatever) is intrinsically-valuable. But there is no objective need or basis for such belief. Perception in general is not belief, though it tends to at least initially prompt belief. But there is considerable scope for ignoring or overruling perception and related prompts to believe. E.g., regarding visual perception, we need not believe a perception, e.g., when it is an illusion (unobjective). Probably at least nearly everyone disbelieves the perception suggesting a stick partly submerged in water is bent by the water. Importantly, this is at least implicitly because that perception is *incoherent with one's inherently coherent objectivity* here, e.g., with the general knowledge that water does not bend rigid materials, as in putting oneself in water and perceiving objectively, e.g., via touch, pain-sensors, proprioception and looking underwater, that one's rigid bits, e.g., leg bones, do not bend, and with the stick-specific knowledge acquirable via one's hands feeling the submerging stick and looking at it underwater. Additionally, some are aware of refraction, of how light is *objectively* bent by water, making the stick seem bent.

So we can *know* that perceptions and thereby-prompted beliefs are in-themselves not necessarily coherent with objectivity. This needs to be applied to emotional perception, in relation to normative objectivity. When pro-objectivity persons know an emotional perception or projection is normatively unobjective, they could be emotionally prompted to believe that the associated object is intrinsically-valuable, but would not believe it is. Here their cognition rationally reflects on emotional perception. This is parallel to cognition rationally reflecting on visual perception, as in knowing a stick is not bent by water.

Via rationally, coherently or consiliently combining the stick-bends perception with those other physical perceptions and high-level knowledge concerning light and human vision, we know that the *objective*, *overall*, highest-level conclusion is that we are perceiving refracted light, not a stick bending. Such knowledge is at least potentially available regarding all physical perceptual illusions. That is, via objectivity's *overall* view, any purely-in-itself unobjective, isolated physical (non-emotional) perception is made coherent with or part of objectivity. But, as indicated by discussions above, e.g., suggesting that pleasure can be emotionally perceived as objectively intrinsically-valuable, this 'made coherent with or part of objectivity' does not apply regarding *emotional* perception in relation to normative objectivity—except sometimes but, with one soon-to-be-mentioned exception or special case, just extrinsically and via a conclusion-overlap needing qualification. (E.g:- Emotionally perceiving or intuiting child-care as good overlaps in-effect with the pro-objectivity conclusion, 'Care for potentially pro-objectivity persons', and is relatedly of potential pro-objectivity extrinsic value. But child-care is not actually pro-objectivity unless in an overall pro-objectivity context. (Nazi child-care was anti-objectivity.)) Relatedly, we can know we *cannot emotionally perceive* objective intrinsic value. The overall situation here means there is no rational ground for believing in any primarily-emotional normative end or theory based primarily on emotion.

Via high-level objective reflection or judgement, we can be open to the possibility that emotional perception can be unobjective, and investigate further here. Our open, rational capacity here is natural, and hence must be evolutionarily advantageous—and it can help us investigate concerning an objective end, and reflect on and discriminate situationally among our other evolutionarily advantageous aspects, including emotional perception. Concerning highest-level objective reflection and that openness, evolutionary advantage is pro-objectivity, though normatively only potentially *extrinsically* so.

Via reflecting on emotional perceptions or emotional-perception-prompted thoughts (emotion-thought combinations), and assessing whether they cohere with the normatively objective end, we can *know* that sometimes something emotionally-perceived to be intrinsically-valuable is overall-objectively-unwarranted. We can also know that in some cases something emotionally-perceived as intrinsically valuable, e.g., a certain type of happiness, can be or is of normatively objective *extrinsic* value—in some cases at least significantly because of the associated emotional perception, via the resulting emotion/feeling helping to motivate further pro-objectivity. A special case is the exception a recent paragraph promised would soon be mentioned. This is when *pro-objectivity* emotion perceives 'Be pro-objectivity', as intrinsically-valuable. Only *this* emotional perception is part of objectivity and where we can know the object *is* intrinsically-valuable, though not because of that emotional perception as such.

Concluding here:- Only via highest-level pro-objectivity cognition can we correctly discriminate regarding which emotions and objects, in which situations, are pro-, a- or anti-objectivity, and which objects are intrinsically or extrinsically valuable. Otherwise, from an objective viewpoint, normativity would be blind, and could easily come from rationally problematic, evolved emotional-perception, or from some socialised or socially-encouraged specific emotional-perception which is just one of many possibilities socially-constructible on the (too-)general evolutionary basis here, typically primarily to benefit an anti-objectivity ruling class, as with Nazism. Again, emotion, feelings and evolution (and such rulers' desires) are not objective normative standards or indicators. Evolved and hence common or any other emotional perception or projection or intuition cannot be the basis of an objective normative theory. We need not be fooled by physical perceptual illusions; we need not be fooled by emotional perception/intuition into believing unobjective normative theories (delusions).

Part II, Section1.4.1.3: Concluding Comments Here So Far

(1) As Appendix 6 and Part II, Section 2.1 argue, pro-objectivity emotion is natural—because it too is evolutionarily adaptive. E.g., at least minimally-pro-objectivity motivation is necessary for many specific knowledge-objects desired by other, associable emotions. (E.g., humanity could not have survived unless humans were naturally motivated to *know*, e.g., how to get food and have heterosexual sex.) Relatedly, significant and further practising of pro-objectivity theory is motivated by that natural, adaptive emotion. So pro-objectivity is naturally motivated, and hence it is reasonable to expect that humans can be motivated to practise pro-objectivity theory, overruling opposing motivations.

(2) It is always rationally problematic, including regarding pro-objectivity emotional perception, to believe, on the basis of emotional perception alone, that emotional objects subjectively-evaluated as intrinsically-valuable are (objectively) intrinsically-valuable. (Inherently) *independent* evidence is needed. It is evidence's dependence on, or its being sought crucially via, *pro-objectivity* emotion, which means the cognition here *is independent*, namely of emotion prompting cognition to be primarily-emotion-based, i.e., normatively problematic.

(2a) Relatedly, obviously, just because someone likes (or dislikes) X, or evaluates X in a certain way, this has *nothing* to do with whether X objectively deserves to be liked (or disliked), or has that value objectively. Emotions and feelings are no basis for or guide regarding what is normatively correct. Knowledge is needed, via inherently independent evidence.

(3) If there is conflict between a cognitive aspect of 'Be pro-objectivity' and

an anti-objectivity emotion/object merely believed to be intrinsically-valuable, the cognitive aspect can and should win. However, in practice, regarding what humans really do, there are no purely cognitive normative aspects: there are emotion-cognition or emotion-thought combinations. Relatedly, the necessity for emotion to be crucially involved in all choices, including the choice of what should win here, does not necessarily mean that the anti-objectivity emotion will win. Again, being pro-objectivity is not a purely cognitive practice:-

If Hume is right in claiming that reason or objectivity is the slave of the passions or emotions, then in any conflict between the cognitive or an objective standard and an emotion, the emotion would win. However, as Part I suggests, there must be pro-reason or pro-objectivity emotion—and this emotion can combine with and thereby direct objectivity to assess, via the hence-emotionally-valued objective standard, what should win the conflict, and hence that the pro-objectivity emotion should overrule the other, anti-objectivity emotion. Here the *objects* of the emotions are important, not just the emotions. Emotional objects at least implicitly involve thoughts, the thoughts in emotion-thought combinations. These thoughts involve the thought of what the object is, that it is desirable, and perhaps reasons why it is desirable or should be achieved. Pro-objectivity emotion's object involves the thoughts (knowledge) that the normatively objective should be achieved and why. Here there is a passion for reason or truth (objectivity), and the inextricable passion-truth (emotion-thought) combination here involves the truth that its associated passion should win here.

When the correctness of the pro-objectivity motivation's object, and the unwarrantedness of its opponents, are fully appreciated, this gives pro-objectivity emotion increased power (ability to motivate) in order to overrule its opponents. Again, the *object* of an emotion is the crucial factor in the emotion-object, emotion-thought interrelation(s): if the object can be known to have objectively important warrant, the associated emotion tends to be(come) more powerful and hence highly able to overrule any conflicting emotion. There is an objective, evolved, natural basis for this: neurophysiology shows that the normal brain's frontal cortex has neural connections with the brain's emotional parts, and can weaken, permit or increase an emotion's strength. Those connections and interactions mean emotion-thought combinations physically exist. For such and other reasons, it is reasonable to expect that humans can be motivated to *maximally* practise pro-objectivity. (Appendix 6 concerns issues raised in (3).)

Part II, Section 1.4.2: Regarding Indirectly Pro-Objectivity Emotions/Feelings

The just-previous discussion of pro-objectivity emotion tended to explicitly concern *directly* pro-objectivity emotion, namely the emotion, internal to our objective faculty-system, which directly motivates pro-objectivity cognition. Part I argues there are other, *in*directly pro-objectivity emotions, and feelings, external to objectivity. (These could help in any conflict between an anti-objectivity emotion/object and pro-objectivity.) Some revision and further points regarding indirect pro-objectivity emotions:-

Among our mix of emotions and their objects, many can be indirectly pro-objectivity. As Part I, Section 2 suggests, various things subjectively regarded as intrinsically-valuable can be of pro-objectivity extrinsic value, including various emotional, subjectively-desired objects. That sentence is pro-objectivity knowledge, and the pro-objectivity end involves practising pro-objectivity knowledge. So, experiencing those emotional objects, including various feelings, is also an aspect of achieving the pro-objectivity end. As Part I, Section 2 said, various emotional experiences and their objects can be *both,* (i) from one's subjective viewpoint, intrinsically-valuable, and (ii) from (pro-)objectivity's overall, primarily cognitive viewpoint, objectively extrinsically-valuable, as with Jim's pro-objectivity improving generally via him loving and enjoying his new soul-mate. Such love and enjoyment are indirectly pro-objectivity. They do not directly motivate the acquiring of (potentially) pro-objectivity knowledge, but they make it easier for directly pro-objectivity emotion to do so, e.g., via helping Jim avoid cognitively-disabling depression. Similarly regarding motivating Jim to act on that knowledge, and avoid activity-disabling depression.

Such combinations of (i) and (ii) are '(pro-objectivity) subjective-objective evaluation-combinations'. From pro-objectivity's overall viewpoint, such *end-achieving combinations*, the *overall* situations here, are objectively intrinsically-valuable. They involve pro-objectivity emotion-thought combinations.

Concluding here:- Such coherent combination of the non-cognitive and cognitive is an aspect of maximal pro-objectivity. Again, being maximally pro-objectivity cannot be an overall dull, narrow, cerebral task. Being dull, narrow and cerebral would be anti-objectivity in that we'd not be motivated sufficiently to be pro-objectivity in even minor ways; or we'd be negative towards pro-objectivity. A *flourishing* of *positive* pro-objectivity emotions and feelings is crucial. Indirectly pro-objectivity emotions and feelings are among those crucial factors. Partly because positive emotion is overall more effective in motivating pro-objectivity than is negative emotion, pro-objectivity requires the above-discussed pro-objectivity-universal benevolence. This benevolence inherently aims at that positive flourishing, among direct and indirect pro-objectivity emotions and feelings. However, the ideal, perfectly positive state here is unlikely to ever be achieved. As the next subsection, and Part II, Section 1.4.7. and others suggest, a realistic (objective) or real-world benevolence aims at a mix of positive and negative motivation, though the balance should be positive overall.

Part II, Section 1.4.3: Negative Pro-Objectivity Emotions/Feelings

That need for emotional flourishing applies only to positive pro-objectivity emotions. There can be negative pro-objectivity emotions, namely emotions helping to cause a pro-objectivity effect but experienced as dislike, disapproval, disappointment, unhappiness and so on. (In an absolutely ideal pro-objectivity world, because there'd be nothing to dislike etc, flourishing would not involve the negative emotions/feelings which co-exist with and hence limit the absolute maximum degree of pro-objectivity flourishing in the real world.)

Some issues concerning negative pro-objectivity emotions/feelings:-

Pro-objectivity Pat, trying to get pro-objectivity-needed sleep, gets annoyed, especially at night, at loud traffic noises. Such emotions tend not to be evaluated as intrinsically-valuable.[11] But they can be of objective value, e.g., if such annoyance motivates Pat, a mother, to soundproof the room, resulting in sleep improved enough to help her give her children better pro-objectivity care.

Similarly, an endnote to Part I, Section 2 suggested that being *un*-happy can motivate seeking pro-objectivity knowledge, e.g., unhappiness regarding diseases can motivate searching for cures. However, it was also pointed out that here there'd also probably be a type of pro-objectivity happiness due to self-respect from knowing oneself is at least seeking useful knowledge, and potentially more pro-objectivity happiness for oneself long-term if one discovers cures. And Pat would be happier due to better sleep and giving better child-care. So, negative pro-objectivity emotions are at least potentially associated with *positive* pro-objectivity emotions/feelings and (inherently objectively positive) pro-objectivity achievements.

But some such negative emotions can be(come) so strong that they are problematic or counter-productive. Because, for motivatability, pro-objectivity needs to be at least primarily an emotionally positive experience, pro-objectivity negative emotions here need to be controlled, so they remain pro-objectivity, rather than increase so as to flourish in anti-objectivity ways. E.g., pro-objectivity rational dislike should not be allowed to develop into anti-objectivity extreme and hence irrational, cruelly violent hatred. Or it may sometimes be pro-objectivity to avoid situations where we are likely to experience emotions/feelings which are likely to so develop (—as opposed to being anti-objectivity by avoiding situations in order to put a pro-objectivity need "out of sight, out of mind").

Part II, Section 1.4.4: Pro-Objectivity Compassion, Caring And Social Harmony

A (com)passionate desire to ensure all have pro-objectivity fair access to pro-objectivity food, health, housing, employment, leisure, legal help, political participation, affection, education etc is needed, along with, negatively, dislike of unfairness here. Being pro-objectivity means a great deal of (action-motivating) compassion or sympathy, including for anyone treated unfairly here—as billions presently are (2010). Indirect pro-objectivity-optimal emotions include the compassionate, unselfish pro-objectivity-directed universal benevolent caring or love discussed in Part I, Section 2.

Pro-objectivity societal and related normative coherence or harmony among persons is best achieved if they universally affectionately care unselfishly for each other, and find affection for each other subjectively intrinsically-valuable (and objectively highly valuable). Regarding receiving care here, childhood is the most important stage, though the following applies to an at least significant degree throughout a person's life:-

Probably the overall most important aspect of pro-objectivity-directed universal care involves sympathy or compassion for children, due to them being overall the most vulnerable humans and long-term most important at least potentially pro-objectivity beings. Adults who are parents, teachers or similar can be vulnerable to abuse by certain here-anti-objectivity children, especially some teenagers. However, mostly it is children who are most vulnerable. Their vulnerability means they on-average need much more help than adults do regarding having their pro-objectivity needs met. So, all else pro-objectivity-relevant equal, children at least often need more sympathy when in need than do adults with the same need. Luckily, via evolution, normal human emotion/intuition tends to harmonise with that difference. Another difference, also and relatedly naturally normally emotionally harmonised with, concerns children having some other major needs at least much less needed by adults, or non-reciprocal needs. Different types of love and thereby-motivated general care-types here are crucial, and the care cannot properly occur without adults feeling compassion.

Relatedly:- The only coherent, evidenced definition of 'child abuse' is 'anti-objectivity practices towards children'—and among the worst such practices, involving an inherently anti-objectivity lack of compassion, is neglect:-

It is well known in psychology that unloved children often literally shrivel, become physically ill and often die.[12] This lack of compassionate care[13] is often associated with a lack of physical and psychological stimulation and related development. E.g., unloved children tend to lack the hugging, stroking, tickling, playing, story-telling, language-teaching, language-practice and other cognitive education which loved children get from parents/carers. If unloved infants survive infancy, they greatly lack the physical and mental health needed to benefit as much as loved children can from education, food, medical care and so on. Clearly, these are areas where emotions are crucial pro-objectivity factors. Here, those with the power to ensure children get caring attention, stimulation etc need to be motivated by compassionate love if they are to optimally provide that care. Providing it will greatly help give children the motivation and ability needed to be at least potentially significantly pro-objectivity.[14]

There is overwhelming evidence that if humans grow up feeling isolated, alienated or uncared for, they are highly likely, all else equal, to be at least somewhat anti-social long-term, often committing in-effect anti-objectivity acts, e.g., violent crimes. It is pro-objectivity for all to feel part of a close-knit, caring community. We evolved as groups, as social animals. If a naturally-needed close-circle is denied a human, the human is likely to be un-social and relatedly anti-social, which tends to mean anti-objectivity effects overall (on-average).

In sum:- To optimally achieve pro-objectivity's cognitive and related emotional etc practical aims, we need to in-practice recognise that a crucial emotional need here is only achievable via that pro-objectivity-universal benevolent care.[15] (This would help develop the universal social harmony maximal pro-objectivity needs. This would facilitate the world peace needed here.)

Yet it would be emotionally at least extremely difficult, and physically impossible, for an individual to be *equally* optimally caring to *all*. And no normal person could have a pro-objectivity effect on anyone if the person tried to care equally and benevolently, let alone optimally, for each of the billions of humans. Here lies another qualification of 'pro-objectivity-directed universal': it would be anti-objectivity to try to be universally equally benevolent:-

If normal persons tried to be universally equally benevolent, this, at least initially, would probably be experienced as an obligation. (Here an 'obligation' is a duty one does not like. The most general term here, 'duties', can be divided into three types, negative, neutral and positive—respectively: (1) obligations, (2) duties we do not mind performing, and (3) duties which are a pleasure.)

That probable experience of obligation would occur because *universal equal* benevolence tends to not come naturally to humans. The natural tendency here seems for one to be very fond of persons in one's close-circle, especially one's closest family and certain friends, but be from less to far less fond of others, and not fond of strangers, with one's motivation to be benevolent *differing* accordingly. Nearly all people are strangers to any individual. Many people are at least sometimes somewhat benevolent to at least some strangers in various situations. But many people are at least indifferent towards at least nearly all strangers. Many people are wary of or hostile towards the strangers and others they typically basically-naturally tend to perceive as outgroups. Socialised views concerning outgroups tend to be built on a natural pre-dispositional basis, because human evolution occurred crucially via small groups, e.g., tribes, as opposed to via humanity *universally*. One's *group*, not humanity universally, was most essential regarding passing on one's genes, and this genes-survival was made more likely if other groups were eliminated, dominated or kept out of one's group's perceived territory, so they could not use often-scarce resources one's group (and its genes) depended on for survival. Hate can be naturally helpful here.

Within such groups, individuals tend(ed) to have a most-preferred, close-circle. That natural tendency to prefer one's close-circle would probably apply to a major degree to the most pro-objectivity of persons. But they'd not be indifferent, wary or hostile towards non-close-circle people—because their pro-objectivity-directed universal benevolence would involve overruling any indifference, and overruling any ingroup wariness or hostility and related desire to eliminate, dominate or exclude, and involve redirecting any natural small-group groupist tendency somewhat to persons *universally* here, viewing no-one here as belonging to an out-group.[16] (Comments here need to be qualified regarding that tiny minority, the irredeemably and hence at least highly[17] anti-objectivity.) With this, pro-objectivity persons would not view themselves as belonging primarily or only to a small in-group. (This universalisation would facilitate world peace). However, that universalised redirecting would not be equalised:-

An optimal pro-objectivity balance here would involve some prominence given to the normal, natural preference to be more caring towards one's family than strangers. (This discussion regarding family applies similarly to friends.) Here, that which is naturally normally subjectively-evaluated as intrinsically-valuable seems capable of also being optimally extrinsically-valuable as far as possible, i.e., within or given the naturally-limited range of human emotional etc capacities. Family-based and certain other close-circle love is about the best type regarding affection being helpful regarding acquiring and practising pro-objectivity knowledge, and is a crucial aspect *of* that practising. Again, e.g., unloved children are unlikely to achieve their otherwise maximum pro-objectivity potential—and the naturally best (and naturally viewed as intrinsically-valuable) love here typically involves family and physical proximity. So, all else pro-objectivity-relevant equal, it is more motivationally harmonious with (the rest of) pro-objectivity to love one's family and others in one's close-circle instead of, e.g., abandoning them and only helping loved-from-a-distance strangers, or in-effect abandoning them by trying to universally help equally. Such abandonment etc would tend to have anti-objectivity emotional effects on the helpers and their family. For pro-objectivity theory to be practicable, human capacities and deep natural needs such as the need for a small close-circle must be considered. (An important conference, on "The Science Of Well-Being", discussed in Part II, Section 2.3, gives further evidence or arguments here.)

A general issue here is that, though normal humans can redirect and in that sense control various emotions to various important degrees, we cannot do much redirecting with some emotions/objects. Pro-objectivity involves considering which emotions, feelings and objects are naturally the most powerful and valued; then, whichever are redirectable towards or potentially helpful regarding pro-objectivity should be used thus. But, apart from a-objectivity ones, if any lack that redirectability or potential, it is pro-objectivity to overrule them to the appropriate degree, if possible. It seems to me that caring for one's family moreso than for strangers greatly (but not totally) lacks that redirectability, but has that potential. So here the balance should normally or on-average be weighted in favour of family, i.e., depending on the situation. E.g., one's family may be safe and well-fed but strangers you can help may be unsafe or starving, so here you should temporarily alter that balance, acting on the presumption that the strangers are at least potentially pro-objectivity. (Previous discussions suggest that the vast majority of persons are at least potentially pro-objectivity. Thence, strangers, those one knows nothing directly of here, would almost certainly be at least potentially pro-objectivity. So, compared to the opposite presumption, at least provisionally that is a reasonable presumption. And if you help strangers, this may help them actualise that presumed potential.)

Within one's close-circle, a similar flexible balance is needed. E.g., obviously, all-else-equal, babies normally need more care than adults.

That weighted balance applied pro-objectivity-directed universally would diminish the groupist conflicts which seem somewhat of a natural tendency, as in bitter rivalry or war among tribes, nations, socio-economic classes, races etc. A pro-objectivity balance here means a close-circle (as opposed to 'clos*ed*-circle') of intimate love, plus increasingly 'distant circles' of at least compassionate caring. It means that, because it is naturally subjectively-evaluated as intrinsically-valuable and hence much more motivating to most love your family and friends, and manageable to directly love only them, it is most practicably pro-objectivity to do so—along with indirectly loving or at least caring for all humanity. ('Direct love' is personal and intimate: it involves such things as hugging, sharing meals and talking with the loved ones. 'Indirect love or care' is such things as sending aid to starving strangers on the other side of the world.)

If each person achieved that weighted balance, everyone would be directly loved by those most meaningful for them, and indirectly loved or cared for by all. Thence, world-wide, universally, the most motivatable and practicable optimal pro-objectivity result could be achieved. [18]

An economic implication here:- That balance does not mean, e.g., a parent is warranted in ensuring that, compared to other children, this parent's children get more resources *other* than that direct-love, e.g., toys, money, medical-care and education, than is pro-objectivity-fair. Persons universally need to share all resources in an overall pro-objectivity-optimising way, i.e., world-wide, long-term. That balance here only means, e.g., that children have a pro-objectivity (need-based) right to get most of the pro-objectivity direct love they need from those who most directly care for them, i.e., normally, parents.

If the parents die or similar, other suitable persons should become the in-practice parents. Relatedly, that weighted balance should allow for anyone lacking sufficient care in a distant-circle to be brought or adopted into one's close-circle if it has the capacity to do so. E.g., if distant children lack direct carers, say through being orphans, and if adults distant from them could best provide that care, they should. All children have an objective right to pro-objectivity loving care. All able potential carers have a duty here. Close-circles need to be flexible, or significantly open. This fits best with the universal social cohesion or harmony required by pro-objectivity theory. (This paragraph's points apply *universally* among at least potential pro-objectivity persons, e.g., to lonely adults here—and to non-human animals with social needs, e.g., various farm animals and pets, animals which can have pro-objectivity effects on humans.)

Concluding comments here:-

Via some such balance, care, openness and universal social harmony, those future potentially most-important pro-objectivity beings, children, would get the start in life they need to fulfil that potential. With this, children normally love a parent/carer who loves them, and hence wish to copy and thereby please their parent/carer. Thence, such loving close-circle relationships can be naturally positively motivationally (causally) related to children being pro-objectivity, in the optimal human overall way. Similarly regarding teachers caring for their students. Thence, parents, teachers and other carers can better motivate children's pro-objectivity. Again, pro-objectivity theory's end-aim involves an interrelated cognitive-emotional *flourishing*, and for humans this would crucially involve a caring close-circle for each person, children being most important here.

Flourishing of and via a balance involving such close-circle love and pro-objectivity-directed universal benevolence is crucial regarding a pro-objectivity societal aim—namely universal, loving or caring harmony (regarding achieving the normatively objective), and hence peace. Such love, care, peace etc is involved in the only objectively-warranted, ideally universal, harmonious flourishing and society.

Regarding that flourishing and balance, ideally any feeling of obligation here, e.g., to care for all distant strangers (while also maintaining one's close-circle love), should be replaced by practices here becoming pleasurable duties. It is important to remember that normally we can (re)train at least many emotions. By reflection and related pro-objectivity-motivated cognitive control (autonomy), assistable by pro-objectivity meditation, plus any needed conditioning or habituation, we can often come to enjoy duties we were originally emotionally neutral or negative about. Positive care for all strangers is significantly possible.

That discussion of pro-objectivity love or care, and other recent discussions, further support the important general point that pro-objectivity requires a coherent interrelation (harmonising) among our cognition, emotions, emotional objects, feelings and other practices. More practicable specifics here:-

Part II, Section 1.4.5: Concerning Some Other Emotions/Feelings/Objects

Sexual emotions and their common manifest objects, e.g., feeling pleasure, can be pro-objectivity. This is particularly so when they are associated with pro-objectivity love. They at least need to be associated with pro-objectivity-directed mutual caring. Sex can help bond (cohere) pro-objectivity close-circles together. Sex can also be pro-objectivity via producing children needed to continue humanity's ability to be pro-objectivity. And people may get so frustrated due to lacking a desired sex partner, that they cannot optimally acquire and/or practise pro-objectivity knowledge. For them it is pro-objectivity to have such a partner.

Enjoying exercise, music, food, meditation, leisure, pets, art, nature, sleep, wine, various (other) indulgences, and so on, can also be pro-objectivity, depending on the overall situation. E.g:- A healthy body is needed for a maximally pro-objectivity brain, because the brain is part of and affected by (the rest of) the body. So morally correct persons would be motivated to enjoy healthy foods, to exercise and so on in physically healthy ways, along with meditation, some indulgences and other practices helpful for pro-objectivity psychological emotional etc health. However, e.g., suppose a student is motivated to exercise vigorously during a pro-objectivity lecture, and so cannot concentrate on the lecture. That motivation, and its object, 'exercise', would be pro-objectivity in certain other situations, but not there.

Wine, sex, music, meditation, art, nature, exercise, sport, pets, literature, comedy, playfulness, indulgence and much else can be aspects of pro-objectivity leisure or recreation. E.g., suppose Mike works hard making pro-objectivity (safe, durable, recyclable etc) bike helmets. He cannot do this 24 hours, 7 days a week. He needs rest and recreation (and food etc). Recreation means re-*creation.* Mike needs to recreate his mental, emotional and physical energy and other personal resources, so he can optimally make the helmets. Such re-creation should be very enjoyable. We often need to "stop and smell (enjoy) the roses".

In sum, to be maximally pro-objectivity, one needs certain quantities and qualities of a vast range of things (in on-average balance), including many pleasurable sexual, leisure etc duties. Many can be social, helping to cohere pro-objectivity close-circles and bonding among strangers. This means flourishing in all possible pro-objectivity ways, emotions and feelings being crucial here.

Part II, Section 1.4.6: Some Summarising And Concluding Comments Concerning Emotions As Discussed So Far

(1) Directly pro-objectivity emotions directly motivate one's cognitive pro-objectivity capacities. A desire to have (potentially) pro-objectivity knowledge is the central directly pro-objectivity emotion regarding cognition. There can be great, often enjoyable passion here. Pro-objectivity flourishing here involves loving a challenge, and enjoying solving problems or discovering truth.

E.g:- It is challenging to learn to drive more safely, thereby preserving potentially pro-objectivity persons you may otherwise kill. It could and should be a motivating challenge to solve the problem of understanding how to best ensure all humanity has access to optimally pro-objectivity food, clean water, health-care, affection etc. Such directly pro-objectivity motivation can be associated with indirectly pro-objectivity emotions and feelings naturally subjectively-evaluated as intrinsically-valuable, e.g., parental-type sympathy-related pleasure due to seeing oneself has helped distant starving, ill children get such access.

(2) Managing and intentionally experiencing emotions in pro-objectivity ways are pro-objectivity practices. 'Be pro-objectivity' is a (practice-focused) *cognitive-emotional* or emotion-thought end (with the cognitive aspect the (directly pro-objectivity motivated) ultimate judge or decision-maker, including regarding emotions and their objects (here practices)). As with ends such as 'collect stones', 'Be pro-objectivity' is at any time both presently and in-future achievable, hence cumulatively achievable. Relatedly, the end-practice of enjoying acquiring and practising pro-objectivity knowledge can also be a means to motivate cumulatively doing so. Such cognitive-emotional-practical harmonising cumulatively across time is an aspect of overall, maximal pro-objectivity.

(3) Emotions discussed so far often involve happiness (or at least an avoidance of unhappiness). Again, happiness can be indirectly pro-objectivity, an aspect of normatively-objective cognitive-emotional flourishing. So we've a right to the freedom (ability and opportunity) to achieve what makes us objectively-deservedly happy. There is a related pro-objectivity duty regarding happiness as a motivator here. One piece of pro-objectivity knowledge is that, all else equal, humans are more likely to persist at something if they are happy, rather than unhappy, to do it. Happiness is what various Utilitarians argue to be the ultimate natural end-aim of all normal intended practice, an end hence experienced as intrinsically-valuable, and this seems partly, qualifiedly, true. A more than sufficiently motivating amount of happiness subjectively experienced as intrinsically-valuable can be associated motivationally with achieving the pro-objectivity end. So this achievement is within the naturally possible and desirable.

Still, history, sociology and the like show that at least many persons can achieve various very difficult ends which do not seem to involve happiness, and via apparently experiencing little or no happiness—meaning that such achievements are also within at least the naturally possible. The often distressing responsibility of caring for terminally-ill, fatally-starving or fatally-wounded persons in great pain is one probable example—common through history due to disease, earthquakes, war, famine and so on. Similarly, most parents and teachers find some child-upbringing responsibilities difficult—obligations rather than pleasant duties. The common achievements in such areas suggest that, even if the pro-objectivity end was unpleasant to achieve, many people could still achieve it. However, fortunately, much happiness can be, often is and ideally needs to be involved in pro-objectivity. (And this book overall suggests that an increasingly pro-objectivity world would increasingly involve happiness, including via lessening many of the just-mentioned difficulties, unpleasantness and similar, or the causes thereof, e.g., disease, war and famine.)

Pro-objectivity theory prescribes avoiding happiness only where happiness conflicts with pro-objectivity. One prescription here is similar to J.S. Mill's significantly pro-objectivity-qualified Utilitarianism (arguably making him rather non-Utilitarian):- He suggests it is better to be a dissatisfied Socrates than a satisfied or happy pig. This fits pro-objectivity theory in that Socrates was often dissatisfied for significantly pro-objectivity reasons, involving his at least implicit pro-objectivity knowledge. Pigs and similar cannot be dissatisfied for such known-by-themselves reasons, and seem, like persons, to be able to aim at and experience much happiness. But for persons the object, 'happiness', can conflict with pro-objectivity—as with persons only dedicated to and made happy via one or more of bottle-top collecting, bingo, sex, eating, jogging, laziness, drunkenness, humour, music and similar objects, many activities here needing not a great deal more than a pig's cognitive abilities, and sometimes less. Mill would here presumably advocate that educating such people to be dissatisfied with the many unwarranted aspects of the world is better than their and any such happiness or contentment involving such objects. (*Deserved* happiness is an issue here.)

Relatedly, a pro-objectivity-optimal degree of psychological peace, an aspect of pro-objectivity mental health, does not involve total, passive, blissful contentment when it is pro-objectivity to be dissatisfied or discontented and hence active so as to increase pro-objectivity and related peace generally in the long-term. (This 'qualified-peace' point relates to the previous discussion of negative pro-objectivity emotions, and is expanded on soon.) This is another aspect of the pro-objectivity duty regarding happiness.

In sum, from an objective normative viewpoint, happiness, contentment and similar can sometimes be unwarranted; but they are often warranted—and achievably-ideally much happiness is required.

Part II, Section 1.4.7: More Concerning Happiness And Unhappiness

As Part I, Section 1.2 and Appendix 4 suggest, as maximal anti-objectivity means one soon dies, one cannot get happiness from maximal anti-objectivity, except briefly. But, ignoring maximal anti-objectivity, people can get much happiness from anti-objectivity. Yet such happiness is objectively morally wrong (and arguments above indicate we could probably achieve more happiness overall via pro-objectivity). A general issue here is that there can be anti-objectivity positive emotions, and these need retraining. E.g:-

Suppose Linda is emotionally positive in that she is always blissfully happy. She maintains this by only doing and thinking about things that make her happy. (Bliss can mean ignorance, and ignorance can be bliss.) She hence never feels worried or dissatisfied about the unwarranted. She ignores impoverished people's undeserved anti-objectivity poor health, education, diet, housing and so on, and ignores her friends' hate-filled racism, their and her selfishness, and so on—all of which she could alter in pro-objectivity ways. So her positive, enjoyed emotions and feelings are anti-objectivity. They need to be retrained, so she enjoys being pro-objectivity. As recently suggested, it would also be pro-objectivity for her to experience enough of certain negative emotions, such as dislike of the unfair way impoverished people often do not get the same healthcare etc as the rich, enough to motivate her to act in a warranted way here. Then she can enjoy improving others' health, education and so on. (This example relates to the recent comment about a dissatisfied Socrates and happy pigs.)

Linda sought egoistic emotional peace and related happiness, partly via cognitively ignoring the unwarranted. Pro-objectivity psychological peace in an achievably ideal pro-objectivity world would involve maximum possible mental or cognitive-emotional harmony and related great happiness and contentment (though not passivity, as activity would be needed to maintain that optimal state). Optimally pro-objectivity psychological peace in the present (2010) and any other less than achievably maximal pro-objectivity world is situationally contexted and hence of a relative degree, involving a corresponding balance. The pro-objectivity-optimal degree of psychological peace here involves less contentment than in that ideal world. Here significant dissatisfaction or discontent is needed, to help motivate the activity needed to increase pro-objectivity and related peace generally, long-term:-

Something like the Yerkes-Dodson curve[19] applies regarding that unhappiness. That is, we can be so *little* dissatisfied or worried, or so *greatly* upset or worried, that, respectively, we either do not bother or are too distressed to do anything effective to change an anti-objectivity situation into a pro-objectivity one. Similarly, hatred, as opposed to dislike or dissatisfaction, would seem to normally be too strong an emotion to be optimally pro-objectivity. A high degree of a negative emotion, such as hate, anxiety, depression or a panicky concern to be pro-objectivity, could lead to counterproductive (anti-objectivity) acts. Occasional, moderate, easily actable-on sadness or unhappiness could be part of an objectively-warranted mental health balance here, in a far from achievably correct world. (Note that such sadness is partly similar to a type of depression, but is not depression defined as a feeling pressing one down, negatively, making one less likely to act in positive, pro-objectivity ways. That easily actable-on sadness concerning a problem would be associated with other some other emotion(s), including, say, annoyance with the problem, and the combination would motivate one to act in pro-objectivity ways, to deal with the problem.)

That presently-appropriate pro-objectivity balance probably requires about an on-average minor degree of concern. This does not mean we should always be in a state of minor concern apart from occasionally experiencing such further, moderate sadness. And it does not mean we should always simultaneously feel somewhat happy and somewhat discontent. Far from it. 'On-average' is an important qualification here. E.g., riotous fun and maximally peaceful and/or blissful recreation, rest, sex, love and meditation can be pro-objectivity in various situations here. The balance would involve a mix over time, including some such positive extremes. (Such balances give us types and degrees of normatively-objective peace and other harmony, as opposed to psychological peace or intended harmony as such or for its own sake.) That balance, around 2010, would probably require only a small proportion of time spent consciously negatively concerned with unwarranted things one can change. (It is impracticable, irrational and hence objectively-unwarranted to be concerned about anti-objectivity things one cannot change.) *Positive* emotion, complementarily related to or arising from and largely replacing explicit negative concern, is needed most, as being positive seems on-average more effective in motivating *pro-objectivity* action. (Negative emotion may be more effective in motivating *anti*-objectivity action, as in the way racist hatred was used very effectively by Nazis.) However, that complementary positive-negative mix could involve emotions which could plausibly be viewed as either positive or negative, e.g., an aggressive determination to end injustice (an emotion helpful in writing this book). To me it seems a matter of degree. E.g., up to a point such aggression seems positively motivating, the negative emotion here being dislike of that injustice, but beyond that point the aggression starts becoming rationality-disabling hatred.

Part II, Section 1.4.8: Some Reviewed And Related Other Conclusions Concerning Emotions

(1) Again, the above discussions and others below here may need significant revision. They include some claims I only provisionally think probable—awaiting further evidence. And a claim applying to many people or normal situations or on-average may not apply to certain individuals or in abnormal or different situations; and vice versa. Again, flexibility is needed.

(2) Such just-discussed (probable?) optimal pro-objectivity balances or interrelatedness among our emotions, and an emotional-cognitive harmonising, are aspects of a pro-objectivity overall integration (harmonising or coherence) of a person, i.e., of pro-objectivity integrity. 'Coherent' means 'integrated'. (Ap-

pendix 4 further discusses the overall coherence involved here.)

(3) The normal human brain naturally projects colour onto visible things, so we have the illusion that colour is objectively "out there". Similarly, as David Hume pointed out, normal persons (inter)subjectively naturally project certain emotional evaluations onto certain objects "out there". Thence, normal persons naturally tend to believe, e.g., that torturing children is objectively wrong, and that it is intrinsically-valuable that one's child looks safe and happy. Many such natural evaluations or projections, suitably qualified, are at least potentially pro-objectivity. Some are anti-objectivity, e.g., the above-discussed groupist ones, and the one concerning religion as discussed in Part II, Section 1.4.1.1.

(4) Pro-objectivity critical reflection on such evaluations is an aspect of pro-objectivity *autonomy*. This autonomy is objective and pro-objectivity-directed, and such reflection enables us to *normatively-objectively autonomously* choose whether to practise in accord with a subjective, emotional perceptions or projections, rather than just be unwarrantedly, unfreely, directed by them. That autonomy involves *knowledge* of which subjectively-evaluated as intrinsically-valuable (and other) emotions, feelings and other objects are pro-objectivity, which are anti-objectivity, and which are a-objectivity, in this or that situation. Thence, each knower here, at their highest reflective level of thought, is a normatively-objective *judge*—ideally hence achieving a pro-objectivity-optimal balance (harmony) overall, among emotional, cognitive and other practices.

(5) So pro-objectivity (inherently autonomous) judgement needs to oversee the (re)training of potentially anti-objectivity emotions. This judgement involves the cognitive, motivated by and hence involving pro-objectivity motivation, having priority (autonomy) over the (rest of the) emotional,[20] via objective cognition being the effective decision-maker (ultimate judge)—though the decisions include promoting certain emotions and are of course (warrantedly) motivated. So, because of its crucial, primary decision-making role, the cognitive needs further discussion. This will be done soon. In order to prepare a suitable, sufficiently overall context for that discussion, more needs to be said about a-objectivity:-

Part II, Section 1.5: More On Pro-Objectivity Society, Regarding A-Objectivity

(As just suggested, in at least some cases research is needed to discover precisely which things and which aspects of a given situation are a-objectivity, and any situational relativity here.) (This subsection is only part of the rest of the book's discussion of a-objectivity freedom. After other subsections below develop a suitable context for more points here, those points are discussed.)

(It is only a reflective, autonomous, highest level of objective thought which can correctly (objectively) make judgements such as those discussed below.)

As Part I, Section 3 explains, the pro-objectivity standard implies that whatever is irrelevant to pro-objectivity is normatively-objectively neither warranted nor unwarranted. So standards used in a-objectivity choices are neither objectively warranted nor unwarranted. Here, each alternative is objectively equal in that each has an equal, neutral causal relationship regarding humanity's ability, motivation and opportunity to be pro-objectivity. Relatedly, these choices' equal irrelevance regarding the normatively-objective means there is no objective warrant for *not* allowing maximum pro-objectivity-possible a-objectivity freedom. (Again:- Frank's freedom to do X here, say, sing, ceases to be a-objectivity if X begins to affect others in anti-objectivity ways, e.g., if his singing disturbs others studying pro-objectivity knowledge. That is, regarding something which can be a-objectivity, pro-objectivity cognitive judgement allows the 'maximum pro-objectivity-possible' freedom here; but there are limits to freedom here.)

Because (within the very broad limits) here it is *normatively objective* that there is no warranted reason to not be free to do whatever you like, we've an indirect normatively objective duty to protect that freedom. Everyone has an indirect right to that freedom. To do otherwise is to treat the a-objectivity as if it is not the a-objectivity—which is overall-objectively-unwarranted, e.g., as shown in Part I, Section 3.1. Another example concerning treating the a-objectivity as a-objectivity, involving a directly pro-objectivity situation:-

If a scientist places objectivity above all else, the associated values include treating impartially all those aspects of fellow scientists irrelevant to their objectivity. E.g., inherently, a pro-objectivity scientist would not reject or accept a theory because it is proposed by someone of this or that race or gender. (Karl Popper makes a similar point.[21]) (Here, at least implicitly, scientists use pro-objectivity judgement to treat the a-objectivity thus, and, perhaps, to cognitively direct the overruling of any emotion tempting them to decide otherwise.)

So, to do the obviously directly objective as in science, we need to implement that freedom, here from racism, sexism and so on, i.e., have pro-objectivity values here. This has implications for society generally:-

Primarily, people living by those non-racist etc values would be unified. (This fits Popper's suggestion[22] that science's and all objective disciplines' internal values are unifying.) That is, primarily, here those people would live harmoniously in relation to the objective and related a-objectivity here. What would it mean for all to be in *overall* or universal harmony (coherence) with the non-racist, non-sexist values inherent in objective, scientific knowledge? It would include all accepting that in *all* situations, *all* would act via the rule that it is rational and pro-objectivity to treat the a-objectivity *as* a-objectivity.

Along with one's race and gender, many things either are or can be a-objectivity. These could include preferences regarding music, art, sport, clothing, sex, food, family-type and various other lifestyle choices. The following simplified trivial example makes generalisable important points regarding such areas. (Trivial examples can be the best way, an initially non-controversial way, to get a general point and its other, important, often controversial implications accepted, e.g., regarding sex.):-

Consider hypothetical equally pro-objectivity fruits F1 and F2. They are equally so because, from a metabolic view, both supply the same nutrients, fibre and so on needed by pro-objectivity persons in the situation in question, and the fruits' production uses the same or equivalent pro-objectivity resources overall, e.g., the same amount of water. And so on. Suppose the only differences are flavour, shape and colour, and these differences are a-objectivity. From an objective normative viewpoint, here all is equal. The standards via which pro-objectivity persons choose between F1 and F2 would be a-objectivity.

Here the standards concern differences associated with equally pro-objectivity alternatives. Pro-objectivity judgement permits persons to have innumerable a-objectivity ends/standards. Thence, e.g., via a-objectivity flavour-standards, a person could either always eat only F1, switch between F1 and F2, or mix them together, perhaps in differing proportions, and so on. Whichever secondary, a-objectivity flavour-standard is applied, or temporarily applied, primarily it is only the ultimate pro-objectivity standard which is always applied. The pro-objectivity judgement thought-level here knows that permitting freedom regarding choices irrelevant to the objective normative end is not incoherent with that end. To *not* be permissive (liberal) here would be to prescribe, unobjectively, that, e.g., F1 is the only fruit which objectively should be eaten. Any such prescription is incoherent with the objective situation, namely that F1 and F2 are equally pro-objectivity and so it objectively does *not matter* which we eat, as long as we eat at least one. If it objectively does not matter, we are objectively free (permitted) to do whatever we (subjectively) like here. It is objective that subjective standards should be permitted here.

Overall, again, this means a type of pluralism along with singularism. Only a single, pro-objectivity standard is objectively ultimate, so here singularism is objectively warranted. But this is irrelevant regarding anyone having a vast plurality of a-objectivity, secondary ends and associated standards. E.g., regarding just F1 and F2, along with flavour-standards one may also like to apply a-objectivity shape- and/or colour-standards, with various combinations thereof, and change among them. (This orthogonally-systematic interrelation of the single pro-objectivity standard and plural a-objectivity standards is indicated by Part I, Section 3.2's diagram and its discussion thereof.)

This means an extremely free, permissive or liberal society here, and not just in somewhat humanly-unimportant areas such as fruit preferences. Various a-objectivity areas concern preferences far more humanly-important, e.g., as discussed later, various sexual preferences. Some such areas concern issues history shows have involved highly humanly-important, great personal, social, political, military etc conflict due to non-pro-objectivity people's intolerant values and associated lack of pro-objectivity knowledge. Treating the a-objectivity as a-objectivity here, via permitting that liberality or freedom, would bring peace here, a highly humanly-important issue.

Pro-objectivity persons would be unified (one or singular) regarding not conflicting over each others' differing a-objectivity non-options and preferred options, because these would be viewed as neither right nor wrong, just different. If *pro-objectivity* persons differ over a collective a-objectivity choice, this type of persons would resolve the issue in a pro-objectivity fair, peaceful, friendly way. Sometimes voting would be appropriate, namely a-objectivity democracy (discussed soon). Sometimes ways other than voting would be appropriate:- E.g., consider pro-objectivity Mike and Julie, having different a-objectivity preferences regarding, say, which tree to plant in their yard. They can decide by various means, none of the means having an anti-objectivity effect via, e.g., causing resentment due to unfairness. E.g., they can toss a coin, or agree that one of them will choose the tree and the other make some other similar a-objectivity choice, say, regarding which painting hangs on some wall. Because, as pro-objectivity persons, they both agree that no choice is right or wrong here, they'd agree via knowing there is no warranted ground for intolerance, hostility or criticism regarding the decision, and that criticism would unobjectively assume the decision is wrong, or may be wrong, and that the critic is right. Similarly, there is no ground for ridicule, silent resentment, jealousy and so on, which are types of criticism. To objectively-warrantedly resent etc concerning choice X, X must be known to be objectively wrong. Regarding a-objectivity choices, via pro-objectivity judgement we can unifyingly know they are not wrong.

Such unity, singularism, agreement, mutual acceptance, fairness, noncriticism, nonresentment etc mean, via orthogonality, social harmony involving diversity, and social diversity involving harmony. Here then, is an objective place for divergent values, each with equal (neither warranted nor unwarranted) status. (For many normative theories, giving divergent values or aspects equal status can mean unresolvable conflicts. Such equality or liberality is ultimately only not a problem for pro-objectivity theory: no other theory involves the here-required normatively-objective orthogonally-systematic non-incoherence plus fundamental, primary coherence; and persons living by that theory would in-practice not conflict over their diverging secondary, a-objectivity values.)

That orthogonally-systematic societal (non-dis)harmony (peace) is an aim of pro-objectivity-directed universal benevolence. With this there'd be types of fulfilment and flourishing, via everyone having the maximum pro-objectivity-possible freedom to achieve or indulge in their most-liked a-objectivity objects or ends regarding music, sex, food, art, leisure or whatever.

This would mean types of happiness. I provisionally propose this involves a probable motivationally important implication of that orthogonal structure:-

It seems likely to me that the optional *objects* within the horizontal dimension, objects among which we are warrantedly free to choose, namely the *contents* of one's choices, are *a-objectivity*—but the overall *method* of choice, namely *freedom* to choose, though it operates within the a-objectivity dimension, is installed there by cognitive, *pro-objectivity* judgement. The objects or contents here are not *installed* there by pro-objectivity judgement. They belong there anyway. Pro-objectivity judgement simply realises that those objects *are* and *belong* within the a-objectivity dimension.

(This is like Australia's government, about the last quarter of the 20th century, legislating against sexist employment, via enough (male) politicians (at last) accepting there are no rational grounds for sexist discrimination in the workplace. This meant that, according to legislation, women gained equal freedom with men here. (The reality did/does not always accord with that legislation, but that is beside the general point here.) Before that legislation, women objectively deserved the freedom and equality anyway, as gender here inherently belongs in the a-objectivity dimension, i.e., regardless of what politicians etc believe(d). When enough politicians became sufficiently rational, and relatedly more pro-objectivity-fair, that (somewhat improved) freedom and equality were instituted via their here in-effect significantly pro-objectivity decision.)

Via the pro-objectivity judgement, the freedom and so on mentioned two paragraphs ago, the free choice-in-itself is a-objectivity, but the thereby-caused *effects* of *being free* to make that choice can arguably be motivationally pro-objectivity. If so, here one's freely chosen object and all other options here belong on the horizontal dimension, but the decision that this freedom or method of choice is warranted is made by the vertical dimension's top section—and so certain effects of the freedom are experienced *by* the vertical. Here, where a person decides, as judge, to institute the person's own a-objectivity freedom, those effects occur because one enjoys the autonomous decision-making, respects the pro-objectivity involved, hence enhancing enjoyable pro-objectivity self-respect, and one knows that oneself will enjoy the a-objectivity freedom due to one's pro-objectivity decision. Relatedly:-

Pro-objectivity persons are integrated beings. And the normal brain's emotional parts are at least somewhat interconnected with each other and with the cognitive parts. Here, parts which are separate from a purely abstract, neurologically-uninformed viewpoint, are, from an objective, overall viewpoint, physically and subjectively or experientially significantly connected:-

The freedom to choose among a-objectivity options is freedom to do whatever makes one happy here. Such happiness is for humans an important *effect* of the freedom. Because this freedom is prescribed and instituted by their ultimate (highest), pro-objectivity judgement level of thought, pro-objectivity persons thereby made happier are arguably more likely to be happy via and with their pro-objectivity judgement-level and its ultimate standard than they'd be with a standard or judge forbidding freedom here. Similarly, people are likely to be happy with a (pro-objectivity) society which inherently prescribes freedom here. Arguably, via the psychological process called generalisation, such motivational effects could spread from that 'here' to 'everywhere (regarding pro-objectivity)'—helping achieve the overall harmony here required by pro-objectivity, and as is possible via our interrelated neurophysiology.

Comments here can be adapted to apply to those not able to make that judgement, e.g., children, but who are given a-objectivity freedom crucially via the judgement of some other, able person(s), e.g., parents and teachers. (Similarly, regarding the recently-mentioned Australian government's legislating against sexist employment, women who resented the previously allowed discrimination tend(ed) to feel happier due to the increased freedom and equality, and happier with the government here, probably including, somewhat, being more motivated to support and be involved in or with the government in a more general way. And rational, here fair men felt happier too.)

Summing up recent discussions:-

In such ways, persons' emotional object-achievements and subjective preferences can co-exist non-incoherently with their and/or their society's highest-level cognitively-arrived-at standard or objective judgement-level. This can make the standard and judgements psychologically acceptable, and societally-instituted judgements here socially, politically and legally acceptable. This should make pro-objectivity even more motivating. This would be moreso when an a-objectivity area is considered important by those involved. E.g., Felicity may be little concerned with fruit, but greatly concerned regarding her a-objectivity sexual preferences and her right to non-racist employment.

The freedom of choice here is a-objectivity regarding the choices' *contents,* and pro-objectivity in that the *freedom* to choose has its source and warrant in the top end of the pro-objectivity diagram's vertical dimension. That is, the *method* of choosing, namely individual freedom rather than via a dictatorially imposed uniform choice for all, is instituted by pro-objectivity judgement, which resides at the top end. This judgement-level knows that individuals objectively ought to be free to choose among a-objectivity options. Pro-objectivity people would respect that right, mutually accepting anyone's choices here.

Concluding comments here:-

1) Pro-objectivity society's educational, political, economic, legal etc systems would need to promote and protect such freedoms, unity, diversity, mutual respect and acceptance, equality, peace, flourishing, harmony and so on. This is suggested further below, along with relating this subsection's discussion of them to the issue of democracy. E.g., such freedoms etc would help mean a society as egalitarian, liberal and fair as is normatively-objectively possible here—as required by pro-objectivity democracy.

2) Recent points concerning suggested pro-objectivity motivational effects of the freedom to make a-objectivity choices can be adapted to apply to pro-objectivity motivational effects of the freedom from discrimination people would experience via pro-objectivity persons treating everyone's a-objectivity *non*-optional aspects as a-objectivity. This freedom would also help mean a society as egalitarian, liberal and fair as is normatively-objectively possible—as required by pro-objectivity democracy.

3) The next few subsections in-part concern a-objectivity, but moreso concern the recently-mentioned crucial need for normatively-objective cognitive reflection and judgement or assessment, and direction. This relates to the present and previous parts of Part II, because it is only via that judgement, suitably informed (knowledgeable), that we can *know* which emotions, emotional objects, feelings and other things are a-objectivity, which are pro-objectivity, and which are anti-objectivity, in this or that or all situations. Only thence can we know specifically whether an a-objectivity option or non-option exists, and hence whether and what type of a-objectivity freedom should apply. (As the above shows, there's a type for options, another for non-options.)

Part II, Section 1.6: Pro-Objectivity Society—More On Its Individuals, Their Judgement And Psychology; Related Democracies And Freedoms

Introductory remarks:-

The unity involved in pro-objectivity society would of course not require totalitarianism. The above shows that pro-objectivity society would only be totalistic in that it would be totally dedicated to being pro-objectivity, which means great a-objectivity individual freedom, and total pro-objectivity individual freedom, namely freedom to be pro-objectivity—the latter often also involving great freedom of choice, speech, expression, imagination, creativity and so on. Direct pro-objectivity freedoms and opportunities here need discussing further:-

These freedoms include any individual being free to rationally helpfully and respectfully inform, disagree with or criticise others, including evidenced diverging from any questionable view held by one's boss or a democratic majority. E.g., suppose only one individual has sufficient evidence regarding some claim concerning whether something is pro-objectivity. Pro-objectivity society and politics would encourage (motivate) such individuals to be and feel free to inform others helpfully and respectfully. Similarly, each individual would be encouraged to feel free to express any rational doubt concerning a view held by all others. The same applies regarding an individual knowing that others hold view V only because they have what understandably *seems* sufficient evidence. Where there is no knowledge or evidence, pro-objectivity individuals should be free to creatively imagine divergent possibly correct hypotheses, and to not have these dismissed by others without serious rational consideration, e.g., if a hypothesis sounds ridiculous to them. As the history of science exemplifies, various ideas, initially appearing ridiculous to perhaps a majority of (alleged) experts, were later confirmed as knowledge. E.g., Einstein's claim that space and time are related and not independent of each other was initially considered absurd by many. (Something similar happened regarding pro-objectivity theory.)

That need for such freedoms implies a need for a type of democracy, and avoidance of totalitarian and similar politics. Pro-objectivity society's citizens would on-average be autonomous and very knowledgeable in some areas, hence objectively deserving a direct say in ruling their society here. And, again, human knowledge-acquisition is at least significantly social, and no individual or small minority can possess all the needed specific pro-objectivity knowledge. So society's decisions need to be made collectively, via a democracy involving such independent rational constructive criticism, combined knowledge or expertise, and so on. Where there is uncertainty or insufficient evidence, that type of democracy is also probably the overall best way for society to become more pro-objectivity-knowledgeable, e.g., it facilitates divergent hypothesising. That type would be in various ways very different from all past and present types. And there'd be a thereto orthogonally-related, a-objectivity type:-

Part II, Section 1.6.1: Orthogonally-Related Freedoms; Two Objectively-Warranted, Direct Democracies

Part II, Section1.6.1.1: A-Objectivity Democracy

Sometimes an a-objectivity collective choice is appropriate. They'd only concern non-personal options, e.g., not anyone's race or central a-objectivity sexual preference. When an a-objectivity collective choice is appropriate, and a majority vote is possible, an a-objectivity democratic vote can be the appropriate way to decide. (Again, some trivial examples, for reasons mentioned above.):-

Suppose Evelyn's sock-colour preferences are a-objectivity, and no-one else is involved. E.g., say she is alone and choices here affect no-one else in any pro- or anti-objectivity way. So she should be free to wear whatever sock-colour she likes. A vote here, by her and/or others, would obviously be inappropriate. But often two or more persons are involved, and here the judgement of pro-objectivity persons would sometimes be that an a-objectivity democratic vote is appropriate. In the example of Mike and Julie, mentioned in Part II, Section 1.5, when they differ a majority vote is not possible, and anyway they could decide the issue by friendly personal discussion or a friendly coin-toss. But, e.g., if an issue involves large numbers of people or where it is otherwise impracticable to conveniently decide by interpersonal discussion, and perhaps where most are strangers to each other, a vote seems appropriate. Here a majority vote is possible, but if there's no majority, a chance-based decision method can be appropriate, e.g., coin-tossing. One issue here involves the recent discussion, in Part II, Section 1.5, of the suggested pro-objectivity motivational effects of the vertical dimension's pro-objectivity judgement-level instituting a-objectivity freedom:-

E.g., suppose it is a-objectivity whether a community hall is built in architectural style P or Q. Each option is of equal, neutral value from a pro-objectivity judgement-level's viewpoint considering just the purely cognitive issue that, e.g., each option in-itself is objectively equally neither right nor wrong. This cognitive 'equal, neutral' criterion might seem to suggest that voting-equality is appropriate, as in one-person one-vote. Yet a pro-objectivity judge's *overall* viewpoint considers more here than just that cognitive criterion. Emotion, the subjective, also needs to be considered. If, apart from that cognitive issue, all else (pro-objectivity-relevant[23]) is equal from that objective highest-level viewpoint, each person involved should get an equal vote, one vote. But, from that overall viewpoint, all else might not be equal. There could be very different degrees of (pro-objectivity-relevant) emotional preference:-

Part II, Section 1.5 made a relevant comment here, concerning the distinction between the *contents* of a-objectivity choices and the *freedom* to choose here—and how being in-practice free to choose what one emotionally prefers can be motivationally pro-objectivity, via our interacting psychological aspects.

That freedom to choose would perhaps be most precisely (i.e., objectively,) and (partly) hence most actualised via the voting (or other non-chance method of choice) representing the varying *degrees* of subjective or emotional preference of voters (or of those choosing via another non-chance method). To be and feel *most* free to express one's preferences would seem to involve being free to express them precisely. There could be anti-objectivity effects due to individuals with differing degrees of preference only being free to express preferences in an extremely approximate, unnecessarily restricted way, e.g., in an imposed, uniform, one-person one-vote way. Here individual liberty would be restricted. An a-objectivity choice is not as free or democratic as pro-objectivity-possible if unnecessarily restricted, or if the individual is not fully at liberty to in-practice express it exactly. Instead of arbitrarily imposing the primitive,[24] one-person one-vote type of democracy on all situations requiring a collective vote among a-objectivity (non-personal) options, a '(subjective) preference-degree' voting system would fit best with (the truth-aspect of) knowledge—e.g., with a voter's knowledge that her/his vote truly or objectively reflects her/his preference in all possible ways, allowing it to be individually distinct from other persons' votes. This then would be both most objective and most pro-objectivity. E.g:-

Suppose a one-person one-vote vote would mean 51 votes for style P, and 49 for style Q. Suppose those preferring style Q do so ten times more strongly. Suppose each person rates their strength of preference from 1 (minimal) to 10 (maximal), and that each person is sufficiently pro-objectivity to honestly rate that degree of preference. This results in 51x1=51 preference-units for style P, and 49x10=490 for style Q. Clearly, some persons could experience anti-objectivity frustration with a society or judgement instituting a one-person one-vote democracy. 'Preference-degree' voting here would probably be most pro-objectivity, especially if the above-suggested motivational effects of the method or freedom of choice apply.

Something like the following should work well. Anyone with zero preference gets zero votes: they abstain. Anyone with preference-level 1 gets one vote; anyone with preference-level 2 gets two votes; and so on. Thence, the previous paragraph's result would be 490 votes for style Q, and 51 for style P. The losers here, because they only minimally prefer their choice, would at most minimally care they'd lost. Highly pro-objectivity persons would not care, or not in any normatively important or practical way. So, regarding pro-objectivity theory's motivatability, this result would be as close as possible to an all-win situation regarding the voters, the pro-objectivity society which instituted the voting system, and regarding the associated theory and pro-objectivity judgement.

Often, such issues would be difficult to solve precisely. But it is probably impracticable for *any* system or theory to "please all the people all the time". 'As far as possible' is all that's rationally expectable, and pro-objectivity theory only concerns the practicable, namely the as-far-as-possible, the as-close-as-possible or the as-far-as-we-know. The pro-objectivity ideal here is a world society or federation where all are entirely unselfish and all know that an a-objectivity choice other than theirs is as right as theirs, namely neither right nor wrong. Here no person would be displeased by group decisions disagreeing with the person's a-objectivity preference. Here there'd be interpersonal peace.

A conclusion concerning recent points:- With preference-degree voting, 'majority' would mean 'majority of preference-votes', as in 490 beating 51. If there is no majority, the fairest decision is via chance, e.g., coin-tossing, or, if pro-objectivity-possible, e.g., where the resources used are not needed for pro-objectivity, alternately implementing each choice or otherwise somehow compensating the losers is probably appropriate. Where not pro-objectivity-possible, the groups with different preferences could agree to take it in turns to have their preferences implemented among any other non-majority voting results.

Some conclusions concerning democracy generally in pro-objectivity society:- It is at least practicable for a pro-objectivity society to show citizens that, via it practising the pro-objectivity-directed universal benevolence needed for a pro-objectivity society, this society is trying as hard as possible to do what seems best on the basis of the pro-objectivity knowledge at the time. It can be greatly motivating to know that the most objectively warranted and relatedly fair possible political system exists, as far as can be known at the time—and that society's rulers are willing to change any system if there is new evidence confirming that a change is warranted. (A pro-objectivity society's rulers would be its voter-citizens.) Here, again, an evidence-based democracy is needed to make society's ultimate decisions. This would consider, among other things, what evidence there is regarding which type of democracy or decision-method is appropriate in this or that a-objectivity situation. I think the present evidence confirms that preference-degree voting would be appropriate sometimes.

Part II, Section1.6.1.2: Pro-Objectivity Democracy

Emotional or subjective, preference-degree voting is not appropriate here. Here decisions or judgements concern the directly objectively-warranted, the evidence-based, not the subjectively-preferred or the neither warranted nor unwarranted. Here decisions need to be pro-objectivity *knowledge* (including the knowledge that the a-objectivity should be treated as a-objectivity). Here it is *evidence* which determines that alternative X, not Y, should be chosen, not whether one likes X or Y. (Maximally pro-objectivity persons would inherently like whatever the evidence points to.)

A normatively-objective society would have a type of *direct* democracy. (The just-discussed a-objectivity democracy was direct too.) This ideally means all adults being legislators, eventually achievable to at least a nearly total degree via education. With direct democracy, also called participatory democracy, all voters participate directly in politics. Here all citizens qualified to vote are directly the rulers, i.e., senators, members of parliament or similar (though in large societies they could not physically properly meet in one place). Here voters represent themselves in the law-making or political institution(s). Voters vote on each *issue*, not for politicians. There is no President, Prime Minister or similar, unlike in indirect or representative democracy. In the indirect democracies common round 2010, voters typically vote only every few years, for candidates most voters do not know and who promise to represent all voters regarding all political issues, many important post-election issues not anticipated by voters, with that promise and their other promises often being fraudulent or broken, their later decisions often being self-serving or according to party dictates rather than voters' or the electorate's wishes. Here only the (alleged) representatives, a tiny minority, make laws and directly rule, not the voters, the vast majority. Here, allegedly, voters rule but only indirectly, arguably *so* indirectly that it is overall hardly democratic.

So direct democracy is far more democratic (inclusive or universal) than indirect democracy. The definition of democracy involves 'rule by the people, for the people': only direct democracy can properly achieve that. The indirect democracies common in the present (2010) world are too much like (medium-term) dictatorships. Often one person has most say, king-like. And here politicians are often less informed than many citizens or voters, meaning that, all else equal, indirect democracies can here easily be more overall-objectively-unwarranted than a direct democracy would be. Relatedly, indirect democracies are unwarrantedly patronising via politicians believing they have a right to make decisions for those voters who are now more pro-objectivity than the politicians. So politicians treat these (and other) adults like children, mostly denying them the freedom to effectively make decisions. Patronising towards a pro-objectivity-autonomous majority would be objectively extremely intolerable.

In pro-objectivity democracy there'd be no separate political parties or politicians with fundamentally differing ideologies or conflicting selfish or groupist interests. (Again, a qualification regarding such comments is that in pro-objectivity society the vast majority would rightly view any irredeemably anti-objectivity persons as an outgroup. Again, the latter would be a tiny minority.) There'd be no typical electorates, or related groupism. Each voter would in a way be their own electorate, but their electorate would be universal. These voters would be impartially pro-objectivity-universally benevolent—toward all humanity, long-term. That is, voting rights would need to be deserved, and earned: voters would need to *demonstrate* such qualities and as in the following:-

Voters would need to make the *long*-term decisions indirect democracies often do not make. Voters would need pro-objectivity autonomy. They'd be independent in pro-objectivity ways, e.g., as recently mentioned regarding an individual constructively criticising all others and expressing his or her view if he or she has evidence no-one else knows of. Voters would relatedly be independent and non-egoistic by being willing to change their view if someone presents evidence showing it needs changing. Voters would need to be fundamentally maximally pro-objectivity and hence unified in that they'd accept the same general guidelines. They'd only differ sometimes regarding any uncertain specific applications of those guidelines, e.g., in cases requiring that just-mentioned critical, individual independence—while being unified and hence peaceful regarding reducing the uncertainty and regarding acting harmoniously together when it is reduced sufficiently to mean knowledge, or regarding acting harmoniously on some consensually provisionally-accepted basis, perhaps a trial-and-error basis, until relevant knowledge is acquired. (This paragraph implies that pro-objectivity democracy can require voters to debate. More here soon.)

Such types of independence, and unity regarding the need for independent possibly-diverging persons, involve the types of freedom involved in pro-objectivity democracy. This is *pro-objectivity* autonomy in that persons here are primarily pro-objectivity and, relatedly, as far as humanly possible, normatively-objectively autonomous in that they are objectively or truly free, e.g., free from believing the unevidenced, and free from being effectively influenced by pressures motivating them to believe the unobjective and be anti-objectivity. Relatedly, as objective statement X's objectivity inherently means X is *independently verifiable*, pro-objectivity requires the recently-mentioned related type of *independently-minded individuals*, i.e., where this independence (autonomy) is pro-objectivity. This autonomy involves unique, important types of freedom, and is essential for pro-objectivity democracy. (Pro-objectivity education would encourage such freedoms and related democracy, via being a most important factor in developing those autonomous individuals.)

Pro-objectivity society would maximise democracy in that, if all individuals had that autonomy, they'd be more happily pro-objectivity, via their free, knowledge-based, hence objectively-independent choice, than if they were ignorant here and had to be persuaded, pressured, intimidated or tricked into outward conformity to pro-objectivity. Universal pro-objectivity autonomy would mean universal social, political etc harmony, and hence peace and happiness. (Appendix 4, concerning there being only one overall coherent mental-system possible, is relevant here.) Only this autonomy can enable persons here to *know* what is warranted, including knowing it is warranted to have universal political, social etc harmony among them and others (e.g., children) guided by them, which means all here would peacefully and happily accept pro-objectivity democracy.

If persons measure up to all such qualification standards to at least a basic level, they'd qualify as a voter in a *general* sense. To qualify to vote on a *specific* issue, they'd need to also demonstrate 'sufficient pro-objectivity knowledge' of the issue. This involves an overall view, i.e., having sufficient evidence concerning all factors involved in the issue to thereby have sufficient knowledge to vote in as pro-objectivity way as far as is possible at the time. (This may only mean voting for provisional acceptance or trial-and-error.) There'll be some unavoidable uncertainty about what 'basic' and 'sufficient' etc mean here, but in-practice some approximate standards to measure them must be at least provisionally used. But flexibility is needed if those standards seem incorrect.

In some areas, sufficient knowledge could be simple enough to allow a conceivable vast majority to vote. (E.g:- Say there is plenty of clear evidence concerning the costs and benefits of having the usual, easily and cheaply replaceable type C1 school-crossing versus the so-far much more expensive, significantly safer C2, but that the cost of C2 becomes greatly reduced due to new inventions, making the cost of replacing C1s with and maintaining C2s about the same as maintaining existing C1's. Virtually all persons could have sufficient pro-objectivity knowledge to vote on such issues.) In some areas, expert knowledge would be needed, meaning just a minority would qualify. Overall, every citizen should qualify to vote on various issues, except perhaps the types of persons present (2010) democracies tend to exclude anyway, for rational reasons.

It could seem that a 'knowledge-degree' system is more appropriate than a 'sufficient-knowledge' system allocating just one vote to each qualifying person. A knowledge-degree system would, say, give one vote to anyone with secondary-school graduation level knowledge, up to, say, 20 votes to Ph.D. graduates. This is a difficult, somewhat uncertain area. But regarding issues requiring expert knowledge, a knowledge-degree system could easily mean that, e.g., 21 voters with the least, insufficiently informed level of knowledge, able to outvote the one expert's sufficiently-informed 20 votes. Here the most or only pro-objectivity decision would not be made, meaning an overall anti-objectivity situation. A sufficient-knowledge system would mean each issue is decided via knowledge sufficient to avoid such anti-objectivity as far as possible.

Concluding comments here so far:- Pro-objectivity-directed direct inclusion in decision-making requires decision-makers to have sufficient relevant pro-objectivity *knowledge*. Here voters would be pro-objectivity-directed informed about issues they vote on. This means being 'sufficiently informed (knowledgeable) in ways directed by and at pro-objectivity'. (Here, decision-makers would not be those with merely the most charisma, or born to power, or who seized power or most skilfully used their wealth and/or the mass media to persuade or fool voters, and so on.) Pro-objectivity-directed universal direct inclusion of those informed citizens in decision-making is an aspect of the pro-objectivity universal benevolence needed for a normatively correct world. This inclusion would involve far more informedness, democracy or inclusiveness than in present political democracies, where in-practice a tiny often uninformed minority make nearly all important decisions, and tend to be voted into power by voters largely uninformed about their alleged representatives. Pro-objectivity democracy's decisions would overall be made by at least nearly all citizens, informed citizens. And pro-objectivity inclusive (democratic) benevolence means those affected by but insufficiently informed concerning an issue would be consulted or considered by decision-makers (voters) here as far as pro-objectivity-possible.

But would that democracy be unfair, and hence normatively-objectively wrong, by not allowing all citizens to vote on all issues? Present (2010), recent and many past societies tend(ed) to have many important decisions made via systems parallel to pro-objectivity's voter-qualification system anyway, and for similar, rational reasons. E.g., modern societies tend to insist that those making the most complex, ultimate decisions concerning bridge construction have the highest relevant qualifications and proven engineering knowledge here—and allow the less qualified to only make simpler, thereunder lower-level decisions, and the unqualified to make no decisions. Not just anyone is allowed to decide or be in charge, or given a vote or a say equal to the relevantly informed. So a pro-objectivity voter-qualification requirement harmonises with the already widely-accepted rational acceptance that, if an important task needs doing, requiring knowledge, it is all-else-equal important to only let the proven-knowledgeable do the task. (Politics, where society's overall, ultimate and hence overall most important issues are decided,[25] is obviously an important task. The more important a task is, the more important it is to have relevant knowledge.)

Similarly concerning individuals rationally deciding who should do various important-to-them jobs. E.g., regarding complex surgery, nearly all are rational enough to choose to be operated on by the most skilled surgeon rather than someone with no surgical knowledge. Again, knowledge-based choices are common, for rational reasons. And to allow decisions to be made by simply anyone, as in all citizens voting on all issues, would be unfair as in it being unfair on the vast majority if anyone was allowed to do or supervise bridge-construction or surgery: most citizens would die much sooner than otherwise. This would also be unfair on the experts not allowed to do their job (properly). So overall it would be unfair. Equality does not necessarily mean fairness, and vice versa.

In sum:- A '(relevant) pro-objectivity knowledge-based' voting system seems best regarding making the ultimate or highest-level decisions regarding society, and most coherent with objectivity. And that system would not be entirely new. It would be what rational persons here do prefer or would prefer, and normatively-objective. Hence it would only be unfair or normatively-objectively wrong from a non-pro-objectivity, irrational viewpoint. (Part II, Sections 1.6.1.3-4 and 1.8.5 at least implicitly discuss this fairness issue further.)

In pro-objectivity democracy, people with insufficient knowledge concerning an issue would have no vote concerning that issue. This would be democratic via affecting every normal adult sometime: no-one can have sufficient knowledge in all areas. (I would get no vote in many areas.) Highly pro-objectivity, inherently rational and non-selfcentred persons would accept their lack of voting rights here. They'd act on their knowledge that it would be objectively wrong and unfair to decide via ignorance. But, again, they would be consulted or considered by decision-makers here as far as pro-objectivity-possible.

This subsection has assumed direct democracy is practicable. More on this:-

There have been direct political democracies, e.g., somewhat in ancient Greece. Many modern families, friendship, educational and other small groups are also direct democracies (non-political ones in that they don't make society's overall, ultimate decisions). They can work well, and some educational, friendship, family and others I know of are at least significantly pro-objectivity.

Some modern indirect democracies allow some direct democracy, namely referendums. Here a referendum's cost and organisational etc complexities could suggest that always having direct democracy in a large society would be impracticable and prohibitively expensive, involving an anti-objectivity waste of resources. But the internet can allow people to practicably and cheaply qualify to vote and to vote on issues they are concerned and informed about.[26] E.g., if academic, professional or trade qualifications are not appropriate regarding being qualified to vote on some issue, or if they are but so is informally-acquired equivalent knowledge, the relevant website here could present material and a quiz thereon here.

The term 'material' is used here because humans are fallible, so the website may contain errors here, not just knowledge. If time etc permit, the quiz material and questions would be provisional and be debated by those qualified to vote, before they vote. All informed people would have a right and duty to appropriately criticise provisional or any alleged information and the questions, and to suggest possible information or questions. The material should include mention of any known uncertainties or controversies, issues requiring skepticism, criticism, further research and so on, and encourage such debate. Via such means, it is highly likely the material will be at least sufficiently knowledge.

Assuming it is:- To qualify to vote, where possible the website would give intending voters plenty of time to understand the material before they do a quiz testing if they have sufficient knowledge to qualify. A 100% score would be needed. If time etc permit, the website could give intending voters chances to improve a non-100% score, via revision and retesting. Voting would be via a related website. (As some persons voting or attempting to qualify as voters might not be maximally pro-objectivity and hence honest here, and as there may be hackers, there would need to be appropriate, sometimes in-person, security and identity etc checks.)

So far, large-scale direct democracy seems practicable now. But the 'if time etc permit' is another practicability issue:-

Votes could be counted electronically, very quickly (and cheaply). Practicable *in*direct democratic parliaments etc often consider or debate issues for ages. There'd often be similar time available for pro-objectivity democracy's debating, improving of quiz material, quiz scores and so on. But a certain type of world is needed to have such time for all political decisions, largely regardless of the type of democracy. The time issue applies generally. In the best achievable world here, there'd probably still be decisions which need to be made quickly, say regarding aiding victims of unexpected earthquakes. In a not-so-good world, like the present (2010) world, there'd be such needs—and more. Among the 'more', military threats are a representative important issue. In a world where a pro-objectivity society is likely to be unexpectedly attacked by anti-objectivity societies, all-else-equal the probably best way to ensure this pro-objectivity society survives is to make at least some military decisions rapidly, not via any slow, gradually improved, internet debating, quiz, learning etc process.[27] (Quick military and related political decisions could be the best or only way here to help achieve long-term pro-objectivity peace.) But, in many areas, there'd often be ample time for such slow processes. It depends on the overall situation. Where urgency seems possible sometime, as indirect democracies have often done, direct democracy could give the relevant public service the right to make quick decisions. Something like an Emergency Service seems appropriate, one ready for any emergency, including military. Its decision-makers would be accountable; their decisions would be critically reviewed later, when time permits. This would allow for any needed improvements in later, similar emergencies. (Again, pro-objectivity is somewhat a work-in-progress.)

Concluding comments here:-

Direct democracy nowadays seems overall about as practicable as the obviously practicable indirect democracies. Regarding the practicability of instituting it, this could be done in indirect democracies by having enough pro-objectivity-educated voters to win a referendum here, or to vote into power a pro-objectivity party which would install direct democracy. Again, education is crucial.

Direct democracy is compatible (non-incoherent) with speedy decision-making in areas where speed is a pro-objectivity need. The quick decision-making easily available to dictators in all areas is not an advantage proving that direct democracy (is so cumbersome in decision-making that it) is an inferior, impracticable type of government. Advantages and disadvantages are so from some perspective or *viewpoint*, regarding achieving some *end(s)*. The overall important issue is: which perspective and related end-result is correct, i.e., objective? Quick decision-making is an advantage only from an end-result perspective such as 'Administrative temporal efficiency' or 'Speed crucially needed to help achieve end E'. Normatively, clearly, only an *objective*-end-result perspective is objective or correct. Here we should situationally-relatively only consider whether X, e.g., speed, is an advantage or disadvantage from that perspective, or, where appropriate, where the balance lies between advantage and disadvantage here regarding achieving end E, where end E is 'Be pro-objectivity'. As just argued, pro-objectivity democracy can use its public service to achieve 'Speed crucially needed to help achieve end E' here. Where pro-objectivity direct democracy can decide slowly, any disadvantage according to a quickness-perspective is outweighed by the pro-objectivity advantages of pro-objectivity-directed inclusiveness, opportunity to increase one's pro-objectivity knowledge, and hence voting rights, and so on, some of which *require* considerable time, not haste. Often, "haste makes waste". (N.B: This paragraph can be adapted to apply to other such 'But X is a disadvantage' criticisms of pro-objectivity politics etc.)

Another important issue for pro-objectivity direct democracy is only irrationally viewable as a disadvantage, in that this issue is *unavoidable* for *any* political etc system or practice, i.e., including any irrational viewer's systems or practices here. However, regardless of any such irrationality, this issue is important and in a sense a practicability issue. It involves the unavoidable fact that some *person(s)* must make ultimate decisions, via their normative theory:-

E.g., in the suggested direct democracy, some persons will need to decide what should constitute the provisional quiz material and questions, judge which later-suggested other material should be included, and hence crucially help decide who votes. Such decisions involve some vagueness or uncertainty, at least some of which is unavoidable and hence pointless (irrational) to be concerned about. Some is avoidable. Here we meet something like the problem raised by Plato's idealised guardians as the ultimate, political decision-makers.[28] They were supposed to oversee and guard (what he believed was) the best society, his Republic, ensuring it stayed best. A central problem is that, in real life, real guardians may need to be guarded against, namely if they err due to normal human fallibility, or err due to believing the wrong normative theory. But if the guardians are the ultimate decision-makers, there is no-one more ultimate, namely with the authority to guard against or control the guardians, or guard the citizens against any erring or evil guardians. This is the ultimate guardian issue:-

Part II, Section1.6.1.3: The Ultimate Guardian Issue

For a society trying to be as pro-objectivity as possible, there will be an ultimate guardian problem: pro-objectivity theory is fallibilist, recognising that "to err is human". But there is an unavoidable need for ultimate decisions and hence ultimate guardians in *all* political, social etc systems. So that problem is not a disadvantage of only pro-objectivity society, politics etc: it would apply *whichever* type of society, politics etc we have, or *whichever* normative theory we practise. The ultimate guardian issue also applies within the mind of *each individual* able to make and implement choices (decisions), which is at least nearly all adults, as each such individual unavoidably at least implicitly makes many ultimate personal decisions affecting politics, e.g., for many, regarding secret-ballot voting, and regarding *whether to obey* decisions made by others claiming to have the ultimate right to decide certain issues for the individual, as in laws made by politicians. The ultimate judge regarding what each individual free to choose (and thereby act) does can only be in the individual's mind. And this ultimate judge issue applies in each area of life. E.g., each driver has the ultimate freedom to choose how to drive, and whether to drive in order to intentionally kill oneself and/or others. In sum, the issue is universally unavoidable.

All that can be done about this for-all-who-choose issue is to have as many safeguards as pro-objectivity-possible to ensure that ultimate judgements are as normatively objectively informed (correct) as possible. This will be difficult, requiring voters/rulers/guardians to have sufficient knowledge here. (In pro-objectivity society the ultimate political guardians would be those voters.) Much more needs to be said and researched here than this book has space for. Briefly:-

First, though there'd be difficulties, from an objective viewpoint, compared to other societies, much in this book suggests that the ultimate guardian issue would be objectively least problematic for only *pro-objectivity* society, e.g., due to its democracy, self-criticism, fallibilism, evidence-seeking and related capacity for objective improvement including regarding pro-objectivity knowledge concerning how to avoid problems here as far as possible, and, centrally, knowledge of what at least provisionally seems the only correct normative theory:-

Each society's (and choosing individual's) ultimate guardianship involves a normative theory. Ultimate decisions concern ultimate ends, and ends are normativity's primary concern. As argued above, all present (2010) (and past) societies' normative theories are too problematic—so problematic that, from that *objective* viewpoint, within modern societies there is major fundamental uncertainty regarding who should make ultimate decisions. The difficulties for pro-objectivity society here would only involve uncertainties as exemplified in this book, namely non-fundamental, sufficiently comprehensible and manageable, often-reducible uncertainty.

Secondly, an ultimate guardianship trying to be pro-objectivity would to a significant degree involve a written constitution, prescribing separation of powers similar to that in various present (2010) democracies which significantly separate the legislative, judicial and executive aspects of government—partly as a safeguard against too much power possibly getting into what they consider the wrong hands, as in corrupt(ed) guardians. Additional pro-objectivity separations of power/persons might involve dispersing armies, having significantly-empowered provincial and local levels of government, and so on. A one-level world-super-State, a State which could not be defeated, and which, if its guardians became corrupt, fascist or similar, would be potentially highly anti-objectivity. Pro-objectivity requires a united world in various important ways, but safeguards, involving some such separations, safeguards against possibly anti-objectivity guardians, are also required. (In a maximally pro-objectivity world, the separated or separable parts would harmonise anyway, via all accepting the same ultimate end, something like pre-assembled, separate parts of a good phone becoming assembled and harmonising to make that good phone.)

Regarding the military capacity of the recently-suggested Emergency Service, a safeguard here, which could also equitably spread any difficult tasks here, is that it should be composed of persons from each of the many provinces, all able persons taking turns, perhaps part-time. And there could be multiple sections of the Emergency Service, separable so that if one section became a military threat, the others could overwhelm it.

The civilian political guardians with ultimate power over the Emergency Service should also come from each province, with as many people as pro-objectivity-possible being such guardians—via the pro-objectivity direct democracy discussed above. A maximum pro-objectivity-appropriate dispersal of power is needed, and would be truly and morally-correctly democratic.

Here, the recently-suggested qualification tests for voters would be a safeguard too. In pro-objectivity society, relevantly-informed persons would of course be the political etc guardians. The constitution would insist on testing them regularly. The tests would be, along with the constitution, a type of provisional written ultimate guardian. Thence, only citizens with pro-objectivity knowledge as overall as possible concerning the most important, overall decisions would qualify as voters here. Via appropriate education and other means, this could still be a large, increasing proportion of the population. And there'd be opportunities for all adults to vote in some other, at least many, less-important ultimate guardian areas.

Those ultimate, political guardians would oversee guardians of each of society's institutions or public services, e.g., transport-infrastructure. Where public-service guardian numbers need to be small, e.g., so as to make quick military or disaster-relief decisions, various 'potential guardian' groups, empowered to replace the ruling guardians here if they become anti-objectivity, would be "Plans B, C etc", with the institution's at-the-time (provisionally) ruling guardians being Plan A. Where pro-objectivity-appropriate, regularly rotating the membership among and within the Plans A, B, C etc groups, (along with inter-group consultations,) would be a useful safeguard here too, in-effect making the small group much larger over time. Similarly, guardian groups' compositions would change according to the area(s) or institutions where a decision is needed, namely according to different persons' specialist knowledge—giving potentially all the opportunity to vote in at least some area(s). The composition would also change according to persons' increasing or decreasing pro-objectivity. (Yearly or so checks would be needed, e.g., after a certain age, to check if guardians or voters are losing their cognitive etc abilities.) Such rotations and changes would also be safeguards against a minority becoming unwarrantedly powerful partly via being in a position of power for too long.

There is also an ultimate guardianship issue concerning the constitution detailing such ways to avoid ultimate guardianship problems: *persons* must first write it. This would probably initially be a minority—though later a majority should have the right to informedly criticise it and suggest improvements, with the initially-needed minority ensuring this via the fallibilism and pro-objectivity-directed universal benevolence they'd need to include in the provisional constitution—and demonstrate as part of their qualifying for the job.

It can only be persons who interpret and implement, or allegedly implement, a written constitution. Even if a constitution is optimal, persons need to ensure it is acted on optimally, permanently, in every area, rather than be forgotten, ignored, misinterpreted, distorted or overruled. Many real live persons, of a certain type, would need to be permanently involved regarding the written constitution.

Concluding comments here:-

An institution or society trying as hard as possible to rule in as pro-objectivity ways as possible will inherently involve far more evidence, knowledge and hence less uncertainty here than any other. So pro-objectivity democratic society would have various safeguards here regarding its guardians, and, as far as possible, be uniquely, objectively, self-correcting regarding any problems here (and generally).

As far as pro-objectivity-possible, *all* adults should participate in pro-objectivity democracy. (All could easily participate in a-objectivity democracy in that issues there do not require participants to have the knowledge needed in pro-objectivity democracy.) But there can be uncertainty regarding who is irredeemably anti-objectivity and who is sufficiently pro-objectivity, i.e., regarding who should participate in pro-objectivity democracy. More on this:-

Part II, Section1.6.1.4: Who Should Participate Politically Etc? Maximising Participation; Some Educational Implications

Consider this expanded version of 'Be pro-objectivity': 'As far as possible, all should always be pro-objectivity'. This requires universal application of and by that standard among persons, as far as possible. The implied or expanded version of 'possible' here is of course 'pro-objectivity(-directed) possible', meaning, e.g., that if it is not possible for certain persons to have sufficient pro-objectivity knowledge to help make decisions regarding pro-objectivity society, they need to be pro-objectivity(-directed) via being directed by others with pro-objectivity knowledge. Here they'd be included in pro-objectivity society except that, though they'd be considered and where appropriate consulted regarding its political and other important ultimate decisions, they'd not be directly included in making them. (In various areas, say highway-construction, I would be excluded here.) *Total* exclusion from politics and society (except its prisons or similar) is only warranted when there is no objective ground for inclusion, or when as far as maximally-knowledgeable pro-objectivity people can know there is no possibility of inclusion or redemption. Much evidence would be needed. As mentioned in previous endnotes, irredeemably anti-objectivity persons are at least highly anti-objectivity and if there is reasonable doubt that someone is irredeemably anti-objectivity, extra pro-objectivity education and/or counselling should be given, to give them a reasonable opportunity to become pro-objectivity. (Part II, Section 1.6.3 discusses this further.) This is an aspect of pro-objectivity-directed universal benevolence.

Again, the number of irredeemably highly anti-objectivity people is a tiny minority,[29] consisting of much the same types modern (2010) societies typically remove from society anyway—to protect the vast majority, e.g., murderous psychopaths lacking the brain parts needed for sympathy. Such crimes and associated permanent lacks are sufficient evidence for exclusion. Various modern democracies also exclude such and various imprisoned or detained persons from voting, often on similar, rational grounds. (Pro-objectivity, benevolent, knowledge-involving democracy would investigate whether genetic, stem-cell, electrode, drug or similar technology could alter psychopathic brains so the person has the sympathy etc needed to be pro-objectivity. Via such means perhaps eventually *no-one* will be irredeemably anti-objectivity, a pro-objectivity aim.)

As inclusion in pro-objectivity politics depends on the individual's pro-objectivity knowledge, education is crucial regarding including as many as possible. As far as pro-objectivity-possible, e.g., in balance with society's other pro-objectivity needs and resource-availability, all should:- (i) Know pro-objectivity theory's basics and general guidelines. (ii) Be at least moderately informed in or about all important areas. (A crucial, often-neglected area is history. This would include studying war, racist hatred, poverty, religious faith, nationalism and so on, to learn how anti-objectivity they are or can be, and to learn how to avoid them. E.g., all should study 20th century Germany or similar.) (iii) Have deeper knowledge in at least two major discipline-areas,[30] say the environment and health. (There'd also be (iv) an a-objectivity dimension to the curriculum.)

Via some such education, all normal people should qualify to vote in some areas. (If the sufficient knowledge is simple, many persons about 16 years old could know it. But voting should probably wait till they are older, more knowledgeable about the real, adult world, and when a person here has the pro-objectivity-needed frontal-cortical control over his/her emotional impulses etc.)

To further maximise participation, people lacking skills widely expected and focused on in many modern Western societies and education systems, e.g., literary skills, should as far as possible have vote-qualifying information (and all other educational content) presented in non-literary ways too. E.g., someone with poor reading skills should be able to hear the information and, where possible, have it pictorially or diagrammatically presented, and be assessed via quizzes using the appropriate media, e.g., speaking and drawing.

A type of hard case regarding pro-objectivity participation concerns universal participation in voting being an at least largely achievable ideal *only for certain types of persons* in a certain type of *society* (—types achievable crucially via education). Most modern (2010) citizens of countries such as Britain, USA, France, Germany and Canada seem capable of soon achieving major advances here. But there are parts of the world where there is a very long way to go. Here specifically lies that hard case: in such societies the pro-objectivity democracy described above is at present inappropriate, except for small minorities. Importantly, the most pro-objectivity alternatives here would be *temporary*. They probably include: (a) other, more pro-objectivity countries helping such much less pro-objectivity countries, e.g., via pro-objectivity media and educational input, (foreign aid would normally need to be an *overall,* pro-objectivity package, not just e.g., food); and/or (b) a somewhat non-democratic government in those overall insignificantly pro-objectivity countries, a government ruled by among-themselves-democratic pro-objectivity ultimate guardians—whose primary task is to educate the rest of the population to make them fit for pro-objectivity democracy as soon as possible, hence ending those guardians' small-minority rule. (This is what, in general, the best educators in any country would do anyway regarding young and any other students lacking pro-objectivity knowledge or acting in anti-objectivity ways. Partly similarly, parents often are and need to be dictatorial with children.)

So, this small-minority government would not be the totalitarian or dictatorial rule Part II, Section 1.1 suggested is always unwarranted. The pro-objectivity rulers (ultimate guardians) here would not have total power over the ruled in that these rulers' primary task would be to increasingly empower the ruled, giving them autonomy from dictatorial rule. From the very start there'd be at least some of the ruled who should be at least slightly empowered and so also somewhat rulers, those who have some at least implicit pro-objectivity knowledge. And reasonably soon, political participation could be greatly increased.

So the main aim of education, democracy and guardians here would to maximise the number of those autonomous individuals (and hence guardians):-

Part II, Section 1.6.2: More Concerning Normatively-Objectively Autonomous Individuals

These individuals would have the crucially needed pro-objectivity overall view, namely, as far as possible, an objective biggest-picture involving all pro-objectivity general guidelines along with much specific knowledge, including expertise in at least two areas. Thence they'd be highly qualified to make ultimate judgements (prescribe) in those areas; and they'd insist on those general guidelines being in society's political constitution. (Relatedly, this discussion has implications for legal judges and legal workers and systems generally.):-

Because one's judgment-level is ultimate, namely because it is one's *highest* level of thought, one can thereby reflect on and assess all one's other thoughts. One can also reflect on one's judgement level via one aspect of that level placing another aspect, or all other aspects, temporarily at a lower level, where they can be assessed. One's judgement level can thereby (self-)assess the evidence for its right to make ultimate judgements. (The ultimate guardian issue, and Appendix 2's discussion of unavoidable, rationally non-problematic circularity, are relevant here.) Pro-objectivity autonomy involves that highest level autonomously objectively assessing that right, that evidence.

So, that highest thought-level involves meta-thoughts, i.e., thoughts about other, hence (at least temporarily) lower-level thoughts and other mental events. As argued above, an overall view of 'thought' realises a human thought is part of an emotion-thought combination. Those lower-level events include the emotion-thought combinations directly prompting possible intended practices. So one's judgement-level has the ultimate freedom to decide whether oneself ought to practise via such promptings, including impulses, and, e.g., whether to practise only in one way, or whether oneself ought to permit oneself to practise whatever one (perhaps impulsively) likes among certain alternatives. When the highest level is pro-objectivity, this is the self-governing freedom involved in pro-objectivity autonomy.[31] Here, motivated via the pro-objectivity emotion-thought combination, one governs oneself, i.e., one's judgment-level governs the rest of oneself, including all other emotions, and promotes one's pro-objectivity emotion, as far as possible. Thence, as far as possible, pro-objectivity autonomy gives one the ability to encourage and revel in various emotions and feelings, and to flourish cognitively too. (Cognition occurs via emotion-thought (emotion-cognition) combinations.)

Regarding cognition, one's judgement-level, if it is pro-objectivity knowledge, would where appropriate involve or prescribe the fallibilism, provisionality, skepticism, self-criticism and so on, stressed above. This involves that highest thought-level being the most objective and least fallible level in that, as one aspect of its overall objective view, it alone is the *most general* level:- As Appendixes 2-5 and Part I suggest, it inherently has the only indubitably rationally-unquestionable, general pro-objectivity knowledge, of pro-objectivity theory's basis and related general guidelines. With this, compared to the more specific levels, it can most easily achieve the pro-objectivity aim of being maximally normatively-objective. The *specific,* directly practicable views, e.g., concerning pro-objectivity-optimal diets, are at lower levels of thought, and here is where errors and uncertainty tend to be most likely. To assess those levels, if the judgement-level uses the most objective general assessment methods available, e.g., scientifically-informed reasoning, methods involving some high- but not highest-level thoughts, it would overall have less chance of being wrong than various views it assesses. And, being self-critical, and open to others' rational criticisms regarding specifics, pro-objectivity judgement can increasingly correct mistakes in the lower levels it assesses, thereby and otherwise also improving the high-level scientific etc assessment methods it uses.

Thence, one can (increasingly) have the normatively-objective and otherwise objective autonomy to correctly assess one's own thoughts, emotions and hence practices. Pro-objectivity autonomy also involves assessing *others'* thoughts, emotions and hence practices, e.g., regarding how these affect one's own and others' emotion-thought combinations and hence practices, and whether others need pro-objectivity direction because they lack pro-objectivity autonomy and hence appropriate knowledge. This has direct implications for society. Clearly it applies to raising (educating etc) children, e.g., because they are often impulsive and not rationally reflective, not rationally self-governing, lacking normatively-objective autonomy. Relatedly, because pro-objectivity autonomy means one's thoughts and emotions are self-ruled, they (may be affected by but) are not controlled by other people (which only happens if one *lets* others do so[32]). Hence one will not accept a view *only* or *primarily* because, e.g., a parent, peer-group, friend, teacher, priest, government or newspaper tries to influence one to believe the view. It is a pro-objectivity test of character to ignore all such attempted influences, and autonomously independently objectively assess such views. The normatively-objectively autonomous individual only conforms to others' pressure if that individual has inherently *independent* evidence that what others wish her/him to do is overall-objectively-warranted.

The others' views may be emotionally attractive, e.g., comforting (as with many religion-based normativities). But, as argued above, this also has nothing to do with whether they are correct. Via a pro-objectivity education, individuals would be encouraged to think independently, i.e., autonomously. Clearly this has important implications for society. Pro-objectivity character or psychology involves having the strength of character to objectively asses all views, regardless of their social, political or media etc source, or alleged supernatural source, or their emotionally attractive, comforting nature, or perhaps disturbing nature.

Clearly, such individuals have a high level of emotional maturity, involving, as far as possible, autonomously controlling their emotions rather than being controlled by them, and being emotionally-directed only by pro-objectivity motivation. This maturity and direction can help with the confidence or courage needed, e.g., to resist anti-objectivity parental, peer-group or other social, political etc pressures, or if conflicting with other, hostile anti-objectivity individuals. (There are pro-objectivity virtues here.) Pro-objectivity autonomy involves the knowledge that oneself is objectively-warrantedly in control of oneself, and objectively (truly) free to make decisions, which would have a pro-objectivity self-motivating effect, facilitating such confidence or courage.

Such emotionally mature, (qualifiedly) confident, normatively-objective individual psychology would mean a rather historically-unique type of character, person or self, and hence, as previous arguments suggest, a harmonious society or world. (If such persons were the majority of adults in the world, there'd be pro-objectivity world peace—partly via them independently courageously rejecting objectively-unwarranted beliefs/theories, all religions and so on, hence avoiding the wars and other conflicts history shows they often lead to.)

Part II, Section 1.6.3: More Concerning The Normatively-Objectively Autonomous Individual's Self-Concept And Character (Virtues); Some Societal Implications

A person's essence involves a self-concept. At any one time, in one's self-concept at least one standard has to be considered fundamental, the highest priority. For normatively-objectively autonomous individuals, this would be the pro-objectivity standard. Thence, their self-concept would involve a unique, harmonious or non-incoherent, overall-objectively-warranted psychological security, and hence (qualified) peace. (Appendix 4, arguing there is only one overall coherent (psychological etc) system, suggests this further.) E.g:-

This secure self-concept would not be harmable by irrational criticism by others. This individual would regard any overall-objectively-unwarranted or anti-objectivity criticism, even if hostile, as evidence that the critic needs to be helped to be more pro-objectivity, not as harm done to the highly pro-objectivity individual's self-concept. There is no effective harm here in that autonomous individuals are independent, governing what happens to themselves, namely not dependently and weakly letting others govern them.

This self-concept would not be significantly threatened by oneself finding one was mistaken about any of one's own lower-level views. As these objective-regarding-themselves and hence fallibilist individuals seek evidence to criticise their own lower-level views, especially any provisional views, they'd welcome the chance to improve by eliminating a wrong view. Improvement in objective-warrantedness is inherently no threat to persons attempting to be as objective as possible here. Again, they'd be self-critical and open to others' rational criticism. A highly pro-objectivity individual would not interpret others' rational (i.e., evidence-based) criticism as a personal attack, an attack on one's primary self. This is because this individual's primary self involves *being* pro-rationality, ready to attack one's own errors, welcoming others' rational help here.

Such personal characteristics are aspects of pro-objectivity non-egoism: here one does not regard oneself as something nobody should criticise. One regards oneself as one regards all *other* pro-objectivity selves here, via oneself having the same ultimate aim as the others. (Or, with potentially pro-objectivity persons, they'd be regarded as potentially such selves). In that sense, all pro-objectivity selves would (actually or potentially) harmonise—one would not view oneself as someone deserving special (e.g., non-critical) treatment only for the (selfish) reason that oneself is oneself. This non-selfcentredness is yet another practicable egalitarian or democratic and social-psychological implication of pro-objectivity theory. It is another aspect of pro-objectivity-directed universal benevolence. It means types of peace within and among persons. It means related freedoms, e.g., being as free as possible from personally harmful criticism, and freedom from being affected by perceived threats to one's ego—because, being non-egoistic, one would have no such perception and nothing to threaten. It relatedly means freedom from jealousy and so on. (Such freedoms involve pro-objectivity duties, or virtues.) (The interpersonal interactions here and mentioned recently would be fairly unique in history, especially in some areas. E.g., they are hardly the norm in the many parliamentary and similar political discussions I've observed. Such interactions would help constitute a new type of democracy, the first overall-objectively-warranted democracy.)

Part I, Section 1.4, conclusion (1) argued that the only overall-objectively-warranted (hence ultimate) end/standard is the only truly *intrinsically* valuable end/standard.[33] *Knowledge* concerning the pro-objectivity end/standard is the primary aspect of the judgement-level which is primary regarding a pro-objectivity self-concept. So, that standard and end are *embodied* (embrained) in this person's primary self, and in an important, practicability sense this is the only place the objective normative end/standard could be. This makes this primary self, the essential *person* here, objectively intrinsically-valuable.[34]

Relatedly, regarding achievement here, as opposed to just having knowledge, this self would at least include the aim, '*Try* your hardest to live by that standard and to achieve that end'. This is equivalent to 'Be pro-objectivity as far as is practicable for the individual', which is all this practicable standard requires, and which is an expanded (qualified) version of 'Be pro-objectivity'.

Besides, from an overall view, trying to be pro-objectivity or being pro-objectivity as far as practicable involves being fallible and hence aware one's attempts may fail—and that trying-and-error (trial-and-error) here can mean knowing what not to do next time, and hence more likelihood of success. This self's overall view considers what can or does happen over *time*, in the long-term, not just at an instant, or regarding an isolated act, X. If X was a failed sincere attempt to be pro-objectivity, any criticism from oneself and/or others regarding X would be contexted via one knowing that error X was *unintended*, hence not one's fault, hence not a *normative* shortcoming or mistake, and avoidable in future and probably correctable. Overall, one's primary self would realise one had been overall as pro-objectivity as possible (namely in the circumstances). So, regardless of fallibility, one's primary self here would have been and remain objectively intrinsically-valuable.

Another societal implication here:- Recent points regarding issues such as fallibility and the distinction between a person's highest-level, primary self and other aspects of the person fit a related notion stressed by some psychologists. The notion is: 'If you wish to constructively criticise a person regarding some act they did, you should criticise the act, not their self-concept or them as a whole person.' This, like many notions not intended by their originators to fit with pro-objectivity theory, can be re-interpreted in a pro-objectivity way. Here, even if the person criticised has been extremely anti-objectivity, if there is even the slightest possibility of redemption, pro-objectivity persons would not criticise that person as-a-whole, telling them their self or character is worthless. This is another pro-objectivity duty, an aspect of a pro-objectivity character or self. This self would always benevolently consider redemption possible—unless or until there is overwhelming evidence to the contrary. (And fulfilling that duty would seem more likely to motivate redemptive, pro-objectivity practices by the erring person than if the whole person was criticised, making them feel humiliated, frustrated, uncared-for, stubborn, rebellious, and hence (more) likely to live up to that unwarrantedly negative label, 'worthless'. So that duty would help the criticised become more pro-objectivity, preferably eventually autonomous, hence able to control any promptings to commit anti-objectivity acts.)

Part II, Section1.6.3.1: Concluding Comments Here

As implied above, the only coherent, evidenced, overall-objectively-warranted meaning of 'autonomy' is 'pro-objectivity (or normatively-objective) autonomy'. Regarding notions such as self-control, character, primary self and self-concept, such notions need to involve that autonomy. Otherwise they are not normatively-objective, coherent notions. Similarly regarding 'flourishing': individuals cannot objectively flourish if they lack autonomy and hence freedom, empowerment, independence, individuality and a resourceful, (self-)educated self, one able to cope with and welcome constructive criticism. And so on.

Facilitating something like the individuals and the society they'd flourish in as described above (and below), is the only overall-objectively-warranted aim of psychotherapy, psychiatric drug and other physical treatment of the mentally-ill, social science, corrective institutions for criminals, of political and legal institutions, the economy, child-raising, education, films, literature, art, sport and so on. With this, pro-objectivity theory offers an objective definition of 'sanity', 'maturity', 'wisdom', 'decency', 'integrity' and so on—fundamentally different from presently (2010) widely-accepted definitions.

Part II so far has discussed various general practicable guidelines and many thereunder typical specific applications of pro-objectivity theory. Hence, and because the discussion is rather long, involving many different issues, it seems appropriate to again summarise a version, here a somewhat structural version, of various earlier-mentioned aspects of the overall picture, while expanding on some. That is, the next subsection revisits the structural big picture, the orthogonally-systematic "forest", plus closely examining a few more "trees", as opposed to just looking at, and perhaps getting lost among, many separate "trees". A crucial aspect of pro-objectivity autonomous judgement is the above-stressed overall view, i.e., knowing that big picture—into which all one's specific judgements and thereby-prescribed practices, and thereby permitted a-objectivity practices, need to be coherently or non-incoherently situated:-

Part II, Section 1.7: Revision Of Some Basic Points In Part II So Far, Involving Part I's Big-Picture Structurally; Some Further Implications Of That Structure

Pro-objectivity theory's orthogonal structure shows that, from an objective viewpoint, all a-objectivity things are of neutral value. Hence they are objectively of *equal* value. So, all persons' (and other) a-objectivity options and non-options are objectively equal. (Here there is no warranted criticism applicable and no real (objective) threat to any person's self-concept.) Pro-objectivity theory advocates treating all persons as equal here—another aspect of a pro-objectivity society's liberalism, egalitarianism and democracy.

That orthogonal structure non-incoherently involves *both unity and diversity*, or non-incoherently interrelates both converging and diverging. This relates, respectively, to the notions 'harmony' and 'irrelevance' as involved in one expanded version of 'Be pro-objectivity'. ('As far as possible, according to appropriateness be either harmonious with or irrelevant regarding the normatively objective: primarily be pro-objectivity, secondarily let there be freedom regarding the a-objectivity'.) Pro-objectivity theory advocates all persons converging, namely regarding that end and standard, a standard permitting diverging where this is neither warranted nor unwarranted. That is, primarily, we should be pro-objectivity; secondarily, orthogonal to this, we should be free to do whatever we like in a-objectivity areas.[35]

Regarding a-objectivity, such things as playfulness, uninhibitedness, bizarre art, individual unique expression and eccentricity are acceptable. This has implications for personal and social psychology and hence society. Some psychological theories have a totally or too one-dimensional (convergent) view of humans. E.g., some theories here see playfulness, uninhibitedness and similar as always a sign of immaturity, appropriate for children but not adults—a sign that one's mind is not yet advanced (warranted) enough. But, e.g., Einstein, Nelson Mandela and many other mature, highly intelligent, often very serious, often significantly pro-objectivity persons, were/are very playful and uninhibited sometimes.

Some theories here view, e.g., hair dyed green, spontaneous singing, lone dancing, and any other eccentricity or non-conformity, as always a psychological problem, e.g., as childish showing off by a socially-unskilled or immature person craving recognition inappropriately, perhaps due to low self-esteem or an inadequate self-concept, or as sign of psychosis or somehow being out of touch with the allegedly single-dimension structure of reality, a narrowly-defined normative reality all should conform to. Sometimes nonconformists here are immaturely craving recognition, psychotic or similar. But behaviour they exhibit here can occur in others for very different, mature, sane reasons. Such one-dimensional theories lack the pro-objectivity overall view of reality: they are ignorant of the normatively-objective, two-dimensional *orthogonal* structure of human life. From an objective viewpoint, it is the psychologists and others who believe such theories who have the psychological problem and an inadequate self-concept or inadequate concept of what a self-concept normatively-objectively should be. They are, objectively, deluded.

So, such limited pro-conformity or anti-individual-liberty theories are only warrantedly applicable qualifiedly, and, within the vertical dimension, to only some areas. E.g., it is pro-objectivity to conform to serious-student behaviour and not play around, but to pay quiet attention, during lessons on pro-objectivity health-care, philosophy and psychology. But those courses would advocate playing around and other diversity often, outside of lesson-times.

Within the a-objectivity dimension, playfulness and silliness can be due to the person here overall being secure and mature in pro-objectivity ways, not insecure and immature. Feeling too inhibited, feeling unfree to be warrantedly free, is normatively-objectively a psychological and social problem. It involves insecurity and immaturity in that here the person is too scared or lacks the independence and strength of character to be an individual, to be what is warrantedly fully human. It involves objective immaturity in that the person lacks the inherently mature pro-objectivity *autonomy* needed to not weakly conform to any statistically-normal inherently unwarranted conformity-demanding rules in a-objectivity (and, often, pro-objectivity) areas. (Such lacks mean such persons are more likely to obey anti-objectivity social dictates, and hence dictators, e.g., a Nazi dictator's command to enter into war, genocide etc, than are autonomous and hence strong-charactered individuals.)

Further, importantly, playfulness, eccentricity, uninhibitedness and the like can also be aspects of *pro-objectivity* fun and other recreation, and the creativity here can facilitate *pro-objectivity* scientific, literary, philosophical and artistic creativity, and so on. Hence they are practices a normatively-objectively responsible and hence mature person would revel in, and flourish partly via. With this, playfulness, eccentricity etc involve freedom:-

Some comments earlier could seem to suggest that the *unity* or *convergence* involved regarding pro-objectivity means that here freedom is unwarranted. However, other comments above show that much freedom or autonomy is needed in order to be pro-objectivity. The unity here only involves the ultimate, *general guidelines* and *end,* and the warrant of converging regarding *them*. Relatedly, the guidelines are *meta*-statements, and include: 'All should be unified regarding the need for pro-objectivity types of freedom and diversity'. Freedom and diversity will often be needed regarding the *specifics* of achieving converged-on general aims here:-

E.g:- People need to converge regarding being free to diverge from any mainstream-converged-on wrong, limited (non-overall) or otherwise problematic viewpoint. And, importantly, advances in knowledge often require free, divergent imaginative or uninhibited thinking: to think of possible new knowledge, we must be *free* to think of new possibilities—of *alternatives* to our present errors or ignorance. This means we need to be *different*, different or diverging from what is already thought, conventional or societally converged-on. So there can be a need to be unconventional, non-conformist or non-convergent, and for the freedom to be so. 'Eccentric' means something like 'very different or way out from the norm'. If a norm is wrong, as is typical regarding normativity, then eccentricity can be just what is needed to acquire normative knowledge and become pro-objectivity—which can then become the new norm(ativity) here.

The freedom needed to diverge intellectually in pro-objectivity ways is more likely to flourish if freedom is encouraged *universally* wherever doing so is pro-objectivity. E.g., if free expression in pro-objectivity comedy, dance, fiction, art, play etc are encouraged, then, all else equal, this seems likely to indirectly facilitate the free thought needed to discover new pro-objectivity knowledge. (Einstein said something like that.) 'New' can mean unusual, and being secure concerning and familiar with behaving and relatedly thinking unusually, including in silly[36] ways, should facilitate the thinking needed to discover unusual new knowledge. (Einstein's objective unusual ideas seem(ed) silly to many.)

Arguably, if we also freely practise being divergent in a-objectivity areas, this freedom as such, as opposed to the a-objectivity objects freely chosen, could be pro-objectivity in that it gets one used to thinking freely, creatively, imaginatively wherever appropriate, which can be useful within the vertical dimension. Anyway, freedom in a-objectivity areas is also *pro*-objectivity in that, orthogonally, it is pro-objectivity knowledge/objectivity which understands the *nature* of and *institutes*, or prescribes there should be, a-objectivity freedom.

Pro-objectivity unity regarding the general aim, 'Be pro-objectivity', can further involve diversity in that in many areas there could be different equally pro-objectivity *specific means* to help achieve that single end. Different family types, different foods, different types of exercise, different sexualities and so on, could be equally pro-objectivity overall. Here too, you are warrantedly free to choose whatever option(s) you like. The choice among equally pro-objectivity alternatives is a-objectivity. The differences among them are a-objectivity. So here too there needs to be freedom of choice, imagination, experimentation, mutual-acceptance of diversity, and so on.

Pro-objectivity fundamentally-unified society would also require diversity in that a great diversity of skills and other knowledge, occupations and so on are needed. Relatedly it would often be pro-objectivity for individuals to freely move (diverge) among different disciplines, occupations etc, each involving different knowledge areas. Imaginatively interrelating different, in-important-ways divergent knowledge areas has often led to new knowledge. (E.g., computers were invented by combining diverse knowledge areas such as those concerning electricity, valves, Boolean algebra, binary maths, engineering, human hand and visual capacities.) Relatedly, pro-objectivity society needs the freedom (ability) to fulfil the diverse dietary, educational and other needs of each individual. Relatedly, all need a very broad (diverse) education (along with depth in some areas). Otherwise persons will lack the knowledge needed to be, as far as possible, pro-objectivity *overall*, namely, here, over all the diverse areas of life.

In sum, an overall view sees that (1) the needed unity or oneness basically only concerns the *one* primary *general end*, but (2) plurality or diversity, requiring freedom, is often involved in *specifically achieving* that end. There is fundamental unity, but because of the nature of the world, including humanity and knowledge, the *application* of that foundation to the world needs to involve much diversity, which requires freedom.

This unity-involving-diversity would mean peace. Because the unity concerns the end, the primary consideration for pro-objectivity persons, they'd *primarily* be *united*: the primary general nature here of society would be unity and hence peace. In pro-objectivity politics, the judgemental, highest-level thinking of all directly involved would ensure peace via all having the same ultimate aim, and via all respectfully considering what any at least significantly-informed person thinks is evidence regarding achieving that aim. All here would be united via being self-critical and accepting others' rational criticisms too, removing a potential source of conflict among persons. Similarly, diversity as in (2) above would involve peace. E.g., all would harmoniously accept the need for the divergent thinking often needed to acquire new pro-objectivity knowledge.

A-objectivity diversity would clearly involve peace among pro-objectivity persons. As they'd consider each others' a-objectivity aspects as neither right nor wrong, these would not be a source of conflict. Regarding persons' unalterable or non-optional aspects here, e.g., racial origin, there'd be unity via all accepting, e.g., that the unalterability means unchoosability and hence that there's no rational point in having preferences here and in not accepting persons' non-optional a-objectivity aspects as merely different. Regarding choosable, optional a-objectivity aspects there'd be unity in that all preferences here would be seen as *equally acceptable*, as opposed to there being mere *tolerance*[37] of preferences different from one's own. (The same applies to a-objectivity personal aspects.) Here 'acceptable' refers to a type of meta-acceptance. It means one agrees positively that everyone has a right to be free to have whatever a-objectivity preferences they have, as opposed to oneself finding all a-objectivity preferences as acceptable to oneself in that oneself emotionally or subjectively evaluates them as positive and hence would practise via them. E.g., Pam might not like someone else's a-objectivity music preferences.[38] Mutual meta-acceptance here, with the resulting interpersonal peace, is another example of how pro-objectivity non-selfcentredness would affect society. Regarding such acceptance, pro-objectivity highest-level judgement and self-governance is crucial.

In sum, the unity and diversity in both pro-objectivity and a-objectivity involve peace, or lack of conflict within and among pro-objectivity persons.

What could seem a possible problem here is that the diversity involved in the orthogonal structure could seem to suggest that a-objectivity freedom and diverging a-objectivity choices involve incoherence or conflict within a theory based on coherence or harmony. Reviewing and expanding on that issue:-

If there are diverse things to choose among, one choice could contradict another. E.g., say, if there is space for only one tree in a couple's front yard, and one of them wants a birch and the other a eucalyptus, the difference between the trees being a-objectivity, there is a type of conflict. So a critic of pro-objectivity theory could say the theory involves incoherence and is hence overall-objectively-unwarranted. But there'd be no *normatively significant* or practical conflict here among pro-objectivity persons, and overall-objective-warrantedness and pro-objectivity theory concern normativity, and normativity ultimately concerns only the practical. That 'interpersonal-(non-)conflict' issue was covered in Part I, Section 3.2 comment (3d) and elsewhere above, so won't need reviewing much here. But some related issues need more discussion:-

It would be possible for a powerful dictatorship to impose uniformity (unity) concerning public a-objectivity tree, music and food options, clothing styles and much else, hence avoiding what the dictators view as problematic diversity (and freedom). E.g:- Consider again the a-objectivity choice between pro-objectivity fruits F1 and F2. (Again, this trivial example's general point applies to various other, important choices.) F1 could be the only fruit allowed to be grown, though it would be equally permissible to also grow F2. A more than superficial view of pro-objectivity theory shows that imposed uniformity here, i.e., *non-inconsistency*, would be *inconsistent with the objective normative standard*, 'Be pro-objectivity'. So *inconsistency* here is coherent with that objective standard. It is not true that F1 is the best or only right choice, the most pro-objectivity fruit. It is the imposed *uniformity*, not the *objectively-permissible diversity or inconsistency*, which would conflict with the normatively-objective: it is normatively-objective to *not* treat only one option among the neither warranted nor unwarranted as warranted, and hence all other, therewith-inconsistent options, as unwarranted in that they (allegedly) should be forbidden. Or, it is incoherent to act as if it is true (objective) that, among things which are objectively *neither right nor wrong*, it is *right* to have only *one* of them, and *wrong* to have the others. This situation involves treating the a-objectivity as *not* a-objectivity. Arguments above show that *this* is what is overall-objectively-unwarranted and incoherent with objectivity here. It would also contradict normatively-objectively autonomous persons' *autonomy*: such autonomy involves knowing it is overall-objectively-warranted to be free to choose between in-themselves conflicting a-objectivity alternatives. And objectively it is only among the alternative *things in-themselves* that there's inconsistency. Again, there would in-practice be no normative conflict among pro-objectivity *persons* non-selfcentredly etc choosing among those alternatives.

With this, if something, including an inconsistent plurality, is *irrelevant* to the pro-objectivity standard/end, it cannot *conflict* with that standard/end. Again, there is no normative conflict. One expanded version of 'Be pro-objectivity' is: 'As far as possible, be harmonious with the normatively objective'. But, as the normatively objective prescribes freedom regarding the a-objectivity, a further expansion is: 'As far as possible, according to appropriateness be either harmonious with or irrelevant regarding the normatively objective: primarily be pro-objectivity, secondarily let there be freedom regarding the a-objectivity'.

Both the irrelevant and the harmonious are involved, i.e., orthogonally interrelated. In other words, the inconsistency-involving, irrelevant-to-the-ultimate-end is independent of the ultimate end, so cannot be incoherent with it. And that *pro-objectivity-prescribed* a-objectivity *freedom* involves freedom to be inconsistent and have inconsistent options. Relatedly here, i.e., orthogonally-relatedly, the cognitive judgement that there is only that one objective *primary* end/standard also judges that *any* end/standard is permissible among those inconsistent ones irrelevant regarding achieving that primary end. Here it is permissible to inconsistently change from one standard and/or end to another, conflicting alternative, e.g., from a certain sexual practice today, to another tomorrow. (A-objectivity flourishing involves revelling in the inconsistency, the diversity, the freedom here generally.)

In sum:- Any inconsistency within the a-objectivity dimension is *not incon-*

sistent with pro-objectivity: there is no incoherence within the objective, and hence not within an objective normative theory. Pro-objectivity non-incoherently *requires* a-objectivity inconsistency.

Concluding here:-

There is no warrant for trying to avoid conflicting choices here by dictatorially enforcing uniformity. A-objectivity liberalism is warranted. *Everything* within the a-objectivity dimension, including the inconsistency, is neither warranted nor unwarranted. This means the inconsistency is not unwarranted.

And it seems probable that enforcing uniformity within the a-objectivity would lead to anti-objectivity frustration and so on, hence decreasing persons' motivation and ability to be pro-objectivity. (Some people may prefer F2, and know it is unwarranted to forbid it, understandably finding any forbidding here frustrating.) If so, here too, achieving *consistency* or uniformity would be incoherent with the normatively objective.

Part II, Section 1.8: More On Unselfish, Caring, Non-Conflicting, Pro-Objectivity Individuals, Their Society, Its Economy, Inclusivity And Egalitarianism; Some Hard Cases For Them

The first discussion below gives special attention to interrelating various issues above with the notions, 'unselfishness and, by implication, selfishness', (and hence the notion, 'pro-objectivity-directed universal benevolence').

Part II, Section 1.8.1: Unselfishness And Selfishness; More Concerning Discrimination; Situationality Here

Two introductory remarks concerning unselfishness and selfishness:-

(i) Here and elsewhere, where appropriate, those notions can be adapted to apply to groups. 'Group selfishness' is not an accurate term because 'selfishness' primarily refers to just one self aiming to satisfy just that self's desires. The term 'groupish' is appropriate when referring to a group or some member(s) of a group aiming to satisfy the group's desires. Groupishness is, e.g., when a parent tries to earn more than other parents so as to financially benefit his/her family group, in-effect at the expense of other families. Below, 'groupish' is sometimes used, but for convenience 'selfish' is normally used when a discussion could refer to individual and/or group greed.

(ii) The discussion beginning after this paragraph further confirms that selfishness is always overall-objectively-unwarranted. However, *un*-selfishness is not necessarily pro-objectivity[39] (and hence a theory prescribing altruism or unselfishness as such is not normatively correct). E.g., consider Harriet. If she has various non-cognitive resources, e.g., time, energy and financial independence, she is cognitively capable of doing medical research potentially of unknown-to-her significant pro-objectivity benefit to humanity. Yet Harriet personally is highly anti-objectivity: she is religious. Her religion prescribes unselfishly devoting her time and energy, and the money able to give her financial independence, to be used to help print religious propaganda used to try and persuade more to believe the religion. She does this unselfishly, not hoping for or expecting any reward.[40] She abandons her medical research, meaning she is in-effect anti- that potentially pro-objectivity medical knowledge, and this abandonment has other anti-objectivity effects. E.g., she will not get the further biological and other scientific insights which, all else equal, are more likely than religious belief to help one and thereby one's family, friends etc to become pro-objectivity. Unselfishness is only morally correct when pro-objectivity-directed—when it involves distributing resources which, as far as is possible to know, will achieve something normatively-objective overall. Pro-objectivity persons are inherently unselfish via distributing (directing) their resources thus.

Next, that just-promised discussion:-

The first issue here further concerns criticism and self-concepts. When a pro-objectivity person criticises someone, the pro-objectivity person is unselfishly only trying to help make the world an objectively better place, for all humanity. Pro-objectivity persons would not criticise others in order to belittle others and make themselves feel superior. That would be self-centred. Similarly, pro-objectivity persons would not criticise others on the basis of the others having an a-objectivity non-optional aspect or preference different from one's own. The other person would not be viewed as primarily, e.g., someone with a certain skin-colour, and hence of negative value. Such aspects would inherently not be, self-centredly, part of a pro-objectivity individual's normativity-related concept of other selves—or of that individual's own self-concept. Relatedly, importantly, the directly objective(ly-warranted) as such, as in scientific and normative knowledge, has no colour, gender and so on.

The second, related issue here concerns discrimination. Discrimination can be objectively either warranted or unwarranted (or neither[41]). This is clear in some areas, e.g., it is warranted to discriminate against stating '1+2=4' in a maths test. Yet these days (around 2000) it has been sometimes suggested that *any* discrimination regarding any aspect of a person is wrong, and self-centred. The above distinction between a-objectivity non-optional aspects of a person, e.g., one's racial origin, and a-objectivity options, say certain architectural building-styles, arises here. Because humans are normally conscious, many might be affected emotionally by others' criticism (negative discrimination) so as to feel like making anti-objectivity choices. Buildings and so on lack such capacities. It is not anti-objectivity, e.g., to discriminate via emotional preferences regarding an a-objectivity architectural style. (The perhaps to-some apparent selfishness here by pro-objectivity persons has been suggested above to be merely apparent. The next subsection suggests this further.) It is anti-objectivity selfishness or groupishness to act on (including express) any emotional preferences regarding any unalterable or unchosen a-objectivity aspect of a person, when such action will have an overall anti-objectivity effect on the person and/or others.

Regarding a-objectivity non-options and options, here objective scientists do not discriminate towards or against others' knowledge or reasonable hypotheses on the basis of the others' race, gender and so on, or their a-objectivity optional clothing etc preferences. Unselfishness is involved here, e.g., when, due to greatly preferring to mix with gender 1 socially and in sport, a scientist feels like generalising from this self-centred strong preference to preferring hypotheses suggested by gender 1 persons—but does not discriminate here via that self-centred preference. Here, the warranted preference concerns only the directly objective, namely knowledge, or the possible objectivity of a hypothesis. Here, discrimination towards or against a gender would be clearly overall-objectively-unwarranted, and selfish.

In such situations gender and certain other things are a-objectivity aspects of a person. However, importantly, the overall issue regarding discrimination and (un)selfishness can involve situationality. In other situations, gender for example might not simply be a-objectivity. Gender here could be either a *pro*-objectivity or *anti*-objectivity *preference*—as opposed to simply being an a-objectivity *non-optional aspect* of a person. E.g:-

Suppose, regarding sex, it is overall most pro-objectivity for Lucinda to have a life-long monogamous heterosexual partnership. She emotionally prefers only a male sex partner, subjectively evaluating that type of sex and partnership as the only intrinsically-valuable type(s). Here it would be anti-objectivity for Lucinda and anyone involved to regard gender as a-objectivity, as neutral, and for Lucinda to, say, toss a coin to in that sense non-discriminatingly decide the gender of her life-long monogamous sex partner. She might get a female. Here gender is not a-objectivity. Here, Lucinda's strong subjective preference for a male sex partner is pro-objectivity. Here, to discriminate against a male would overall be unwarranted. Here, as explained soon, Lucinda is pro-objectivity and unselfish via discriminating against a gender, against females.

Suppose Maggie feels discriminated against here, because she wants to be Lucinda's sex partner. Part II, Section 2.4 argues that whether homosexuality is pro-, a- or anti-objectivity is situational. For Lucinda homosexuality would be overall anti-objectivity. 'Overall' in such cases refers to the on-average result across all beings and/or things concerned, (as far as can be known,) e.g., here, say, the major anti-objectivity effect on Lucinda from having Maggie as her partner would outweigh any pro-objectivity effect on Maggie from having Lucinda as her partner, which, if there was any pro-objectivity effect, would be small and only initial, mainly because Lucinda would be an unhappy, unwilling partner, whose health would probably suffer, and so on, eventually affecting Maggie in anti-objectivity ways—overall outweighing that possible small initial pro-objectivity effect on Maggie. Via Lucinda's pro-objectivity overall view, Lucinda realises it is objective (true) that those are the overall most likely effects. So here Lucinda is pro-objectivity via discriminating against females.

If Maggie becomes more pro-objectivity here, she will be unselfish and overcome that initial desire, redirecting it to where it is warranted. First here, she will unselfishly not let her desire for Lucinda affect her actions. She will unselfishly accept that, overall, i.e., over all the time and persons involved, the most pro-objectivity thing is for Lucinda to have a male partner, and for herself to seek another, willing woman. Then Maggie can gradually replace and lose that selfish, potentially very anti-objectivity desire for Lucinda.

With this, true love or caring is entirely unselfish, only aiming at what is truly best, i.e., most normatively-objective, for the loved or cared-for person(s). (So, importantly, true love is only fully possible via being maximally pro-objectivity, which involves the pro-objectivity-universal direct (and indirect) love and hence unselfishness etc discussed above.) A pro-objectivity or morally-correctly caring Maggie would want Lucinda to be (warrantedly) happy.

Concluding here:- Persons' non-optional aspects include gender, or at least the gender one was born with.[42] It may seem incoherent that gender is a-objectivity in some situations but not in others. But it is the ultimate normative *end* achieved in each situation which is, for a normative theory, inherently the ultimate consideration. In the 'Lucinda's sexuality' case, the pro-objectivity end is achieved via discrimination. And via not discriminating regarding gender, scientists correctly treat gender as a-objectivity when assessing persons' views for objectivity. Here the pro-objectivity end is achieved in that objective beliefs are assessed as objective and no-one suffers due to anti-objectivity, unfair discrimination. And so on. In every such differing type of situation here the differing treatments of gender are coherent with pro-objectivity. Relatedly regarding various other things beside gender. Overall, i.e., over all situations here, the general end, 'Be pro-objectivity', remains constant and is achieved. But, again, there can be different means of achieving it in different specific situations.

Another pro-objectivity implication concerning unselfishness, explaining further why Lucinda is unselfish:-

Part II, Section1.8.1.1: Pro-Objectivity Unselfish Self-Care

Being entirely pro-objectivity-unselfish need not conflict with doing certain things for oneself. It is situational: the overall view is that doing things for oneself can be pro-objectivity unselfishness. Here, what you do for yourself also creates or maintains resources you need to optimally serve *other* persons in pro-objectivity ways. Here one's ultimate central focus is pro-objectivity-directed *universal*. This is pro-objectivity 'unselfish self-care', involving a balance between (1) duties to oneself and (2) duties to others, where (1) is a means to help perform (2). E.g., you cannot optimally help others if you are overtired, malnourished, lacking energy, unhealthy, highly sexually-frustrated or disablingly miserable. So we all have a duty to eat well, rest, exercise, be healthy, not overwork on-average, to have some person(s) to directly and deeply love and be loved by, to have friends, fun, desired sex, recreation, indulgences and so on in pro-objectivity ways related to one's individual (situational) needs here. Fulfilling such needs, so as to be as pro-objectivity as possible, would normally involve keeping oneself at least moderately happy on average, a general need here. (This would also help motivate people to be pro-objectivity.)

The previous paragraph suggests it would be pro-objectivity unselfish self-care for Lucinda to act on her preference for a male sex partner. This would better enable her to give unselfish pro-objectivity care to *all* at least potentially pro-objectivity beings etc as far as is (pro-objectivity) possible, including herself. The pro-objectivity self's judgement-level would impartially understand that *any* pro-objectivity person has various general self-care needs, e.g., food, and that *anyone* in one's specific situation has certain specific pro-objectivity needs, e.g., say, via being allergic to a specific food, or via having a certain sexual preference. In fulfilling one's own needs here, one is only doing what one would unselfishly do for *anyone,* as far as pro-objectivity-possible.

Someone could try so hard to be optimally unselfish that they pass the optimal point and become sub-optimal. E.g., Malcolm could work so hard and give so much away to try to help others, that he has not the energy and other resources available to in future optimally help others (or himself). Not caring for oneself here, via such excessive, morally incorrect unselfishness, can involve as much anti-objectivity discrimination against persons, namely oneself and, here, in-effect against those Malcolm could have helped more, as would discriminating towards oneself via being selfish. To not practise pro-objectivity self-care is one type of anti-objectivity neglect or abuse of a person.

Part II, Section 1.8.2: Pro-objectivity Unselfish, Fair Sharing: Further Economic Implications

The only overall-objectively-warranted economy is where, as far as possible, all resources are distributed unselfishly only so as to create and/or maintain the overall most overall-objectively-warranted possible world, permanently. Pro-objectivity-directed universal caring involves pro-objectivity-directed universal sharing, an aspect of morally correct economics. Relatedly, pro-objectivity-directed distribution (sharing) of resources and resource-related benefits and costs means normatively-objective economic fairness. Such pro-objectivity fairness, caring, sharing and hence economics is needed for an overall harmonious, maximally pro-objectivity society and individual life:-

Pro-objectivity caring and fair sharing rules out economies such as Stalin's allegedly communist economy and, for somewhat related reasons, inherently selfishness- or greed-promoting capitalism. Still, some other important pro-objectivity needs have been significantly fulfilled in Western and Western-influenced democracies with part-capitalist, part-socialist economies. E.g., among those democracies there is much open, critical rational discussion, much freedom of thought, expression, evidence-seeking and independent research, much non-sexism and non-racism. So at least some significantly capitalist and hence overall non-pro-objectivity economies are not entirely incompatible with an often at least significantly pro-objectivity *society* overall.

However, discussions above imply that it is the socialist (or public) parts[43] of such democracies' economies which inherently have at least most potential to maximise pro-objectivity. To help maximise pro-objectivity, the capitalist parts would have to change into being pro-objectivity caring and fair sharing, i.e., become socialist. So, e.g., there are for-profit, non-public or non-State-owned universities and media which somewhat promote in-effect pro-objectivity, but to do so maximally and hence coherently they would have to explicitly promote that pro-objectivity caring and fair sharing, i.e., socialism. But this would probably be opposed, probably successfully, by their aiming-for-profit owners.

Often those societies' public or socialist educational and media institutions have intellectual independence and are highly rational, critical and evidence-seeking. So they could, with no such opposition, successfully and coherently advocate full socialism and pro-objectivity generally in those societies, reducing the greed-promoting aspect of those societies, increasing that caring and fair sharing. (They would need to advocate *directly democratic* socialism.)

However, as much in the above implies, even in the presently most pro-objectivity societies, there is a long way to go here. With this, there has never been anything close to an optimally pro-objectivity, socialist economy. To achieve one, we can only do what is possible, and so we must work with whatever economy is available:-

To be pro-objectivity, one needs certain material resources, and if the only source of most such resources is a strongly capitalist economy, then one needs to use this—partly in order to ultimately end capitalism and promote unselfishness. This situational, provisional, qualified acceptance of capitalism would be merely a temporary means to a morally correct end. There is no conflict here with the objective normative end, because capitalism is here the only available, practicable economic means to that end. Any apparent selfishness involved here in acquiring resources capitalistically is needed to help achieve, in the longer-term, an unselfish, normatively-objective end. (This acquiring would be similar to pro-objectivity unselfish self-care.)

More specifically, what is the long-term economic end-aim here?:-

Unselfish, pro-objectivity-directed universally benevolent persons would try to ensure they and all others only get a pro-objectivity-fair share of resources. This fair share is whatever quantity and quality of resources is coherent with humanity overall being as pro-objectivity as possible, crucially including via economic resources enabling each individual to be educated and motivated to the maximum pro-objectivity-possible degree individually needed to optimise humanity overall having and thereby maximally practising pro-objectivity knowledge. (This has implications for Rawls's theory concerning fairness.[44])

It is obviously overall-objectively-unwarranted for any individual to have either more or less than their share here. Each only objectively deserves whatever proportion of resources is needed for him or her to help create and/or maintain pro-objectivity overall, namely over all individuals, or for and by all—including in oneself or any one individual or group to the degree that this does not conflict with humanity overall being as pro-objectivity as possible.

All future generations need considering. 'Overall' also implies 'longest-term'. So, e.g., in relation to a pro-objectivity-optimal population size, a pro-objectivity economy would try to ensure a sustainable pro-objectivity resource-use and environment for all future generations, e.g., avoiding health- and agriculture-threatening UV-radiation, pollution and climate change.

Concluding comments here:-

Capitalism lets some profit at the expense of others: its primary aim is not to promote, fairly for all, everyone's ability, motivation and opportunity to be maximally pro-objectivity. If some have a selfish proportion of resources, others would be denied an otherwise available degree of, e.g., pro-objectivity education, or, as often happens, survival-necessary health-care and food. (This paragraph can be adapted to apply to any unselfish but overall-objectively-unwarranted economics, e.g., other versions of socialism, and recently-mentioned Harriet's economic unselfishness.)

Successfully selfish or rich persons often get their anti-objectivity, unfair proportion of economic resources because they are at least moderately rational, but use their rationality and related objectivity here in a merely instrumental, greedy way[45]—as opposed to using it to learn which economic etc practices are (objectively) right. Such selfishly instrumental rationality is another case of objectivity being used in anti-objectivity ways. It is morally-objectively another selfish waste of cognitive resources, one related to the anti-objectivity immense waste of economic resources typical through history and the modern world.

Part II, Section 1.8.3: Some Other Representative Hard Cases And Related Issues

An objectively unfair distribution could also be via giving immense, disproportionate educational, housing, medical, entertainment etc resources to the most poor, the most ill, the most aged and so on. As a hypothetical example, consider severely intellectually disabled people who, given present (2010) medical knowledge, can improve cognitively only marginally, temporarily or not at all. This book argues that such people need decent, kind, humane treatment (which I gave when teaching such persons). However, from an normatively-objective, overall (long-term etc) viewpoint, that hypothetical *disproportionate* resource distribution is unbalanced and hence unfair to the degree that there'd hence be insufficient resources for normatively-objectively deserving others, including, in the present world, others dying of starvation. There'd also be insufficient for overall more productive pro-objectivity uses—including training enough able persons to develop medical science so as to increasingly avoid intellectual disability in *future* generations, or to quickly develop new biochemical, gene or stem-cell technology which might help those now-alive disabled persons' brains change so as to at least significantly remove their disability.

Choices regarding such resource distribution can be, for at least many people, hard. E.g., many could be upset due to believing that those disabled persons would suffer or be treated unfairly if some of their immense resources were taken away. But, as far as we can know, it could be most likely there will be much *more* suffering overall medium- to long-term if they get massive resources in the short- to medium-term, and that this distribution would be less pro-objectivity-fair *overall*, including via there not being enough left to optimally pro-objectivity-benefit future disabled persons. And so on. Here, discrimination towards those presently-disabled persons could be in-effect overall anti-objectivity discrimination against disabled persons long-term, and against the vast majority or society overall, or against more-suffering, e.g., starving, others.

Relatedly, discrimination towards such resource-waste is likely to be primarily emotion-based rather than rational or pro-objectivity. Similarly, often, regarding finding choices here hard. In general, hard choices or moral dilemmas often occur when each alternative seems important, and the chooser cannot easily decide between what seem at least nearly equally correct alternatives. The perceived importance and indecisiveness can involve emotion which in-effect greatly reduces one's rationality or objectivity.

From a rational, pro-objectivity viewpoint, choices are only hard if there is insufficient knowledge for pro-objectivity-directed choice and the issue is important regarding pro-objectivity—which includes being emotionally important regarding pro-objectivity. (Maximally pro-objectivity persons have pro-objectivity-directed emotions as far as possible, often making otherwise emotionally hard choices less hard or not hard.)

Regarding resource-distribution, to the degree that pro-objectivity persons lack knowledge of an optimally pro-objectivity balance and hence resource-distribution overall, to that degree there will be uncertainty. Uncertainty makes it hard to know precisely what to do. However, again, objective persons do not find it hard to not worry about any at-the-time unavoidable uncertainty, and they know that uncertainty will decrease as our knowledge and hence other, economic and, hence, medical finance, technology etc resources grow. Thence, the hardness of resource-distribution choices will decrease for those choosing via a knowledge-involving, objective normative theory.

It is pro-objectivity to accept that hard choices or normative dilemmas will always somewhat exist for pro-objectivity theory. However, it seems likely that in various areas there'd be at least implicit hard choices *whatever* normative theory one has. E.g., any at least moderately rational person, whatever their normative theory, can understand the simple fact that, if you spend X here-needed resource-units, e.g., money or time, on to-the-theory-important P, you will have that much less to spend on to-the-theory-important Q—because overall resources are limited. So the holder of any normative theory will have to make some hard resource-distribution choices.

Also, all normative theories have hard choices involving the fact that, whatever you do regarding choosing among any alternative means to achieve a theory's end(s), you could and perhaps should have chosen to do something *else* to achieve the end(s). E.g., consider Kant's and Rawls's theories prescribing of the end: 'Act via absolute respect for each individual's absolute right to life, i.e., regardless of the consequences'. This can in-effect mean regardless of the consequences for *other individuals*. (This issue parallels the just-exemplified *general* (e.g., capitalism-relevant) issue of whether certain persons have a right to receive, and certain (perhaps the same) persons to allocate, massive resources to be used largely non-productively (e.g., for capitalists to have unneeded luxuries), regardless of the consequences concerning what's morally right.)

Suppose that (alleged) absolute right to life is a theory's single ultimate end. This can mean hard, indeed impossible choices:- Suppose food and drinking water are short on a crowded, isolated life-boat, and either only one person can be kept alive or all will die. To preserve any one life, one person must be chosen, which at least implicitly means choosing to *not* preserve the others. But such theories claim that *each* life as such is of *absolute*, *intrinsic* and hence *equal* value. Such theories can offer no way they can rationally call 'fair', 'correct' or similar, to prioritise or decide whose life is most valuable here. (Pro-objectivity theory does not regard each life as necessarily equally and absolutely intrinsically-valuable. E.g., pro-objectivity theory would regard Hitler as inferior to most people, and irredeemably anti-objectivity, so he should be sacrificed if in that life-boat among at least potentially pro-objectivity persons.)

In sum, such theories are fatally incoherent. And, as shown previously, this applies even more to theories with two or more ends regarded as ultimate, as with the previously-discussed 'equality' and 'freedom'. Such ends will conflict sometimes, as will specific types of or ways of achieving equality,[46] or freedom.

For such reasons, let alone other, previously-discussed reasons, each of the many such single-end and all plural-ends theories are incoherent, self-contradictory. Where it is impossible to properly achieve a single-end theory's end, or each end of a plural-ends theory, this means more than just *hard* choices. It means impossibly hard choices, and insoluble problems. Normative theories inherently need to be practicable—not incoherently prescribe that we should do what is impossible to do. So theories here are not really normative theories.

Concluding remarks here:- If whatever normative theory one holds means there can be choices which are at least hard, it is incoherent or overall-objectively-unwarranted to reject pro-objectivity theory because it can involve hard choices (and some associated, reducible uncertainty). This book is arguing that all other (sometimes only allegedly) normative theories have too many problems, and that pro-objectivity theory is the (objectively) best available: pro-objectivity theory can involve hard choices but it alone is objective and knowledge-related, hence involving an overall, coherent view—meaning the hard choices here are overall the *least* hard among all normative theories.

Part II, Section1.8.3.1: A Pro-Objectivity-Handled Medical Hard Case

Sally is 20 years old and William is 60. Both have a fatal but curable disease which will kill within a month unless treated now. Due to limited medical resources, only one can be cured. There are only limited alternatives in life: whichever choice is made in such cases, e.g., here, to either try (unsuccessfully) to save both William and Sally, to save only Sally, or only William, or neither, will be hard from some perspective. All we can fundamentally do is try to discover and apply the best available or most correct perspective, i.e., normative theory. Consider someone trying to apply a pro-objectivity perspective:-

Suppose, as far as we can know, that, if cured, regarding their individual lives as such both will be equally highly pro-objectivity in each future year they live. If cured, as far as can be known, Sally probably has about 65 future years, and William 15. On the basis of that 'separate, isolated-individuals' information, it would seem most pro-objectivity to discriminate in favour of Sally, giving her the cure. Here, because William is highly pro-objectivity, and hence objective, he would impartially accept this. William would be unselfish here, making the ultimate sacrifice. Here this is the pro-objectivity fairest decision. It would be the least hard in that William and Sally would know it is the only normatively correct choice here. But that attempt to apply a pro-objectivity perspective is too limited. The term, 'separate, isolated-individuals', and hence the previous four uses of 'here', are problematic. The information on which the 'sacrifice-William' decision was made is too limited, i.e., insufficiently overall. 'Information' is knowledge and relatedly evidence, and there are important issues here. E.g:- First, evidence *relates* or is *relevant* to something, and the something may not be relevant regarding achieving an objective end. E.g., evidence relevant to how (un)happy all will be if X is done, compared to Y, is evidence directly relevant only to a maximise-happiness theory. It is not in-itself unqualifiedly, directly and fully relevant to pro-objectivity. Secondly, a pro-objectivity (and hence practicable) view is an as-far-as-we-know, *overall* view of the evidence:-

This overall view would be aware that, e.g., emotions are involved in being pro-objectivity, and hence that pro-objectivity and any unavoidable anti-objectivity actual and potential emotional factors involved in William's and Sally's case are important evidence here. Here, evidence concerning happiness or sadness is, if pro-objectivity-qualified, indirectly part of what is relevant. Again, many people regard hard choices as hard at least partly because the options involve for-them-strong emotions. Thence, e.g., many people make what seems for them or all concerned the least sad choice, not relating this to pro-objectivity. Again, we can overrule emotions and somewhat retrain them, and pro-objectivity persons would not make choices on a primarily-emotional basis, as with making the least sad choice—but there will at least often be some negative emotion unavoidably involved in hard cases for pro-objectivity theory. Sadness will often be involved, but here pro-objectivity decision-makers would relate it to pro-objectivity. With this, that discussion of William and Sally only considered them as isolated individuals. An overall view considers more:-

E.g:- That discussion ignored William's and Sally's close-circles. Suppose Sally has only one person, Brian, who loves her directly and who would hence be sad more than insignificantly if Sally died. Suppose there are twenty persons who directly love William and would be sad about his death to the same, major degree as Brian would concerning Sally's death. This degree, as far as can be known, will probably reduce each person's overall pro-objectivity effectiveness by, say, about 40 percent on average, for 3 years. This would mean, say, 40x3 anti-objectivity sadness units per bereaved person. So, for Sally to die, there'd probably be 120 anti-objectivity units, i.e., for one other person, Brian. If William dies, there'd be 2,400, i.e., among those twenty other persons. Suppose we have a fairly accurate likely score for William's potential post-cure isolated-individual pro-objectivity achievements, and add this to that 2,400; and likewise for Sally. Suppose these scores mean that William's death is likely to overall have far more anti-objectivity effect than Sally's would. And, as others might also die, e.g., in car accidents, it is far more likely that Sally's entire close-circle, Brian, will die than will William's. This is further, objective-probability type evidence needing to be considered by decision-makers here.

There is other such and other actual or potential evidence to be considered, but enough has been said to show that the original 'separate, isolated-individuals' related evidence is insufficient. Suppose all the available evidence indicates it is still most probable that William's early death will have far more anti-objectivity effect overall than Sally's would—with emotions playing a major role, especially where some emotion is unavoidable. Emotions such as anger and hate tend to be at least significantly controllable; however, from my training as a psychologist, observing many people, and personal experience, it seems to me that, for a considerable time at least, though there is considerable variation among persons, to an important degree normal humans tend to have little control over sadness felt due to the actual or highly-likely death of or desertion by a much-loved person. And such sadness disaffects one's cognitive ability. So, it seems, discussions concerning what the most pro-objectivity decision concerning William and Sally is need to consider any disabling grief which will unavoidably occur as a result of (and relatedly before) each possible decision.

Here, Sally and Brian, if doing the most normatively-correct thing, would unselfishly decide that Sally should die. (As Sally is objective, she knows that all the available evidence suggests that, after death, there is nothing—all experience ceases.[47] So, as an ancient Greek said, death is nothing to fear. Sally does not fear being dead. She accepts she'd not miss not being alive.[48])

That decision is the most pro-objectivity-directed benevolent and least anti-objectivity-sadness-involving decision *possible* here. An objective normative theory does not ask for more than what is possible as far as can be known:-

Different hard cases can mean different judgements are required—yet all should relate to the one ultimate end, statable as: 'Do what is overall most pro-objectivity as far as you know'. And, of course, there is a problem common to all consequentialist theories, namely, here, we cannot know how to precisely calculate such things as degrees of missing a person, anti-objectivity units, and so on. It is only possible here to act on the best knowledge we have, which may be limited, approximate or probable. And we sometimes err. E.g., it is often only possible to have only probable knowledge, e.g., of the future, and 'probable' means 'somewhat uncertain'. Yet we do know, for instance, that normal persons can for years lose much of their motivation and ability if they lose a much-loved person, through death or whatever. We can also know that some dead persons would be missed much more than others, and that the length and/or type of lives certain people will probably have are very different. We can ask those who could be bereaved to honestly estimate the degree to which they'd be upset in an anti-objectivity way, contexted via knowledge of previous similar bereavements, and can informedly estimate the likely future regarding persons' pro-objectivity.

So, at least often, we can have at least some probable and/or approximate evidence in such cases. And, again, it is only possible here to act on the only available, often-limited knowledge and/or fallible estimates. To expect full knowledge in such cases is impracticable and unobjective, and hence objectively-unwarranted. (It is objective that here we *know* we do not have full knowledge.) If we choose to ignore the often little we do know, and allegedly do nothing, we are thereby still doing something. We have still made a choice. We have in-effect chosen to do something even more overall-objectively-unwarranted and irresponsible, a choice for which we are morally responsible.

Part II, Section1.8.3.2: More Concerning Hard Choices; "Playing God"

An important issue regarding hard choices is that some person(s) need(s) to do what many call playing god, i.e., make the implemented or in-effect decision. Many people consider this role necessarily immoral, e.g., as an abuse of power. Some believe there is a god who will and alone should decide. That belief is in-effect a version of the just-discussed alleged nothing-doers. In my experience, e.g., regarding slowly, painfully dying persons where euthanasia is a reasonable option, the choice to let an alleged god decide would increase and prolong suffering for all concerned, for no normatively correct reason. Such effects would often be anti-objectivity. Here a human choice is *still made* regarding the dying or similar—so the chooser trying to avoid playing god is in-effect playing god.

The general point is that, if a person is aware of a hard case and can influence what happens, this person necessarily makes a choice—either to explicitly prescribe a relevant act other than 'do nothing', or to (allegedly) do nothing, the latter being implicitly also prescribing a relevant act. Similarly, if someone else tries to stop that person allegedly playing god, or criticises the person for doing so, the someone else thereby also plays god.

In sum, unless no-one is aware and able to decide regarding a hard case, a human decision is unavoidable: someone *must* do what many call playing god, i.e., 'must', as opposed to 'should'—because 'should' allows avoidability (as in 'I should exercise daily, but I avoid doing so'). The 'someone' (or group) here is necessarily, unavoidably, responsible.

The ultimate guardian issue, discussed in Part II, Section 1.6.1, is relevant here, and vice versa. The ultimate guardians regarding society, medical hard cases or whatever are also doing what many call playing god. But again, someone must. Suppose people decide a hard case via chance, e.g., a coin-toss. Some person(s) must first decide that chance is appropriate. Still, in an important sense such persons do not play god in that they do not decide *specifically*, e.g., who dies or otherwise suffers, when someone must die or otherwise suffer anyway. (Only if choosing between X and Y via chance is based on pro-objectivity knowledge that X and Y are equally the best available alternatives, would choice via chance be normatively-objectively appropriate.)

Anyway, when a hard decision must be made, the next unavoidable (must) issue involves a 'should', namely, ultimately: 'via which normative theory should the decision be made?'. If the choice is believed to be 'Who will make the best decision?', ultimately this involves choosing the decider(s) via a normative theory, and the decider(s) must implement one. Here, again, some person(s) must be the ultimate guardian(s), doing what many call playing god, and decide via a normative theory.

Sally and William are capable of deciding between themselves who is to die, via the (objectively) best normative theory. However, they may not be allowed to decide. Here someone else must decide, e.g., a medical board.

Someone else must also decide when those the decision directly affects are incapable of deciding, e.g., comatosed. Some directly affected conscious persons may seem incapable of deciding in a way the ultimate guardians deem appropriate. This can be reasonable, e.g., where severely intellectually-disabled persons are the directly affected. Where appropriate, deciders here should hypothetically ask what would be most normatively correct to have done to themselves if they became, e.g., here, comatosed or severely intellectually disabled, and/or hypothetically ask what the comatosed or real disabled person would do if he or she somehow could make a normatively-objective judgement. Again, there will probably at least often be some uncertainty here. Even if all concerned try their hardest to make the most pro-objectivity decision, it is possible some crucial evidence is missing, e.g., concerning how long a comatosed person is likely to stay comatosed, and what future they'll have if they wake. Yet deciding on the basis of the best normative theory and all the available thereto-related evidence, including regarding the available (medical and other relevant) resources, is all that is practicable and overall-objectively-warranted—as far as we can know.

Finally here:- At least much in those discussions of hard cases can be adapted to apply generally, e.g., to easier cases and to the type of democracy which would make the most pro-objectivity decisions, often hard decisions, of ultimate societal importance.

Part II, Section 1.8.4: Returning More Directly To Economics; Representative Issues Regarding A Pro-Objectivity-Directed Universal Or Overall, Macro Context

The following economic discussion involves some mere hypothesising, or some somewhat-educated guesses. I am not an expert economist. However, at least nearly all economists knew or know nothing or little about various highly important economic issues, e.g., regarding predicting and preventing major capitalist economic disasters such as that round 2008, and I can match that level of knowledge. Also, no economist has (in early 2010) the fundamental prescriptive economic knowledge concerning which economy is normatively-objectively correct. Relatedly, much of what various economists consider objective descriptive economic theory involves highly questionable psychological assumptions and related subjective, often conflicting, highly questionable normative views by economists, and by the persons largely constituting the subject matter of that allegedly objective economics, namely those who sell, buy, work, do not work, and so on. Such matters are within my field. And, again, regarding some economic and other specific issues, this book only aims to suggest what seem to me likely hypotheses needing further investigation.

The book's discussions of capitalism concern pure, greed-promoting capitalism, not capitalism defined as the economy of USA and similar, economies which are mixtures of capitalism and socialism, with the socialism somewhat mitigating capitalism's otherwise unmitigated selfishness and groupishness.

Regarding sharing resources pro-objectivity-universally (fairly), we are presently (2010) in a somewhat anti-objectivity situation here in that capitalism has major social, political, health-care, educational etc effects within and among societies. E.g., a small number of countries is enormously wealthy, at least significantly at the expense of the vast number of poorer countries. Capitalist groupishness here means some countries are so poor they cannot even feed all their citizens. So, many potentially highly pro-objectivity persons have died, and are dying. Because rich persons and countries have far more than is needed for their pro-objectivity flourishing (and tend to not use those resources to so flourish), if even one poor person lacks a basic need here, it is objectively immoral for rich persons and countries to not share their excess resources here (with the sharing contexted so as to help all humanity be more pro-objectivity). Capitalism inherently involves an in-effect unfair normative end something like: 'Be free to have resources far in excess of what needy others have' or 'Be selfish (or groupish); don't share unless sharing is either in your selfish (or groupish) interests or you are legally (socialistically) compelled to (as with much taxation)'.

Pro-objectivity-directed universal sharing is contexted via an overall view recognising that fair sharing here is that which, given available resources, seems most pro-objectivity overall, i.e., long-term over all beings, and things, e.g., the physical environment, thereby increasing pro-objectivity resources long-term up to the pro-objectivity optimal degrees, then maintaining those degrees. What each individual would fairly get here relates to the individual's needs in relation to that overall context. Society's relation to the individual, and vice versa, is crucially important here.

The term, 'society's resource-input into the individual', covers all a society gives to an individual, which can temporarily be overall a cost for society, e.g., when the individual is a child. Resources here can include housing, education, safety, the ensuring of affectionate child-care, leisure-time, unpolluted air and other health-care. (The objective, overall view considers all resources, e.g., not just narrowly-defined economic factors such as material income.)

Those inputs should be duties of normatively-correct benefit to the given-to individual, and society's costs here would hence be normatively-correct costs (which, by pro-objectivity persons, would be willingly paid, unselfishly, and in that important sense not burdens). There should be an as-far-as-possible overall sharing of and balance among those benefits and costs, and among inputs and outputs. Thence, via society's educational, health-care etc input, the normal individual can acquire an increased ability for resource-output, including work, namely a type of dutiful or virtuous resource-input into society.

'Work(er)' here is an overall (totalistic) notion. E.g., it would include parents staying home and caring for their children. It covers what is sometimes separately defined as 'help' where help involves volunteering,[49] no payment and unselfishness. But all pro-objectivity persons' work would be unselfish, hence in an important sense voluntary, and helpful (in pro-objectivity ways). Some suggestions regarding payment for work, and some related notions:-

As argued in Part II, Section 1.4.4, to be maximally pro-objectivity, humans need a close-circle. So where a worker has a dependent family, a collective, close-circle (shared) income seems appropriate. A close-circle will only be as caring and hence as close as is possible and optimally pro-objectivity if its members' resources are known to be shared pro-objectivity-fairly among all individuals therein. E.g., if a family has only one adult able to work, that adult's income would be paid to the *family*. Wealth, e.g., a car, would also be shared among the family (with pro-objectivity qualifications, e.g., regarding age).

Every family's needed material wealth, e.g., housing, would be pro-objectivity-directed universally supplied by society. (There should be as much freedom of choice regarding housing, transport and so on as is either pro-objectivity-possible or a-objectivity.) Similarly for individuals. Apart from that 'individual/family-use' wealth, individuals would also be supplied with any needed 'societal-use wealth'. This involves resources an individual uses to serve others outside that individual's family. There'd be situational differences here, related to differing specific needs. E.g., a dentist needing a dentally-equipped plane to serve remote areas needs much more sophisticated, expensive equipment than someone delivering city mail on foot. The pro-objectivity inequalities (differences) here would only be those which are means to help achieve the overall (societal) end, 'Be pro-objectivity', e.g., via the differences enabling each dentist and mail-deliverer to fairly serve every person they serve.

Pro-objectivity-directed universal caring and fair sharing arguably requires all adults having, if all else pro-objectivity-relevant is equal, *equal* individual resource-input by society, or, where there's a dependent family, *equal* family resource-input by society for each family of a certain size and type. Here, e.g., all workers' families would get equal pay.

There are various qualifications possibly needed here, because all else pro-objectivity-relevant might not be equal. Differences or inequalities here would relate to differences in the individual's/family's pro-objectivity needs. Society's wealth- and income-distributing institution's universal focus would include universally catering for pro-objectivity-relevant individual differences addressable via wealth/income. E.g., someone needing a wheelchair and wheelchair access at home has expenditures not needed by those not confined to a wheelchair. Similarly, obviously, a large family needs more than a smaller family, all else pro-objectivity-relevant equal.

So, arguably, a normatively-objective definition of 'fair or just distribution of society's resource-input into individuals' involves 'pro-objectivity-related equality, all else here equal', and involves recognising that often all else pro-objectivity-relevant is not equal. (It would of course be somewhat uncertain what each individual's (overall pro-objectivity contexted) needs precisely are, compared to other individuals, and hence precisely what inequality is needed when all else is not equal here. But, as often indicated in this book, all other normative theories face such and many other, greater uncertainties.)

Part II, Section1.8.4.1: Normatively-Objective Economic Desert

Do all *deserve* economic equality (qualified as in the previous subsection), or do some deserve more income/wealth than others? In an unachievably ideal world, all would know and practise all pro-objectivity knowledge, being absolutely maximally and hence absolutely equally pro-objectivity. So all would clearly be equally deserving. But in the real world, people are unlikely to all be even individually-relatively equally maximally pro-objectivity. Even if they were, this achievable ideal would be another, relative, 'as far as possible for each individual etc', situational notion, involving absolute inequality. E.g., suppose person P1 has less pro-objectivity capacity than P2. If both try as hard as possible, they can be as maximally pro-objectivity as is possible for each. But P1 lacks the capacity to equal P2's achievements or resource-outputs, due, e.g., to being much younger, genetics or an accidental disability—situations these persons have no control over. Does such inequality mean P2 deserves more wealth/income than P1, as capitalism suggests? Is capitalist economic inequality here punishing the innocent by giving them inferior resources based on them having inabilities they cannot help having? (This would conflict with a legal presumption of various societies here, namely that everyone is (equally) innocent till proved (normatively-objectively) guilty.) Or is such inequality in ability/output normatively-objectively coherent with economic equality?

It seems to me that the most objectively-warranted approach overall involves a benevolent 'presumption of trustworthiness' (involving the previously-discussed presumption of at least potential pro-objectivity), something like the presumption of innocence applied by various legal systems. Unless there is evidence, beyond reasonable doubt, that someone is irredeemably anti-objectivity, it seems most pro-objectivity to at least provisionally treat all as if they will work towards being as pro-objectivity as is individually possible—if given the needed resources.

These resources include far more than income/wealth. They crucially include educating all concerning the objectivity (correctness) of the pro-objectivity end, namely the rationally unquestionable reasons why they should try to be maximally pro-objectivity. Another resource here is the motivation an individual needs to make that effort. Achieving less than maximal pro-objectivity may only be due to being under-motivated, which may not be the person's fault. That education would give all an explicit, clear *reason* to be optimally motivated here. As mentioned in Part II's Preliminary Remark (2), many are in-effect implicitly already (2010) significantly pro-objectivity, though they lack *explicit awareness* of pro-objectivity theory. That education would facilitate that motivating awareness. Becoming more pro-objectivity requires individual commitment. But this tends to be at least significantly influenced by societal resource-input, involving giving persons such educational and other help and opportunities they'd otherwise lack. With this, again, an *overall* approach to resources is needed, considering, e.g., health, happiness, affection, leisure and so on. And, I suggest, it would be most coherent with pro-objectivity theory overall, and hence objectively fairest, to distribute all pro-objectivity individually-needed resources equally, all else pro-objectivity-relevant equal—on the unavoidably uncertain but arguably reasonable presumption that all at least potentially pro-objectivity persons, if able to benefit by that trust-motivated equal resource-input, would thereby and via that education etc equally fulfil their individual potential maximally.

That presumption involves at least provisional trust that the individual who, from an objective viewpoint has benefited from society's resource-input, will reciprocate fairly to the best of their ability. (The correctness of such reciprocity would be taught and encouraged by that education.) Relatedly, that beneficial resource-input would be via pro-objectivity society's inherently unselfish, pro-objectivity-directed universal benevolence, namely normatively-objective kindness. All else pro-objectivity-relevant equal, moreso than inherently inequality-involving *mis*trust, it is positivity as in kindness, trust and related respect which tend to motivate the trusted, respected and kindly-treated to do what they have been trusted to do. This would be even more likely if they know that what they are trusted to do is objectively worthwhile, or normatively correct.

If this trust, kindness and presumption fails, then, where possible, individuals should receive counselling, here a type of education, and other reasonable, kind help. Where appropriate, such individuals should be asked to provide *evidence* for why they should be anti-objectivity, as part of a rationally-critical cognitive therapy. If after all such available help a person still seems beyond reasonable doubt irredeemably anti-objectivity, only then should trust and that all-else-equal equal treatment end. (Again, all societies do something similar to their untrustworthy, anti-society inhabitants or societally-defined criminals, often less humanely.) Such persons have shown that, in a negative sense, all else pro-objectivity-relevant is not even at least potentially equal regarding them. In an important sense, they have shown they are guilty (of irredeemable anti-objectivity)—so the presumption of innocence or trustworthiness is disproved, by themselves as evidence.

For all other persons, namely, I think, nearly all, that presumption should be at least provisionally accepted. This would be pro-objectivity in that, *as far as can be known*, nearly all persons can be helped and motivated to become as pro-objectivity as possible for each, and treating them via that presumption is a resource-input into them here which would make it all-else-equal likely they will be so. In that sense, all here are equal, deserving equal economic and all other pro-objectivity beneficial, kind treatment, all-else-equal. (This would mean types of peace among all here, e.g., via all feeling trusted, respected and deserving (worthwhile), and no-one being objectively able to resent an unfair inequality discriminating unkindly against them.) There'd probably be a non-irredeemably anti-objectivity minority who'd selfishly abuse that trust etc, but overall it seems to me best to still give them equal economic input, all else equal. They'd still be potentially maximally pro-objectivity, and may become actually so in time, partly via a version of that education or counselling.

That presumption of trustworthiness, and, relatedly, equal deservedness, fits with the book's other interrelated arguments here, e.g: (1) that all at least potentially pro-objectivity persons should be regarded as highly-valuable, as at least potentially intrinsically-valuable;[50] (2) that pro-objectivity-directed universal benevolence and related democratic inclusivity are required and motivating; and (3) that various pro-objectivity prescriptions at least implicitly prescribe doing what avoids making it less likely non-maximally pro-objectivity persons will accept offered help to become more pro-objectivity.

That presumption of trustworthiness and equal deservedness is partly also based on probable knowledge that normal humans are not naturally selfish, and so can under certain conditions be about equally relied on to do what is right. (Until these conditions are well-established, as Part II, Section 1.8.4.3 suggests, that 'equally' may need qualifying along with those equal payment etc notions.)

Part II, Section1.8.4.2: More Concerning Capitalism's Assumption Of Natural Selfishness; Some Other Economic Issues

Much modern economic theory, especially capitalist theory, involves the normative-psychological[51] belief that the just-discussed (at least provisional) presumption of trustworthiness and related kind treatment would be unrealistic because people naturally normally only or primarily serve their selfish/groupish ends. But, arguably, this serving only appears to be so *because* of capitalism's powerful existing structures—structures which need not exist, but when they do they tend to shape people's normative and related statistically-normal psychology in ways which would not occur if those structures were absent:-

These structures require individuals/groups to compete against each other to acquire wealth/income for themselves, relatedly encouraging each individual/group to try to profit at the expense of others. This inherently involves selfishness/groupishness, involving some getting much more wealth than others, which tends to mean the rich selfishly care more for themselves than for those made relatively poor or bankrupt via the selfishness of the rich. Due to those structures, individuals statistically-normally, as opposed to *unavoidably* psychologically-normally, somewhat compete and are selfish/groupish where those structures apply. This often involves them being dishonest, i.e., untrustworthy, in order to try to profit at others' expense. Partly hence, people here often distrust each other, e.g., because one can easily expect others to treat oneself as one treats them, i.e., unequally, selfishly, dishonestly. And consumers in capitalist societies have ample evidence that businesses, advertisements etc will probably try to selfishly/groupishly exploit them and not be fully trustworthy and honest.

But, where those selfishness-promoting structures *do not apply*, e.g., inside many families, friendship groups, charity groups, social clubs and sports teams, it is often the *same* individuals who are selfish in their capitalist activities who will co-operate and *share unselfishly* here. Here they are kind, rather than just helpful for ultimately selfish reasons. Partly hence, here they *trust* each other much more. Here then are different, rather opposite economic and related moral-psychological structures, structures promoting unselfishness and harmony rather than greed, dishonesty, selfish rivalry and actual or potential conflict.

Children growing up in such families and friendship etc close-circles, but in a strongly-capitalist society, tend to learn to be selfish and untrusting *outside* their close-circles, but unselfish and trusting *within* them—*because* of the different structures. So persons' normative psychology is significantly shaped by *avoidable structures*: humans are not naturally or unavoidably selfish. Up to a major point, if we change the structure, or move from one to another, the normative psychology or alleged human nature changes accordingly.

Further evidence here is that many in modern strongly-capitalist societies at least significantly *resist* capitalist structures' encouraging of selfishness—*outside* their close-circles. People here include many paid workers such as teachers who unselfishly voluntarily work far beyond what they are paid for. Unpaid volunteers working unselfishly to help others, often strangers, are similar. They'd tend to feel insulted, i.e., that it is morally wrong, if they were offered payment, or accepted payment—payment being a capitalist, selfish motive.

Similarly, how many normal persons, e.g., on meeting an unfamiliar child in great need or danger, a child they could help without great difficulty, or perhaps even only with great difficulty, would only help if they were guaranteed payment? Probably at least almost none. Yet capitalism's selfishness assumption implies that payment would need to be guaranteed here, and everywhere, for *all* help by all persons, with increasing payment according to the difficulty or danger to the helper.

Further evidence here is that history indicates that capitalist structures tended to be significantly instituted, promoted and maintained via the at least indirect influence of those benefiting financially the most from capitalism, a small powerful minority—rather than having been chosen freely via the vast majority, a majority far from fully pro-objectivity-informed (educated) here, partly due to the trivial distractions ("circuses") given to them via that minority.

Also, consider the claim that capitalism (normatively-correctly) benefits all and is the best economy because the selfish/groupish competition involved leads to increased efficiencies meaning more economic goods and hence more wealth/income available for all. That claim is normatively questionable in that, e.g., the poorer classes often get only slightly increasing wealth/income relative to the rich, and sometimes get less or also get relatively poorer, and because at least latently the rich tend to pay the poorer ("bread") in order to help stop the poorer seriously considering acting or voting to end the unfair, selfish dominance of the rich. That claim is also negated by facts such as the competition here often involving counter-productive waste, e.g., via expensive advertising and other unneeded repetition among similar businesses.[52] Relatedly, many capitalist enterprises attempt to increase in size, partly because capitalists here desire the economy-of-scale efficiency effect, whereby the more units produced, the cheaper is the per-unit production cost, which can benefit all possessions-wise, including the poor. But here lies one of various incoherences regarding competitive selfishness and efficiency: clearly, only a monopoly can be the largest and hence potentially most efficient and cheapest producer, and a monopoly is not engaged in competition; and monopolies are aspects of socialist economies.

That capitalist claim is also negated by the fact that *unselfish* people often help increase efficiency, as with some purely voluntary workers—and paid workers in part-capitalist societies' *socialist* parts often do. E.g:- Many scientists in State-owned universities have done so, only wanting their moderate university pay though they could get much higher pay working for capitalists. Similarly regarding many paid workers in public works departments and so on. Some public institutions allow or even facilitate selfishness, allowing laziness and hence inefficiency, but this possible problem is not inevitable. E.g., during war, the vast majority of workers in various countries' public institutions, e.g., armies, police, military hospitals and government-controlled factories and farms, tend to unselfishly work very hard, making or prepared to make great sacrifices—where they believe there are good (normatively-objective) reasons to do so, reasons independent of capitalist profit-making, e.g., to save their nation from defeat. So if a well-evidenced, hence truly believable reason to be unselfishly efficient is thereby believed, i.e., as normative knowledge, this would most securely avoid that possible inefficiency or laziness motivational problem. In sum, increasing unselfishness and knowledge of an objectively worthwhile cause would achieve increases in motivation and relatedly efficiency which capitalism claims that inherently competitive selfishness can alone or best achieve.

Concluding here:- As far as possible, pro-objectivity society's structures would highly efficiently fulfil all persons' overall-objectively-warranted needs fairly, i.e., all else pro-objectivity-relevant equal equally, negating capitalism's claims, further facilitating unselfishness. This coheres with the previous subsection's arguments concerning benevolent, unselfish, equal sharing and related trust etc motivating persons to do their best.

Part II, Section1.8.4.3: Some Suggestions Concerning Ending Capitalism; Two Currencies?

(Again, such subsections explicitly mostly discuss selfishness, but can be adapted to apply to groupishness.)

Human nature includes various motivations in contrary pairs, as with the 'fight or flight' motivation(s). As the previous subsection suggests, along with any aggressive, competitive and selfish motivations, normal human nature also involves a contrary powerful motivation to peacefully *co-operate* with and *unselfishly* help others, because, e.g., within one's close-circle or gene-protecting group, co-operation and unselfish care are evolutionarily adaptive. So, any selfishness humans naturally tend to feel is only a situational tendency, not an inevitability. It is a tendency applicable only in certain, avoidable situations, e.g., capitalism, and overrulable via our tendency to co-operate with and care for others. The latter tendency can be combined with our normal natural tendency to be motivated to do what we believe is right: our rightness-motivation. (This combination would be most effective via our *knowing* what is right, via evidence.)

Importantly, many anti-objectivity, inequality-promoting structures, e.g., slavery, feudalism, monarchies and other dictatorships, and sexist and racist institutions, have totally or largely *disappeared* from much of the world. So, capitalism could similarly disappear—via the above-suggested means. (This is one of various reasons why studying history can be important. It can liberate our thinking, showing warranted change is possible, and how to achieve it.)

However, that disappearance would take considerable time, and involve various problems and at least temporary balances between capitalism and long-term achievably ideal pro-objectivity economic structures, and relatedly between the contrary pair, selfishness and unselfishness. (This was suggested at the end of Part II, Section 1.8.4.1.) E.g:-

Until at least a majority is maximally pro-objectivity and hence entirely unselfish, partly like Rawls's Difference Principle,[53] applied among the selfish, might be most pro-objectivity here. That is, to increase the pro-objectivity economic productivity and pro-objectivity nature of society overall, some may need to be at least temporarily motivated by differential tangible rewards, e.g., by higher pay. It may be most pro-objectivity to pay the difference in a different type of currency. Here, all else pro-objectivity-relevant equal, all would get equal income in what could be called 'needs-dollars', spendable only on pro-objectivity needs. Beyond that, people could earn different amounts of, say, 'wants-dollars'. (There'd of course be only an approximate, flexible borderline between needs and wants.) So wants-dollars could only be earned after persons had earned their needs-dollars, which includes after making their fair work-contribution to society's needs. Want-dollars could only be spent on things unable to give one political, economic etc dominance or anti-objectivity influence over anyone else. E.g., one would be allowed to pay for more expensive holidays than are needed, but not (perhaps with others) to buy sufficient control of a mass media to thereby politically influence citizens' thinking.[54] And wants-dollars should not be used so as to allow their earners to selfishly (foolishly) believe they are superior to their neighbours etc, i.e., objectively superior. There'd be a limit on the amount of wants-dollars earnable, say no more than 20% of the needs-dollars income amount. So, no person could work so hard selfishly acquiring wants-dollars that the person becomes even more anti-objectivity, or could not become more than insignificantly pro-objectivity. (Pro-objectivity education would facilitate the ending of any such beliefs and greedy acquisition.)

Even in an achievable maximally pro-objectivity society, a type of two currencies may be appropriate. (I'm only suggesting this tentatively.) E.g:- As suggested in various parts of this book, that society would inherently involve much flexibility and freedom regarding work and life-styles—and one aspect here might be that, after contributing fairly each day to maintain that maximal state, all are free to either indulge in recreation or do limited extra paid work. The extra work could be paid in wants-dollars, the situation here not involving temporarily bribing selfish persons to contribute to society. Those who choose to not work extra would have more *quantity* of recreation or leisure, and would prefer their overall mix of its quality, that extra quantity and their shorter (but pro-objectivity-fair) working hours. Those who work extra would prefer their overall mix of work and quantity and quality of recreation. That preference would have the pro-objectivity advantage that the work would produce more to share fairly among all—one aspect of the worker's pro-objectivity motivation here. (Pro-objectivity workers would inherently also be motivated to avoid putting in so much extra time/effort working here that this would have an anti-objectivity effect, e.g., via them getting too tired, hence irritable and more liable to illness.)

Here, all would equally have their achievable pro-objectivity *needs* met, including via all-else-equal equal needs-dollars. And the related individual-worker related differences via wants-dollars would be beyond that societal need-fulfilment. Wants-dollars would only buy unneeded, a-objectivity wants. So two currencies here and in the other scenario need not conflict with equally supplying pro-objectivity needs via equal (pro-objectivity-currency) pay, all else equal.

Part II, Section1.8.4.4: Economic Aims; Productivity

In pro-objectivity society, increased economic productivity would not be for its own sake. It would also not aim to produce an increase in material possessions as such. In contrast, the inherent central aim(s) of capitalists can be summed up as: 'Put profit and productivity before people, i.e., profit oneself or one's group increasingly, before or instead of considering everyone's overall human needs'. A pro-objectivity economy has all at least potentially pro-objectivity *people* and all their economically-addressable normatively-objective human needs as its primary economic focus. Relatedly, pro-objectivity economic productivity and a pro-objectivity life would aim at an ultimate end involving a human quality of life incompatible with aiming ultimately at increasing one's or one's group's quantity of money and possessions, or thereby one's socio-economic status, and so on.

Similarly, productivity should not be internationally groupish via giving an anti-objectivity nation more ability to dominate other nations, win wars, and so on. (There'd achievably ideally be no nations, hence no military conflicts and economic waste on weapons of war.)

Instead, increased pro-objectivity productivity would only aim at normatively-objective world-wide progress (up to an achievably-maximal stage). It would, e.g., aim at increased pro-objectivity efficiency, including maximally durable, reliable and recyclable, environmentally-friendly products and avoiding waste. This efficiency, would, e.g., give workers more time and energy etc, i.e., more freedom, to do other pro-objectivity (and a-objectivity) things, such as have better education, health, family life and recreation. That progress would involve replacing some workers with robots, freeing these workers to have more time to do such other things and more humanly-meaningful work, including work only humans can properly do, e.g., child-care.

Increased pro-objectivity-productivity would also involve it being easier to maintain a longest-term sustainable pro-objectivity physical environment, compared to the environmental rapaciousness of unmitigated capitalism. This sustainability would include maintaining a great deal of nature as it is, which for many people is greatly subjectively meaningful, and objectively medically, environmentally etc important, in at least potentially pro-objectivity ways.[55]

Occupational health and safety would also be far higher priorities than under capitalism. Boring or meaningless work, death, injury and psychological suffering of workers, and the negative effects these have on their friends, family etc, are disharmonious with the benevolence, human flourishing and social harmony needed for maximal pro-objectivity. Again, all at least potentially pro-objectivity *persons* are objectively highly important, and of at least potential intrinsic value. Capitalist productivity, profit, wealth, possessions and so on are not.

Productivity at any one time has limits, and, partly hence, many other economic, time etc resources are limited. Some always will be. So, hard economically-related choices, as exemplified in Part I, Section 1.8.3, will never be entirely avoidable. Some things, which could be a-objectivity if there were sufficient overall resources, are anti-objectivity due to limited productivity and resources. E.g., suppose that, if overall resources were unlimited, it would be a-objectivity for everyone to have whatever trivial, unneeded cosmetic plastic surgery they liked. Because we do not have unlimited resources, including productivity, the resources required to provide the merely-wanted cosmetic surgery would be needed for pro-objectivity purposes, e.g., education, needed plastic surgery and life-saving surgery. Here it would be anti-objectivity to use the resources for unneeded cosmetic surgery. (This is another case of situationality.)

Of course, if productive efficiency, renewing and conservation of resources increase, we can increasingly have more freedom (resources) to have or do more (thereby) a-objectivity things we want or like, after doing or getting any further pro-objectivity things we need. In that extrinsic sense, increased productivity can be valuable regarding pro-objectivity freedom, progress and flourishing, and a-objectivity freedom and flourishing.

Part II, Section 1.8.5: Expanding On Some Important Recent Discussions, Relating Some To Earlier Discussions

Pro-objectivity requires that, as far as pro-objectivity-practicable, as an aspect of unselfishness, all economic and other benefits and costs of living in a pro-objectivity society should be shared universally. Regarding practicability here, some people are not capable of contributing in various ways, e.g., infants. But, e.g., infants can contribute significantly in other ways, e.g., by having a pro-objectivity effect via their parents enjoying their children, involving parents subjectively-evaluating their babies as intrinsically-valuable, as suggested in Part I,

Section 2, and by their potential future pro-objectivity and hence present selves being appreciated by parents, teachers and others as objectively highly valuable and objectively potentially intrinsically-valuable. Still, overall it is obviously impracticable for infants to achieve the same balance or reciprocity between rights and responsibilities as able adults. Adults have the pro-objectivity responsibility (duty) to provide children with food, education etc. Children have a pro-objectivity right to those resources, but no responsibility to (as far as possible) fully reciprocate till later. They need to learn that, when older, they will have a duty to reciprocate and use their abilities, developed via those resource-inputs, in a pro-objectivity way, to help others. Regarding infants and similar (e.g., the temporarily ill), the overall view here involves a long-term view, namely recognising that as they become more able they should normally increasingly contribute up to a point. Similarly, with obvious differences, regarding persons who through no fault of their own are or become permanently unable to contribute.

In sum, as far as possible, overall there should be universal harmony (reciprocity etc) regarding persons' pro-objectivity resource inputs and outputs. Here, as far as possible, pro-objectivity rights (benefits) harmonise overall with pro-objectivity responsibilities, an aspect of pro-objectivity fairness. More here:-

In a pro-objectivity society all able persons would be employed: they'd contribute their fair share. If, say, a certain shoe factory became unneeded, all its workers would have had other work already arranged for them. There'd be none of the historically and presently (2010) common impoverishment, frustration, humiliation, depression, alienation, feeling powerless, family break-ups, resentment or conflict between the employed and able unemployed, and other negative consequences of unemployment. Relatedly, because work would be as positive, fair, safe, enjoyable, interesting and in all other ways as meaningful, varied, flexible and fully humanised as possible, this would help motivate all able persons to desire to be employed and help or contribute to pro-objectivity society.

Pro-objectivity fairness means all able persons would have a right and associated duty to work (only) as hard as each other on average over the medium- to long-term. Such things would be difficult to measure, but we can only do what is practicable. (Similar unavoidable uncertainty would occur in any society. E.g., in societies with different incomes for different work, non-maximally-pro-objectivity societies, there is no way decision-makers here can measure with even approximate certainty, i.e., normative-objectivity, how much different a teacher's pay should be from, say, a plumber's.) Regarding whether an hour's work by, say a teacher, is as hard as an hour's work by a plumber, large-scale impartial surveys, preferably of people who have been both a teacher and plumber, is the only way to get an as objective as possible on-average measure. Thence, say, for each situation type here, e.g., classes with 25 normal 10 year-old students, versus fixing normal taps, it could be approximately known that, say, per year a teacher should teach 4 hours and prepare etc 3 hours a day for 40 weeks, study for 5 weeks, and a plumber work 8 hours a day for 42 weeks and study for 3 weeks—for the same pay, all else pro-objectivity-relevant equal.

The as-far-as-possible fair-share equality here, in pay and conditions of work, would mean important types of peace. E.g., via educating all concerning what is objectively fair as far as can be known, and acting on this, there'd be no rational reason for resentment or conflict among different occupations or economic classes. Anyway, there'd be no socio-economic classes.

Recent points imply further that a *socialist direct democracy* is the only appropriate political institution for pro-objectivity society. E.g., it is only thereby that, as far as possible, the distribution etc of work, and the sharing of costs and benefits, can be fairly and harmoniously organised among and *by* all involved, and *all* involved can be treated in pro-objectivity-benevolent, decent ways, via that humanising, equalising etc of work. Relatedly, recent points have somewhat implicitly concerned pro-objectivity inclusivity. More on this explicitly:-

A maximally pro-objectivity society would include all its members via treating all as equally worthwhile, as all here would overall pro-objectivity-fairly equally share both the benefits and costs as far as they are able. One's character is of normatively-objective worth to the degree that one tries to the best of one's ability to achieve the normatively-correct. As this is all that is practicable for an individual, this is all that is objective to say here concerning an individual's character. Thence, it is possible for *all* persons to have a normatively-objectively virtuous character. Again, many pro-objectivity achievements can be achieved by persons other than intellectually brilliant persons. This means each person able to contribute something pro-objectivity can be an individually-maximal pro-objectivity achiever, and feel included in society. And pro-objectivity-fairness requires that those unable to contribute would not be excluded.

A very wide, overall definition of 'able' and 'contribute' is needed here. (E.g., I had an aunt able (and very willing) to give me needed pro-objectivity helpful emotional support during various family disasters, including when she was very old, had been largely physically disabled for decades, and had always been significantly intellectually-disabled. Similarly regarding my dog, Midi, whose affectionate company significantly helped make this book possible. For generalised reasons here, and other reasons, pro-objectivity theory prescribes humane treatment of animals. Pro-objectivity inclusivity covers numerous non-human animals (but not, e.g., a human-eating tiger).)

The overall, collective (version of the) end, 'Be pro-objectivity', requires a network (harmony) of achievements, or of causal chains—*each* individual link of which is needed. Apart from individual end-achievements here, and interrelated with them, there is that collective, humanity-overall end. This involves many individuals' differing practices harmonising. That collective end does not require all to be brilliant discoverers of complex pro-objectivity knowledge. It requires only some such persons. It also requires *all* persons to be *practisers* of whichever pro-objectivity knowledge they are able to practise. An individual is achieving the pro-objectivity end if the individual, e.g., simply cares for others by caring for the environment in pro-objectivity ways, e.g., by keeping parklands rubbish-free, thereby helping all here to have an attractive, healthy, safe environment. Pro-objectivity society would need and value *every* able person's (and animal's) pro-objectivity contributions (and not be negative towards the unable).

So, in a maximally pro-objectivity society, all individuals would be included via being normatively-objectively equal via contributing to the best of their ability. The inclusivity, equality and harmony here would mean various types of peace, within and among individuals with often very different abilities.

Anything less than the realistic egalitarianism here is objectively unfair. However, equality as such is not the objective normative end, with priority over all else. Sometimes *in*equality is an aspect of achieving that end. Recent paragraphs imply the context within which a type of inegalitarianism would be realistic and fair in pro-objectivity society:-

Part II, Section1.8.5.1: Pro-Objectivity Inequality And Hierarchies

In various areas inequality and hence hierarchies are pro-objectivity, and therefore overall-objectively-warrantedly fair. We are objectively normatively equal if we equally try to be as pro-objectivity as is possible (for the individual in the situation in question). Yet to *be* as equally normatively correct as others, each person will sometimes need *situationally un*equal rights or power. This relates to Part I, Section 1.3's distinction between someone's general intention to do their best and their specific ability and hence achievement in a certain area:-

Part II, Section 1.6.1.2's discussion of a deserved right to vote or be decision-makers applies here. Similarly, it would be anti-objectivity to give a dangerous driver or a non-driver the right to drive a car, instead of an expert safe driver, and, relatedly, unobjective to regard them as equal here. Another common, above-mentioned example:- If you need life-saving brain surgery, would it be objectively-warranted to trust an expert brain surgeon or a medically-ignorant painter to operate? Or would you insist that all in the hospital (cleaners, clerks etc) have an equal (mostly uninformed) right to vote on what specifically to do at each step of the operation? Or would you insist that they all have a right to equally participate directly in the operation, doing their (unaided) best as far as they are able? If so, this would not be fair, e.g., the surgeon would not have the *objectively appropriate* fair chance to exercise her/his skills and save you, you would have no fair chance of survival, and those who in-effect killed you would know it was unfair for you to have insisted they vote or directly participate, causing them to feel distressed. In sum, a hierarchy, here with the expert surgeon on top, is objectively appropriate and overall fair.

Relatedly, normal rational persons here would be *pleased*, they'd evaluate it as positive and right, that the hierarchy had the surgeon on top, nurses lower down, then clerks and so on. Similarly, pro-objectivity persons fairly placed at each level in a needed hierarchy would inherently non-selfcentredly be pleased, evaluating it as right that the hierarchy exists, e.g., that they are where they at-the-time fairly belong, meaning that the needed pro-objectivity knowledge is directing practices here. All pro-objectivity persons would impartially accept inequality in such cases, i.e., accept the objectively rightful authority of whoever is deservedly in charge, because they'd all accept that the ultimate end alone matters ultimately—and whoever, as far as can be known, is most likely to know how to achieve it should direct the attempt to achieve it.

Normatively-objective hierarchies are situational: they relate to the *area-relevant* pro-objectivity knowledge of those in the hierarchy. That expert surgeon may greatly lack pro-objectivity knowledge concerning teaching, gardening, repairing cars or programming computers, and so belong near the bottom of hierarchies here. (I belong at or near the bottom of many hierarchies.) Pro-objectivity experts in some situation would, in other situations, where they know that someone else is the expert, say to the expert, "Here your pro-objectivity knowledge is best, so *you* should decide or tell me what to do". If someone's knowledge in an area increases (decreases), their position in the relevant pro-objectivity hierarchy would correspondingly rise (fall). Flexibility is needed.

Regarding being pro-objectivity in a *general* sense, all persons can be equal via knowing and impartially agreeing that the most normatively-objective thing ought to be done, which includes having such knowledge- or evidence-based flexible (situational) hierarchies. It is that agreement, that objective general decision, which would context and *lead* to all specific intended pro-objectivity achievements: it comes first. In other words, at the contexting, overall, general-guidelines or meta-level, there can be pro-objectivity-directed universal equality and hence no hierarchy in that all can be totally and thus equally convinced that, regarding specific situations, inequality or hierarchies can be pro-objectivity.

That agreement would involve agreeing there should be only hierarchies such as those just and previously discussed, e.g., in discussions of pro-objectivity-democratic voting rights.

However, the maximally pro-objectivity society needed to produce that universal agreement is only an ideal in that, e.g., many young persons would lack the education, rational decision-making abilities etc to be even significantly pro-objectivity achievers and hence able to understand the fairness of their low position in hierarchies. They could regard their positions as unfair, and the hierarchies as inappropriate patronising. However, any such self-centred irrational resentment is reducible via appropriate education, and via as obviously-fair-as-possible ultimate guardian-instituted tests proving where one objectively-fairly belongs in a hierarchy at the time, as in the above-discussed quizzes. As far as possible, clear such *evidence* for one's position needs to be shown to oneself.

Concluding here:- All specific pro-objectivity hierarchies would come under the (ultimate guardians') general, overall pro-objectivity view, i.e., be contexted via pro-objectivity general guidelines, relate to life-as-a-whole and the pro-objectivity big(gest) picture. One such guideline is that, depending on the situation, area or issue, either equality or inequality can be pro-objectivity.

Part II, Section1.8.5.2: Relating The Previous Subsection To Some Other Issues Above

An often-achievable ideal aim of pro-objectivity hierarchies or authority would be autonomy for the thereby governed, i.e., for them to progress, initially largely via educational hierarchies (others' teaching), to where one governs oneself rather than being governed. Here one acts on one's knowledge that one has the knowledge-based right/duty to be at level L in hierarchy H, and hence to decide X, but, perhaps, not Y. Here one does not need others to position oneself: rights one allocates oneself are those which (other) maximally pro-objectivity persons would allocate oneself. However, some people lack capacity for such autonomy. E.g., in various areas it would not be pro-objectivity for the severely intellectually-disabled or psychopaths to have the rights and freedoms the vast majority could earn. That would be in nobody's (objectively) best interests.

(Such points, and those in the next few paragraphs, have further implications for the legal system and democracies pro-objectivity society needs, and further implications for its education system and child-raising generally.[56])

Among maximally pro-objectivity normal adults, specific hierarchies would involve equality (and hence peace) in that the hierarchies would involve mutual equal helpfulness and respect in relation to all equally doing their best to achieve their equally-accepted end. Equally highly knowledgeable experts in the same area, and across certain different areas, are equal regarding having expert potentially pro-objectivity knowledge as such. But their ultimate end-aim is to be pro-objectivity—not that *knowledge* as such. Thence, again, pro-objectivity persons less able to achieve high-knowledgeability are equal to all other pro-objectivity persons if they all intend to, and do, achieve to the best of their ability. An objective theory and related egalitarianism aiming to be universally practicable does not aim at or expect impracticable equality. An objective theory inherently has a firm grasp on reality, on what, situationally, can be achieved, here by this or that person. We can know that if each person puts in their individually-practicable maximal effort, differences among persons' achievements are due to factors *outside* of a person's control and responsibility, e.g., the genes one is born with, the time one has (been alive and has hence) had to learn, and accidents. So the differences in achievements are due to *normatively arbitrary* factors, i.e., luck. It would be unrealistic and hence unobjective to believe oneself to be objectively superior to another person and hence unfairly exclude and not respect the other person, on the basis of merely arbitrary factors. (Respecting differences existing due to chance or luck is in-effect to respect the normatively arbitrary, which is clearly normatively unobjective, or wrong.) Where each person makes an individually-best effort, all persons in any hierarchy here need to accept that each person's position in the hierarchy is only because of arbitrary, unintended, often temporary factors—and that their positions could have been reversed via such factors, and may change due to future such factors. E.g., someone high in a hierarchy may have a brain-damaging accident, putting them on the bottom.

In sum:- Here there is total practicable or objectively-possible normatively-relevant equality among maximally pro-objectivity persons and within their hierarchies, equality evident to an overall, objective view. (Orthogonally-relatedly, something similar concerning normative arbitrariness (irrelevance) and equality applies regarding a-objectivity aspects of persons.)

That overall view also knows it is unobjective (and self-centred) for one to accept that normative-arbitrariness argument but still regard oneself as superior and hence not equal to others due to what one views as one's *purely individual achievements*. Objectively, overall there are no such achievements. Achievement-based, high positions in hierarchies crucially involve much *societal* input into the individual here. E.g., an engineer supervising car-manufacture could not do so unless farmers grow food for the engineer, miners mine the needed metals, someone removes garbage which would otherwise lead to the engineer dying of disease, someone taught the engineer to read etc when young, someone cared for the engineer when young, and the engineer was born into a society with the history, knowledge and other resources needed for those achievements. And so on.

In sum, the term 'largely societally-dependent individual achievement' is objective, not 'purely individual achievement'. Any individual achievement is inextricably mixed with societal factors, not pure: take away all, or never give any, social input, and there is no individual. They'd be dead. E.g., they'd never have been fed when infants.

Yet an objective view of 'largely societally-dependent individual achievement' leaves some room for achievement via differing individual efforts:- If, apart from genetic luck and so on, societal factors entirely explain individual achievement, then each individual here societal-factor-wise equal and, as with identical twins, initially individually equal, would thereafter, all-else-equal, achieve about the same or equivalently all their lives. This seems to not always happen. Beyond equal societal resource-input, but still at least historically highly dependent on society, via will-power, motivation or effort one individual can achieve much more than another, all-else-previously-equal (as far as we can tell). Here one individual can be normatively-objectively superior to another. However, the former, superior one, if maximally pro-objectivity, would not egoistically feel and act superior. The former would help the latter, partly via facilitating them having more will-power, to reach the latter's individually-maximal pro-objectivity. (Will-strength relates to what the individual believes regarding his/her end aim(s). The more the end-aim is believed to be right, the stronger the will. Again, pro-objectivity-optimal will-power would be facilitated by education imparting *evidence* giving the individual *knowledge* of the right end-aim.)

In sum, a person's high position in a pro-objectivity hierarchy can be significantly due to individually virtuous effort—but that person would as far as pro-objectivity-possible help others less virtuous here become objectively-normatively equal here to that person.

Concluding here:-

Though individual effort is important, a high place in a hierarchy is not purely the individual's achievement, and can change. We, including our individual efforts, are socially-dependent to a major, crucial degree, and dependent on genetic etc factors beyond our control and hence in which it is not realistic (objective) to take pride in. This implies a type of democracy involving recognition of that interdependence and, hence, respect for each individual doing their pro-objectivity best. Here, being proud of persons as in *equal respect for each individual*, which includes equal self-respect among individuals, is appropriate—not an inegalitarian, selfish or arrogant pride. That respect or mutual pride involves pro-objectivity-directed universal, benevolent, helpful, democratic inclusivity, and non-selfcentredness and fairness.

Relatedly, again, pro-objectivity egalitarian fairness and unselfish helpfulness require flexible, open hierarchies. Every pro-objectivity person above others in some hierarchy, due to this person having more knowledge or other ability, or will-power (motivation), would unselfishly try to help the others improve here. So, e.g., again, a pro-objectivity teacher would give students the opportunity to become more knowledgeable than the teacher. If a student proved to have more knowledge in some area, the pro-objectivity teacher would ask this student to temporarily be the teacher here. This is egalitarian in that it involves equality of opportunity and all persons in authority being equally willing to share power with or relinquish it to others who objectively deserve it. Overall-objectively-warranted power is never absolute. It is situational or *relative*, relative to the objectively relevant abilities and motivation. This is objectively democratic.

Part II, Section1.8.5.3: More Concerning Inclusivity; Multi-Culturalism

Another general point regarding inclusivity and hierarchies concerns treatment of beings lacking the knowledge-ability and direct motivation to intentionally be pro-objectivity, though they may unknowingly be pro-objectivity via other, potentially pro-objectivity abilities and indirect motivation. Some animals can be motivated to give us what can be pro-objectivity loyalty, comfort, companionship, affection, enjoyment or fun, plus, sometimes, protection or help with work. E.g., a horse cannot itself choose to help make the world normatively-objective, but, under appropriate human direction (hierarchies), horses can, e.g., provide pro-objectivity transport, help regarding human pro-objectivity vaccinations, be good companions and be part of our pro-objectivity recreation.

Similarly regarding non-sentient life. E.g., at least partly via human direction, e.g., concerning pro-objectivity environmental needs, we can have ample trees to give us needed oxygen, pro-objectivity fruit, aesthetic pleasure, and shade which helps us avoid anti-objectivity skin cancer. Trees can absorb harmful carbon dioxide, help stop pro-objectivity rivers and agriculture being destroyed by erosion, and so on. A partly similar point can apply to non-living things. E.g., a sunrise can give pro-objectivity aesthetic pleasure, warmth and the (small amount of) radiation needed regarding the Vitamin D necessary for pro-objectivity physical and mental health. Somewhat similarly regarding certain food, clothes, art, music, wine and much else.

In such ways, pro-objectivity inclusivity covers countless beings and other things. Pro-objectivity theory covers everything because each thing has either a positive, neutral or negative relation to pro-objectivity. A-objectivity things are obviously included, as exemplified often above. Pro-objectivity theory would, where possible, only exclude things which negatively affect pro-objectivity. (All normative theories inherently exclude whatever conflicts with their end(s), so pro-objectivity theory is not alone and rationally criticisable here.)

Pro-objectivity theory excludes widely exclusivist, inherently anti-objectivity, racist, sexist, socio-economic and similar structures. Capitalist structures are highly anti-inclusivist via not fairly, equitably including the poorer majority via ending their relative poverty. Nationalism is another, dangerous anti-objectivity groupism. (This does not mean one should not help a pro-objectivity nation threatened by an anti-objectivity country. It only means a nation as such should not be one's highest priority. Also, one's nation can be anti-objectivity.)

Similarly regarding culture or society:- 'Culturalism' is a term describing much groupism here, with a non-groupist, inclusivist term here being 'multi-culturalism'. Some multiculturalist normative views prescribe including what pro-objectivity would include; others prescribe what it would exclude:-

Again, including in education a type of multi-cultural perspective greatly helps regarding reflecting in pro-objectivity critical ways on one's own culture. E.g., actual or potential anti-objectivity dietary and linguistic conventions, economic and political structures and related normative values and other beliefs common in one's society can be accepted by one at least largely because what exists is often easily assumed to be something which must and/or ought to exist. Any such hence-unquestioned convention, structure, value or other belief is questionable via the perspective of a culture with a very different convention, structure etc here. Comparison can lead to pro-objectivity critical reflection which otherwise may not have occurred. So educational inclusion of that type of multi-culturalism is important.

But that inclusion does not necessarily mean that each such different culture's conventions, structures, values etc should be included in one's society via being bases of citizens' *practices*—or that persons with simply any strongly-held values and other beliefs have the right to have those beliefs included in society just because these beliefs are the persons' treasured cultural heritage or tradition. E.g., if persons see their primary self as 'Membership of culture C (or race R, gender G and so on)', pro-objectivity is not their primary, highest priority.

Pro-objectivity society would impartially include all cultures' pro-objectivity aspects, allow any a-objectivity aspect of any culture, and include any at least potentially pro-objectivity person practising those aspects. However, in some societies with a multi-cultural policy, (even in some often-significantly pro-objectivity societies, e.g., Australia,) anti-objectivity views and practices of certain cultures are permitted or even encouraged. Some such cultures are sexist, some inhibit the divergent thinking, rationality, skepticism and self-criticism a pro-objectivity society needs, and so on. Here such cultures need altering, not including. (Again, education is the best long-term solution here.)

Still, some part(s) of perhaps each culture could warrantedly be included in pro-objectivity society, along with their a-objectivity cultural differences. There are probably a-objectivity options in every culture. One society-wide a-objectivity practice should be the including of a-objectivity diversity, covering countless multi-cultural alternatives, e.g., for the sake of enjoyable variety and rampant free indulgence or expression (flourishing) here.

END NOTES TO PART II, SECTION 1

1 Here this refers to a type of democracy suited to making pro-objectivity decisions. There is another, a-objectivity type, discussed later.

2 Statements here are not falsely alleged to be knowledge, need not be knowledge, and have no effect on anyone's pro-objectivity knowledge. E.g., suppose a certain fictional story is a-objectivity in situation S. Fiction is of course not true, not knowledge.

3 A simple example:- Zoe sees Bill apparently cruelly forcing a metal object down a distressed dog's throat. Zoe could scream, "Bill, you cruel swine, I'll kill you", and kill Bill. But rational Zoe suspends belief, and politely asks, "What are you doing?". Bill explains the dog has a bone stuck in its mouth and to stop its distress he is carefully removing the bone with pliers. Kindness to animals is pro-objectivity, as explained later.

4 Via objectivity's overall, coherent view, objectivity can know that perceptual illusions are in-themselves unobjective, but also only unobjective from a non-overall view, and relatedly that, e.g., a perception that a stick partly submerged in water is bent by the water is an objective perception of *refraction, not* of a stick bending. That is, illusions, if interpreted via high-level rational reflection, still relate to reality—and the isolated illusory observations as such do too, though unclearly so, and more indirectly, unless so interpreted. Part II, Section 1.4.1.2 discusses this further.

5 E.g., the frontal cerebral (cognitive) cortex is linked with the limbic (emotional) system.

6 Emotions/objects here can have a beyond-themselves purpose the person involved may be unaware of, or ignores. Emotions tend to have an evolution-installed purpose beyond themselves in that they motivate object-achievements, e.g., having sex and caring for children, which help serve the evolutionary purpose of passing on and preserving genes. But this purpose is extrinsic and external to the person in that it is at least often not the person-experienced, direct reason for the person's practices here. This reason involves the emotional experience and associated person-intended object being subjectively-evaluated as intrinsically-valuable by the person. Here evolution can predispose (fool) persons into have person-unchosen values.

7 E.g., my experience is that music and sunsets can be indirectly pro-objectivity. And collecting bottle-tops and similar could be as anti-objectivity as counting all pebbles.

8 If, as some religious people claim, a god used evolution to create humans etc, then because evolution is mostly errors, involving immense suffering, this casts doubt on the also-often-claimed intelligence, all-knowingness and benevolence of the (alleged) god. This relates to the above-discussed issue of evidence regarding religion and hence religion-based normative theories, and to 'intelligent-design' religious theories here.

9 Fodor (1983) discusses such encapsulation.

10 As explained further soon, some intuitions are potentially pro-objectivity. None are in themselves actually pro-objectivity, but become so via combination with relevant pro-objectivity knowledge. E.g., the common intuition that bravery is morally good could be religiously contexted, facilitating many being willing to bravely fight for their religion, but that intuition could also be pro-objectivity contexted, facilitating pro-objectivity bravery being correctly viewed as right and a virtue.

11 Previous discussions of emotions/feelings/objects can be adapted to apply to emotions/feelings/objects not subjectively regarded as intrinsically-valuable, and which involve disliked experiences.

12 This was discussed in David Suzuki's TV series, "The Nature Of Things". In some orphanages, e.g., in late 20th century Romania, there was plenty of evidence for this. Similarly regarding a documentary on modern Bulgarian institutions for children (Aus-

tralian TV, SBS channel, Cutting Edge, May 13, 2008). See also Shaw in the Psychology and Aging journal, March 2004. Harry Harlow's famous (somewhat controversial) experiment, where infant monkeys only had two types of substitute-mother as company, one only a food-provider, the other, preferred one, cuddly, suggest a general need for young primates to be loved.

13 Those directly caring for children here may be very compassionate but lack resources needed to practise their compassion, especially in poor countries. This is ultimately because rich persons/countries who could increase those resources lack sufficient compassion, being selfish or groupist.

14 See Holt (1969) and (1970). Parts of many such books can be re-interpreted in pro-objectivity ways.

15 Some feminist and masculinist commentators describe a primarily cognitive normative theory as a 'male thing', and a primarily emotional, pro-caring normative theory as a 'female thing'. Pro-objectivity theory suggests that such descriptions are not the overall, objective picture. Pro-objectivity theory interrelates the cognitive and emotional, and sees rational cognition and passionate caring as normally combinable in the same person, regardless of gender.

16 Importantly, a type of meditation can help greatly regarding facilitating pro-objectivity-directed universal caring, including via turning off any groupist hatred towards perceived out-groups, and so on, as well as via turning on compassionate universal benevolence. Here one's frontal cortex controls those unwarranted emotions, via the brain's interconnections and the (motivated) cognitive decision to do so. This decision-making can include effectively deciding to feel more benevolent. Such meditation was discussed on the Australian ABC TV show, "The Big Picture: Primal Instincts", 8:30 pm, March 3, 2004.

17 A Part I, Section 1.2 endnote explained that irredeemably anti-objectivity are at least highly anti-objectivity.

18 Helpful here would be a universal scheme of world-wide travel exchanges and similar—an expanded version of the sister-cities scheme practised by some countries. The internet could help greatly too, e.g., instant mutual video-communication can mean fairly close, personally-meaningful contact among geographically distant people.

19 See, e.g., Gaudry and Spielberger (1971). Parts of many such books can be re-interpreted to become pro-objectivity knowledge.

20 Again, brain research suggests a physical basis enabling this, in that the frontal cortex has neural connections with the limbic (emotional) system, and can thereby inhibit and hence overrule at least many emotions or emotional-perceptions. Again, this is similar to how our higher-level, flexible cognition can overrule primitive, encapsulated physical perceptions as in not believing illusions. Similarly, higher-level cognition can overrule an emotion when we believe the emotion ought not to be expressed. E.g., one can stop oneself attacking someone one is motivated to attack.

21 Popper (1966) p 225 and 238

22 Popper (1966) p 225

23 Again, this 'pro-objectivity-relevant' qualification applies to all this book's (often implicit) such 'all else equal' qualifications of a notion. 'All else' covers more than the pro-objectivity-relevant. Anything a-objectivity is not pro-objectivity-relevant.

24 The book's discussions of democracies imply that each past and present (2010) political democracy I know of was/is a primitive historical stage.

25 These decisions are not always made only via formal institutions, e.g., by Parliament or in Parliament House. They can in-effect be at least somewhat made via informal or implicit politics, outside of such explicitly political institutions and buildings, often by a tiny minority.
26 Pro-objectivity persons would know they have a duty to be concerned and informed about all important issues as far as pro-objectivity-possible—namely in optimal balance with other duties. This is implied further later, e.g., when discussing education.
27 A pro-objectivity peaceful world would remove the motivation and excuse to have the less democratic but more efficient governments often best able to wage war.
28 Discussed in Plato's *Republic*.
29 Part II, Section 1.8.4's discussion of 'presumption of trustworthiness' is relevant here.
30 I suggest at least two because advances in (voters' pro-objectivity) knowledge can occur via interrelating two or more knowledge-areas. E.g., the combination of maths and biology gave humanity much new knowledge or created new areas, e.g., genetics.
31 This is clearly only somewhat similar to Kant's and others' notions of autonomy. There are fundamental and other differences.
32 E.g., one may be upset and thus affected by a relative's tearful demand that one lends them money for anti-objectivity drugs, but not let this pressure one to actually lend it.
33 An objective ultimate end is by definition intrinsically-valuable. In general, an ultimate end is viewed as intrinsically valuable, and vice versa.
34 This is similar to, but fundamentally different from, Kant's notion of persons as intrinsically-valuable or ends-in-themselves.
35 Again, because it is anti-objectivity to discriminate against a person's a-objectivity non-optional aspects, e.g., race, pro-objectivity persons would not allow themselves to be free to do whatever they like here if this means acting on a preference regarding a person's a-objectivity non-optional aspect.
36 Here, of course, as recent comments imply, 'silly' does not mean silly as in being unobjective in anti-objectivity ways, as with sexist Sam above.
37 'Tolerance of X' means one thinks X is wrong, (perhaps arousing annoyance in one,) but not so wrong (or annoying) that one will oppose X. A-objectivity things are not wrong (and pro-objectivity people would not get annoyed concerning them).
38 If the someone else imposed this music on Pam, this would be anti-objectivity. For the situation to remain a-objectivity, Pam would not have to hear it unless she chose to.
39 Above, when discussing (un)selfishness, the need for qualifications was mentioned.
40 Her religion offers no reward for such acts, and teaches there is no after-life and no heavenly reward. (If a religion teaches there are after-life rewards for obeying its morality, believers here can never be known to be as purely unselfish as possible, adding to the religion's and morality's incoherence, especially one prescribing unselfishness.)
41 It would be 'neither' when someone discriminates (chooses) in an a-objectivity way, i.e., towards an option here such as fruit F1, and hence against F2.
42 Some aspects which can be a-objectivity are permanently unalterable and hence unchoosable, e.g., one's age. Other aspects, at-the-time not quickly alterable, can later be altered, e.g., often, gender, and in that 'later alterable' sense they are choosable.
43 Socialist parts include free or by-government-highly-subsidised public education, libraries, museums, art-galleries, parks, beaches, playgrounds, roads, medical care, police-help, and a guaranteed basic economic living standard for all, e.g., via unemployment benefits, which is socialism up to a point. Beyond such points there is capitalism. But there is obviously so much socialism in economies often labelled 'capitalist', that there is considerable hope for an entirely socialist world, a pro-objectivity need.

44 Rawls's and other fairness-prescribing theories do not have that aim. 'Fairness' is an abstract term: regarding practice it must relate to some specific practicable end/standard. The only standard to which fairness can normatively-objectively be related is a normatively-objective standard. If it's not pro-objectivity fairness, it's objectively not fair.

45 Rawls's and other theories' rational egoists inherently also only use their rationality egoistically (selfishly). This is another reason why such theories are wrong.

46 E.g., to achieve intellectual equality over all living persons, many persons below the (average?) standard required would need an enormous, unequal share of resources to help them achieve that standard. Many others would need to be inequitably killed because they could not rise, or fall, to the decided level of intellectual equality.

47 E.g:- Consider when, due to non-fatal injury or removal, part of a person's brain ceases electro-chemical activity, a part operating a certain function and whereby persons have conscious experience of the function. Here the person's conscious experience of that function ceases, as does the function. E.g., one becomes blind or loses short-term memory. All such evidence suggests that, when the whole brain's electro-chemical activity ceases, due to death, all the person's thoughts, consciousness, memory etc functions etc cease. (This is evidence against religious beliefs in an after-life, and hence against religion-based normative theories here.)

48 However, if one dies, others may miss one, with anti-objectivity effects. It is a pro-objectivity duty to avoid death if one's continued life would probably mean a more pro-objectivity world than if one dies.

49 In a maximally pro-objectivity world, volunteering would only be as in being helpful company for a sick friend, for no payment or other tangible reward. Volunteering would not be as in raising money for Red Cross to help the poor, because in that world all persons' financially buyable needs would be provided. There'd be much helping, but no need for charity in that sense. E.g., there'd be no poor needing handouts, and no-one denied pro-objectivity-needed medical care.

50 Argued near the end of Part I, Section 2, and added to later.

51 'Normative psychology' here refers to an (alleged) aspect of human psychology (allegedly) predisposing humans to in-effect believe a corresponding normative theory. This predisposing does naturally tend to occur regarding the above-discussed survival-necessary core values which all viable societies share. But one problematic claim here is that we are naturally psychologically at least predominantly selfish, so would naturally tend to act on and in-effect believe a 'Be selfish' theory, e.g., capitalist theory.

52 E.g:- Suppose ten companies making much the same shirts each have a shirt designer, meaning that nine designers could be used more productively elsewhere. Similarly regarding shirt advertising, salespersons, shirt-factory building, administration etc.

53 Rawls, J (1999)

54 Pro-objectivity (and a-objectivity) media would be democratic, e.g., in ways implied by Part II, Section 1.6.1's discussion of democracy.

55 E.g., experience suggests it is likely we will discover more cures for diseases in as-yet uninvestigated species/places, cures unavailable if we destroy the species/places. Also importantly, the aesthetic appeal of natural environments, including flora and fauna, can be subjectively-evaluated as intrinsically-valuable, and this and the freedom to enjoy them, exercise in them, and so on, can be indirectly pro-objectivity.

56 Pro-objectivity democracy would encourage all concerned with a decision to be involved in the decision-making. If persons lack pro-objectivity knowledge others here

have, only the latter people would make the decision, but they'd consider the formers' views, as with informed adults considering and in that way involving children's views.

PART II, SECTION 2: OTHER FURTHER ISSUES AND APPLICATIONS

Part II, Section 2.1: More Regarding Motivation/Emotion And Feelings

Introductory paragraph:- One aim of the book is to show that pro-objectivity is sufficiently motivating to be practicable by at least the vast majority. (No other (non-survival-necessary-core part of a) normative theory has been practised world-wide by anywhere near a majority, perhaps at least partly because all other theories lack evidence or knowability, hence being insufficiently convincing and hence insufficiently motivating except for people socialised into unquestioning, rewarding acceptance of their minority group's theory.) There is a for-us necessary minimal natural degree of pro-objectivity motivation, often in an overall (on-average) anti-objectivity context. But there naturally tends to be more than that degree, and can be much more, enough for maximal pro-objectivity:-

One aspect of that necessary minimal pro-objectivity motivation exists because we are naturally motivated to be pro-objectivity in that, to survive, humans need to know many things, e.g., how to get food. If beings needing survival-necessary knowledge genetically lacked motivation to acquire knowledge, they'd not live to pass on those unadaptive genes. So such pro-objectivity motivation is natural via being survival-necessary for us.

The survival-necessary degree includes a normative aspect. In relation to the human necessity to make innumerable choices and hence at least implicitly believe some normative theory, there is the survival-necessity to have a group normatively cohesive enough to facilitate its members' survival, including by passing on its genes. This cohesion requires a group normativity. Here there is a simplistic, primitive degree of the rightness-motivation mentioned above, e.g., in Part II, Section 1.8.4. This is simplistic and pro-objectivity in that it tends to motivate people to unquestioningly (irrationally) do what they *believe* is *right*, i.e., normatively-objective, and they tend to only believe it because their group socialises them to believe it, to achieve that cohesion. Here people are only pro-objectivity via believing, without evidence, that they *know* what is right (objective). It is a normal *general* motivation, i.e., not directed specifically to any normativity in that *any* of the many different group-cohesion-producing normativities will do, all else equal. (They all include the survival-necessary core.[1])

Rightness-motivation here is another aspect of *minimal* pro-objectivity motivation, involving that *simplistic* emotion-thought combination. This general pro-objectivity rightness-motivation can and often does specifically only involve false beliefs (delusions). Here one would only be *intentionally* pro-objectivity or right, as opposed to being *successfully* pro-objectivity in that one has normative knowledge. But, beyond its necessary minimal degree it can become motivation, as part of our (soon-discussed) highly open curiosity instinct, to *really know*, via evidence, which normativity is right, or if some specific normativity, often that which one's socialisation tells one is right, is right—or if any is right.

Survival-necessary motivation and its simplistic rightness-motivation combine with a further natural amount to produce a naturally common, larger degree of pro-objectivity motivation. The further amount typically involves achieving much regarding objectivity, but normative pro-objectivity is not necessarily achieved. As with those survival-necessary types, the only necessary pro-objectivity achievements here are the *non-overall,* objectively-warranted *type-A,* discussed in Part I, Section 1.2. (One's pro-objectivity motivation achieves *normative* pro-objectivity only via motivating an overall-objectively-warranted, type-B achievement.) That further type-A-related motivation involves achieving knowledge, but typically only achieves knowledge merely instrumental for achieving non-pro-objectivity, non-survival-necessary ends people delusorily believe to be right. (E.g., beyond the survival-necessary, persons intentionally achieve various ends, e.g., bottle-top collections, so normally they must *know* how to achieve them.) As ends here are not the objective end, in-practice this is *merely instrumental* pro-objectivity. So, being motivated to be somewhat pro-objectivity can be contexted in being overall (on-average) anti-objectivity.

Yet one can also be overall normatively pro-objectivity. This involves another natural common pro-objectivity motivation beyond the minimal and other instrumental type-A amounts discussed so far here, a motivation involved in a non-simplistic, rationally-critical emotion-thought combination involving rightness-motivation. Here motivation helps take one beyond typical type-A achievements, to acquire at least basic potentially pro-objectivity knowledge, namely of an objective end. This motivation-knowledge or emotion-thought combination can move one from type-A to type-B achievements:-

Humans seem to have evolved a normal tendency to at least sometimes believe it is *intrinsically valuable to discover knowledge fairly generally*, and hence find doing so *powerfully motivating*. E.g., we can naturally find it *challenging, worthwhile*, to solve a problem, i.e., to acquire knowledge. Challenges can greatly motivate. That is, normal persons have a powerfully motivating *curiosity* instinct (though various types of society, education or culture stifle this greatly, because it threatens their unwarranted, often-comforting beliefs). When normal young children are not stifled here or stopped from doing so, they tend to investigate their environment and ask frequent questions, exhibiting such motivation. Many ask something like 'Why (should I do that)?', which can implicitly mean: 'Give me evidence to show why it is objectively right to do that'.[2]

That is, from very early in their lives, unless anti-objectivity socialisation or education successfully intervenes, normal humans tend to be naturally motivated to seek knowledge very openly, often including about normativity. Again, it is an evolutionary advantage to have a highly *open* desire and capacity for knowledge, because our survival depends on adapting to our environments—and, when unborn, one cannot know which among the many different possible environments one will be born into, and later one cannot know what one's at-the-time environment might change into, or where one might move to, and so on. For such reasons, this Type-A-related highly *open* pro-objectivity motivation to acquire knowledge somewhat generally is, on-average, adaptive. So our curiosity instinct has an 'at least potentially survival-necessary' basis. But it can take us far beyond the survival-necessary. E.g., some seek knowledge of Roman art. Many are interested in philosophy, 'the love of knowledge'. So this general, open love or desire (motivation) leaves the way open for seeking normative philosophical knowledge, knowledge about that overall most-important and hence highly-motivating issue, 'How should one live?'. That investigation is made at least somewhat likely because normal human rightness-motivation at least potentially directs humans to investigate that issue anyway.

So this natural curiosity (pro-objectivity) of normal children can continue into adulthood, often more insistently, with adults also asking 'Why?' regarding some X, and not being satisfied with answers children may accept. When anyone asks this, it at least implicitly means 'Tell me *objectively* why X?', i.e., 'Why is it *true* that X?' and hence 'Give me *evidence* that X is true'. This is at least the potential beginnings of adult pro-objectivity critical rationality, involving serious openness, e.g., to the possibility that the normativity one's society teaches one might lack evidence, or not be correct. Here one may in-effect ask, 'Why should I live that way if you cannot give me evidence sufficient to show why I should?'

So, that insistent, increasingly rationally-sophisticated curiosity and openness etc can mean one becomes *significantly* (normatively) pro-objectivity. It can mean one is motivated to go beyond that to being maximally pro-objectivity. Here, rightness-motivation works *coherently* with that open pro-objectivity motivation—explicitly rationally-critically seeking *evidence* and hence actual (rather than imagined) knowledge of what is normatively right; and one acquires that knowledge, and practises it. (Appendixes 3-5 are relevant here.)

In sum, there is ample natural motivation potentially available for at least all normal persons to become at least highly pro-objectivity (in and via a certain social(ising) or educational environment).

Concluding comments here:-

Motivation to seek knowledge involves natural rewards for acquiring knowledge, rewards which are further motivating here. E.g., one is pleased one has solved a problem, or one finds at least many facts interesting (motivating). Also associated with the motivational general object, 'Acquire knowledge', is something like what Kant suggests is a natural 'respect for reason'. When we intentionally acquire knowledge we are rewarded by naturally respecting ourselves for being successful(ly pro-objectivity). Self-respect is motivating. We can also be rewarded here self-respect-wise via feeling pleased we've overcome a challenge, and not given up, motivating us to later do more thereof. So, along with specifically rightness-motivational rewards, we can be motivated by that general pro-objectivity motivation, becoming increasingly pro-objectivity. Motivational rewards will be greatest if associated with acquiring knowledge about the issue of greatest overall human importance: 'How should one live?'.

Relatedly:- We are naturally motivated to avoid cognitive dissonance, i.e., the frustrating realisation that there is incoherence or contradiction among our beliefs. Similarly, many are motivated to avoid doubt or avoid thinking something that is untrue or unevidenced. We feel rewarded if we remove the doubt, dissonance or frustration, the psychological conflict. This reward is clearly most securely achieved in the long-term by achieving overall harmony and related non-incoherence, only achievable via having *knowledge* regarding all areas one deals with.[3] And one must make choices in and hence deal with the normative area. (Appendix 4 argues this further.)

As Part I shows, people can learn there is sound theoretical and related empirical evidence for only a *pro-objectivity* normative theory, and that this evidence shows that alternative theories are unobjective, i.e., not right. Further motivational rewards are available here if one can *know* that, as far as one can know, one is doing what is either right or rightly permitted, and that there is rationally undeniable evidence for at least the general guidelines here. This would give one great cognitive and related emotional security and (qualified) peace—a major aim of normal natural human motivation. Other normative and any associated religious beliefs can give emotional security, but as these lack evidence, this security is delusory and highly vulnerable to rational skeptical attacks.

Finally here:- This subsection did not mention *indirect* pro-objectivity motivation. Consider educators trying to increase the just-discussed normative direct pro-objectivity motivation in students. Pro-objectivity-directed unselfish, fair, kind care by those educators would indirectly help motivate that direct motivation. It would also be motivatingly rewarding for the carers. And such help and benevolent care would help fulfil those and other, psychologically-interrelated emotional security etc needs—providing yet more motivation. In sum, all direct and indirect motivation considered, normative pro-objectivity can easily be at least sufficiently motivating for practicability among at least nearly all persons.

Part II, Section 2.2: More On Virtues, Including Regarding Animals

(As overall pro-objectivity means maximal pro-objectivity longest-term, pro-objectivity dutifulness should be an inherently *permanent primary* aspect of persons, namely a character-trait, a virtue.) 'Virtue' means a character-trait one (objectively) *should* have, a normatively correct trait—and, as argued above, the only coherent, evidenced meaning of terms such as 'normatively correct' is '(normatively) objective'. So something claimed to be a virtue cannot really be a virtue unless it is pro-objectivity. Virtues have traditionally been non-pro-objectivity notions, with all the problems these involve.[4] Yet at least some qualities often regarded as virtues can be pro-objectivity in certain situations, or they can be defined or qualified so they describe a pro-objectivity duty. Bravery is often regarded as virtuous. If Pam is brave to question her cherished, comforting anti-objectivity beliefs, this bravery, if long-term, is a pro-objectivity virtue. Similarly for pro-objectivity-directed bravery in war against an anti-objectivity enemy. Unless an alleged virtue helps achieve an objective end, it cannot correctly or objectively be called a virtue. E.g., Nazi soldiers were often amazingly brave, but such bravery is overall-objectively-unwarranted, hence not a virtue. More on pro-objectivity virtues and that implication that they are hierarchical:-

Pro-objectivity bravery in war involves and comes under another, higher-level virtue, the above-discussed qualified pacifism. Sometimes the best or only way to achieve pro-objectivity peace long-term could be via bravely fighting enemies who cannot or will not be persuaded to become peaceful, pro-objectivity persons. Such qualified pacifism, aiming to achieve an objectively just peace, can reasonably be viewed as the overall, most important specific pro-objectivity virtue here. It could also reasonably be viewed as coming under pro-objectivity-directed universal benevolence, in that this benevolence's long-term aims include peace. (Regarding practice, differences among views here would not matter, making the differences a-objectivity.) Anyway, importantly, all such virtues come under the ultimate, highest-priority and hence highest-level, or overall or *most* general pro-objectivity virtue, 'Being pro-objectivity'.

Crucial under this is (the less general) pro-objectivity-directed universal benevolence, involving protecting and promoting the pro-objectivity freedoms and rights of all to rationally criticise, be educated, fed, cared for and so on, including be securely (qualifiedly) peaceful. And bravery may be needed to in-practice achieve any of those rights. If virtue-related terms such as 'honourable' have any normatively-objective meaning, they'd involve fulfilling such duties.

That benevolent-care virtue also covers benevolence to all at least potentially pro-objectivity non-human beings:-

In Part II, Section 1.8.3, it was pointed out that if persons are upset by what happens to someone they love or even indirectly care for, this can have anti-objectivity effects. Many persons are upset if they know animals are treated cruelly. (As suggested at least indirectly above, all-else-equal, such persons can be those with the most pro-objectivity potential overall, e.g., due to their natural widespread benevolence and associated sympathy for the most vulnerable.) Getting upset can lessen persons' ability and motivation to be pro-objectivity. So kindness to animals is needed here, to develop that potential or maintain/increase that ability and motivation, and to free the ability and motivation of persons here so they can fulfil other pro-objectivity duties.

Further, as many psychologists point out, if children grow up knowing that animals are treated cruelly, the children can come to accept this as normal and hence acceptable. This can generalise so these children come to accept cruelty to persons. Again, cruelty seems always anti-objectivity.[5] Kindness (benevolence) is one of various virtues that are best learnt at as early an age as possible. (Education is important here, including via parents/carers.) As kindness can also generalise, it is pro-objectivity to encourage children to be kind to animals, as training for later treating their own children, parents/carers and all in optimally pro-objectivity ways. (Similarly, a virtuous mass media would not, e.g., show films which can promote acceptance of generalisable cruelty. This especially applies to media for children, who are on-average less discriminating, less reflective and more impressionable than adults.)

Another reason why kindness to animals is a pro-objectivity virtue is that, if treated in a kind (and, often, relatedly, firm) way, various animals are more likely to do their best to help provide in-effect pro-objectivity companionship, therapy and other help for many persons.

In sum, for such reasons animals have the indirect pro-objectivity right to be treated kindly, which means that long-term kindness to animals is a pro-objectivity virtue. In a pro-objectivity world, as far as possible there'd be harmony and hence peace universally among human and non-human animals.[6]

Various of those points regarding non-human animals can be adapted to apply to humans who also unavoidably lack the pro-objectivity capacities of normal human adults, e.g., their health, awareness, intelligence, rationality and hence accountability. Various of those points can also be adapted to apply to such lacks avoidable by others than those disaffected, e.g., to poor persons' lacking, due to selfishness of the rich, the resources needed to have the diet, healthcare, education etc needed to become maximally pro-objectivity. (In a pro-objectivity kind, fair and otherwise virtuous society there'd be no rich and poor.)

Another virtue issue concerning kindness:- Pro-objectivity requires social harmony and hence consideration and appreciation regarding the costs and benefits of pro-objectivity society. This means types of social manners, e.g., always saying 'Please' and 'Thank you' regarding the care, sharing and helpfulness involved. Such manners are a pro-objectivity virtue. Relatedly, the rewarding nature of manners can help motivate people to be more pro-objectivity.

Concluding here:- The most general virtue, 'Being pro-objectivity', is in a sense also an abbreviated description of an objective definition of 'integrity'—in that the more specific virtues are integrated under 'Being pro-objectivity', becoming mutually-coherent only thereunder. (Appendix 4 explains this further.) 'Integrity' is also often defined as general moral rightness, which also fits here.

Part II, Section 2.2.1: Virtuous Exceptions To The Rule? Conflicting Virtues? Potential, Conditional (Aspects Of) Virtues

It could seem plausible that honesty or truthfulness is inherently, necessarily, a pro-objectivity virtue. Truthfulness can seem coherent with being pro-objectivity because the objective is the true. However, life and pro-objectivity are not that simple. Unobjectivity as in making *errors* is objectively-unwarranted and clearly not a virtue (though in that errors as such are unintentional they are not a normative issue[7]). But unobjectivity as in inherently intended *lying* can be either normatively-objective or not, so the pro-objectivity virtue here involves correctly judging whether to lie or not. As Part I, Section 1.3 suggests, being objective as such does not necessarily mean being normatively at least significantly pro-objectivity. (Type-A is not Type-B.) There are different uses of truth or objectivity, and it is pro-objectivity to discriminate among these uses. Here 'uses' involves 'stating'. Stating some truths, in some situations, can be anti-objectivity. This means that total honesty, or truthfulness as such, is not necessarily a virtue, namely not an unqualified aspect of moral integrity:-

To achieve the end, 'Be pro-objectivity', in some, typically rare situations we would need to lie—so as to instil a pro-objectivity false belief in some person(s). This could seem paradoxical or incoherent, involving a lack of integrity. But there is no conflict with the normatively-objective *end* or standard. E.g:- Consider pro-objectivity parents, as far as they know unable to stop a murderer murdering their children except by lying to the murderer concerning their children's whereabouts. These parents lie, with the expected result that their children live to develop their potential to be highly pro-objectivity. This lie, this unobjectivity, crucially helped achieve the pro-objectivity end. The murder would be anti-objectivity, and, from an overall, objective view, a virtuous parent here would lie to the murderer. To be truthful to the murderer would be anti-objectivity: here there'd be incoherence with the normatively-objective. Here the parents, needlessly sacrificing their children, would lack integrity. They'd not have done the right thing according to both a common moral intuition and pro-objectivity theory. (Saving those children would also result in more pro-objectivity happiness overall, making pro-objectivity theory more motivating here. In such cases, it is unlikely that parents and most people could be motivated to obey rules such as 'Always be truthful', or Kant's 'Never lie'.)

Importantly, lying in such situations is *not* 'making an exception to the (correct) rule', because the only normatively objective or correct ultimate or overall rule is 'Be pro-objectivity'. (As suggested above, the only objective definition of 'correct rule' is a coherent, evidenced and hence pro-objectivity prescription (rule).) Only if a theory's *basis*, and hence its fundamental end/standard, is or includes or implies the rule, 'Never lie' or 'Honesty is a virtue', would lying be an exception to that rule—and hence wrong according to that theory. Pro-objectivity theory's basis is not, and does not include or imply, that rule. In the child-murderer example, those parents have *not* excepted themselves from practising a normatively-objective *rule*. And it is the *circumstances* which are exceptional, at least in societies such as Australia.[8]

That example is also not a case of conflicting (non-cohering) virtues, each virtue being in-itself normatively correct, namely, here, 'truthfulness' and 'parental care' or 'saving innocents' or similar. From an overall, pro-objectivity viewpoint, a practice is only what virtuous persons would do if it coheres with (helps achieve) the objective *end*. E.g., normally truthfulness coheres best here, but in that example untruthfulness does, or, more basically, 'parental care' or similar does. In both cases, the ultimate, overall or absolutely fundamental, unconditionally warranted virtue is 'Being pro-objectivity'. Honesty, and dishonesty, are only '*potential, conditional aspects*' of the virtue here. They relate to or are subsumed under that unconditional virtue. They are situational: the overall virtue here involves flexibly practising via such situationality.[9]

In sum, with pro-objectivity theory, as opposed to various virtues-based or virtues-as-ends theories, there are no conflicting virtues, each correct, an (equally) ultimate or unconditional end. Such conflict would mean incoherence within the associated theory. An objective theory has no incoherence.

Some related issues, involving trustworthiness, a character-trait related to those just-discussed merely alleged virtues, hence needing qualification:-

'Robert is trustworthy' implies others know Robert is reliable in ways commonly deemed positive, ways normally coherent with being pro-objectivity, e.g., a promise-keeper and punctual. Yet trustworthiness is a virtue only when qualified via general points in recent paragraphs and before, expansions thereof, and the following:- Sometimes it is not pro-objectivity to keep promises and be punctual. Sometimes it is not practicable, or something of more pro-objectivity importance unexpectedly needs doing urgently or first. E.g., a promise to mow a friend's lawn by noon might be broken because the mower did not work; and your promise to attend your friend's concert may need to be broken because on the way you notice a car accident, and it is overall more pro-objectivity to help save the victims' lives than to attend the concert.

A solution here is to qualify, conditionalise or situationalise all promises except the promise to be pro-objectivity (or, equivalently, to follow all pro-objectivity general guidelines). ('Be pro-objectivity' is the objectively ultimate and hence *un*qualified, *un*conditional end). E.g., regarding those promises involving punctuality, it seems best to say something like: 'I promise I'll try my best to finish mowing by noon, if all goes well' and 'I promise I'll come to your concert if all goes well (implying e.g., 'unless something more important urgently needs doing')'. Such qualifications involve promising that X will be done under conditions which presently seem to the promiser at least likely, e.g., unless something unexpected (presently unknown) makes X impracticable or a lower priority. One is not responsible for the unintended or unforeseen. If one intends to and will keep one's promises unless certain events occur which one is not responsible for, one remains a morally responsible, virtuous person here. With this, by doing whatever is at-the-time highest priority regarding achieving the pro-objectivity end, one can be trustworthy regarding always being as morally correct as possible. And pro-objectivity persons being promised to would not object to what others may view as broken promises. They'd unselfishly be pleased the most pro-objectivity thing was done. Here the pro-objectivity promiser always (trustably) keeps that most important, highest-priority, overall promise: 'I promise to be pro-objectivity. Specific conditionalised promises here would not be broken anyway. E.g., regarding the mowing, all did not go well.

Concluding comments here:- Regarding character-traits commonly (in 2010) regarded as virtues, such traits are not absolutes: they are relative to some normative theory/end. E.g., according to Nazi theory, Nazi bravery in war was a virtue. From a normatively-objective view, bravery, like various other character traits, is only a potential, conditional virtue. To correctly describe virtues, terms such as 'pro-objectivity bravery' are appropriate, rather than, here, 'bravery'.

Part II, Section 2.3: More On Flourishing, Including Via Education

'Flourishing' means something like 'well-being, fulfilment, involving optimally developing one's capacities, and involving related happiness or pleasure'. When qualified via pro-objectivity theory, flourishing is a right, duty and virtue. ('Be pro-objectivity' means being pro-objectivity overall (totally, long-term), so it is an unconditional duty only achievable by all one's character-traits being either virtuous or a-objectivity.) Many points above can be or were interpreted to concern pro-objectivity flourishing. So only a few comments here:-

In 2003 there was a conference titled "The Science Of Well-Being".[10] This involved research into people's sense of long-term well-being via examining their satisfaction with their lives. It reported that pleasure, as can be gained from food, sex, wine, luxury and so on, is not in itself a factor in such satisfaction or long-term, overall happiness. Rather, meaningfulness and interpersonal engagement are the crucial factors here. Pleasure without those factors present is not regarded as important, or meaningful. Pleasure, when it exists *along with* those crucial factors, becomes an important factor. The combination of them all leads to the most satisfaction with life, via a multiplier effect.

The meaningfulness and engagement can be pro-objectivity, and a-objectivity. E.g:- Part II, Section 1.4.3.1's discussion of the pro-objectivity need for close-circles fits here. So does Part I, Section 2's stressing that various naturally subjectively-evaluated as intrinsically-valuable experiences are important regarding pro-objectivity, because certain such experiences involve naturally meaningful harmonious interpersonal engagement. (We are social animals.) Importantly, much in Part II, Section 1.8.4.2 also coherently relates to various points here and below, e.g., concerning capitalism.

The conference reported that increased economic productivity, hence material prosperity and associated pleasures as under modern Western capitalism, does not seem to have increased happiness here. There is some evidence there has been a decrease. Social-psychological and anthropological research on modern small village-type communities, and historical research on previous ones, indicate that, before material prosperity and related mass urbanisation and hence anonymity increased greatly, persons seem to have been happier or more satisfied due to living in small village-type communities, i.e., more-or-less natural, physically-close close-circles, where all knew/know each other well, mostly working for purposes mutually deemed worthwhile (meaningful). Here, interpersonal engagement and a type of meaningfulness are naturally quite easy.

The conference findings potentially cohere somewhat with what is needed to achieve the flourishing and social harmony needed for maximal collective pro-objectivity. But the conference lacked an overall pro-objectivity view. E.g:-

The meaningful interpersonal engagement easy in small communities is often via comforting, groupist normative and related religious beliefs, i.e., delusions, which a normatively-objective flourishing would exclude. A small society would be excluded too, as pro-objectivity social harmony requires a world-wide society, and that flourishing needs a society large enough to have the universities and other educational/research institutions needed to avoid those delusions. In this world-society, all should practise Part II, Section 1.4.3.1's suggestion that it is probably most pro-objectivity if each person has, beyond a small family-and-close-friends close-circle, a larger, village-size close-circle of caring, along with at least indirectly caring for all other persons. There'd be no groupism in a pro-objectivity world, and hence no outgroups. There'd be universal flourishing, often via people being interpersonally engaged, often passionately, in doing the both objectively and subjectively meaningful (or, regarding a-objectivity, the subjectively meaningful). (Village-size local government would help here.[11])

Complete pro-objectivity flourishing would involve balance. (A-objectivity flourishing inherently need not involve any specific balance, because of the freedom here.) The following concerns a suggested needed balance, among pro-objectivity factors, involving the individual and the overall, collective pro-objectivity needs of humanity. (Again, there is some unavoidable uncertainty concerning precisely what such balances, needs and so on are and involve.):-

Again, for the individual, most importantly, as far as possible this balance involves a pro-objectivity-philosophy contexted education developing all one's general pro-objectivity capacities, cognitive and non-cognitive, to an at least moderate degree—except that one's highest, judgemental, general-guidelines-including thought-level should be developed as far as possible, including via that philosophy's justification thereof, and one should have beyond-moderate knowledge of at least two general academic areas, e.g., maths and biology. (There'd also be an a-objectivity dimension in the curriculum, allowing flourishing here.)

Those general pro-objectivity capacities, representatively suggested above, are exemplified by general physical capacities such as walking, running, jumping, lifting, climbing and swimming, involving associated general and sometimes widely-generalisable capacities such as endurance, will-power, strength, flexibility, co-operation, friendliness, helpfulness, unselfishness, fairness, willingness to try something new, risk-taking, bravery, adventurousness and determinedly taking on difficult challenges. These capacities do not require playing any specific organised sport(s), though various sports can fulfil the same general needs here, as long as the sports involve pro-objectivity (social harmony etc) guidelines. Similarly concerning various other, non-physical general capacities.

As mentioned previously, I suggest beyond-moderate knowledge in at least two general academic areas because advances in knowledge often occur via interrelating (cohering or consiliating) two or more areas. E.g., the combination of maths and biology gave humanity much new knowledge and created new knowledge areas, e.g., genetics. Pro-objectivity cognitive flourishing involves flourishing via venturing into and/or creating new knowledge areas, or expanding one's horizons, combining knowledge areas as far as pro-objectivity-possible, thereby acquiring a more overall, integrated view.

Normatively-objective flourishing also includes being educated to reflect critically on one's own culture. Again, this is achieved better if the reflection includes comparisons with some different culture(s). E.g., practices, values and other beliefs common in one's society can be unreflectingly accepted by one at least largely because what exists is often easily assumed to be that which must and/or ought to exist. (Here one can remain stagnant rather than flourish.) Cross-cultural comparisons can lead to (self-)critical pro-objectivity reflection freeing one to flourish in new pro-objectivity (and a-objectivity) directions such comparisons suggest. (Similarly regarding studying some other language(s). E.g., comparisons here can show English can and should be more coherent (less irrational), and help to develop the common language (a rational, New-English?) pro-objectivity *universal* harmonious(ly communicating) flourishing needs. This would end much wasting of time and other resources, e.g., in translating and learning presently (2010) too-difficult hence too-frustrating English (and Chinese and so on), freeing persons' resources to flourish more and generally.)

Concluding here:- Some such liberal, pro-objectivity overall education should be understandable by at least the vast majority. Each specific developed capacity or expertise here is a (potential) virtue. If some such educational combination is achieved, individuals here should next develop (flourish) further in one or more such general or some specific area(s), (in the flexible, meaningful, socially-engaging ways discussed above,) to achieve a society-wide balance among society's need for a flexible mix of types of workers, experts, artists and so on, while catering for individual interests and abilities. Fulfilling individual responsibilities to society here would help society generally flourish.

Part II, Section 2.4: More On Sexual And Related Matters

Sexual and related matters are important regarding pro-objectivity (and a-objectivity) flourishing. The following suggests how sex can be a virtue here:-

First, importantly, regarding sex there needs to be pro-objectivity-informed free consent—unless certain highly unlikely, exceptional circumstances arise, such as:- The only humans alive are a few fertile, willing pro-objectivity females and one anti-objectivity, fertile homosexual man who will not consent to give them sperm, even without sexual intercourse. The only way to ensure a future pro-objectivity world is to rape him. This would be normatively correct, unselfish rape, not done for the rapists' pleasure. The man's refusal would be selfish, and anti-objectivity in other ways. (Part II, Section 2.2.1's discussion of exceptions to the rule or situationality is relevant here.)

Returning to the most likely situations:-

Warranted, informed free sexual consent means decision-makers here[12] have relevant pro-objectivity autonomous judgement. E.g., an adult having sex with an allegedly consenting child, a child deciding this sex is acceptable, would involve the adult selfishly using hence-unwarranted power, and the child being insufficiently informable and lacking pro-objectivity autonomy. This adult would lack it too, involving having anti-objectivity mental illness and social problems, involving not relating appropriately to normal adults regarding sex, and probably other areas, and perhaps involving the self-deceptive delusion that this adult-relationship-lack and sex with children are acceptable, and that what are objectively an illness and abuse of power are not. Pro-objectivity requires no-one here to be mentally ill in such ways, and so on.

For in-part somewhat similar reasons, celibacy and attempts to enforce it are normally[13] anti-objectivity. Arguments elsewhere above also suggest this, as do the many cases of Catholic priests sexually abusing children.

Next, heterosexuality and homosexuality. Clearly, neither as such is *inherently* or irredeemably anti-objectivity, because there is overwhelming evidence that persons of either sexuality can be as objective and pro-objectivity as the other. Still, as also suggested above, depending on the overall situation, any sexuality can be *situationally* anti-, a- or pro-objectivity. Some points here:-

Human existence is a basic need for even a slightly pro-objectivity world. Suppose that, somehow, all of one sex turned homosexual (or celibate) and would not help with reproduction. If heterosexual intercourse was the only way to reproduce, as humanity would become extinct, homosexuality would here be maximally anti-objectivity. (Or, suppose all of one sex died, or were killed or de-sexed by the other, and so could not help reproduce. If both sexes are needed for reproduction, here it would be maximally anti-objectivity to have just one gender. Here a person's gender is not a-objectivity.)

So if a type of heterosexuality is necessary for humanity's survival, here that type has priority over homosexuality—though homosexuality would not be ruled out in many circumstances. But that type of heterosexuality includes both heterosexual intercourse and impregnation without sexual intercourse, via some (perhaps simple) medical procedure. Here, as long as at least a viable sperm-egg meeting occurs, it can be normatively irrelevant (a-objectivity) whether persons are heterosexual or homosexual. It is normatively irrelevant if all else pro-objectivity-relevant is equal, e.g., regarding fulfilling child-care needs.

Interestingly, the 'Here' two sentences ago does not cover the overall situation: reproduction now seems possible via manipulating female DNA, meaning there is now no reproductive need for heterosexuality, or males. Here just females would be fine, and they could all be homosexual. Yet the 'if all else pro-objectivity-relevant is equal' applies, including regarding there being functions of sex apart from reproduction:-

Conceivably, all else could be overall equal regarding fulfilling those child-care and various other pro-objectivity needs. But, e.g., if babies here could only be produced via using far more resources than are used to produce babies via sexual intercourse, those costly resources could be needed for *other* pro-objectivity purposes. E.g., perhaps the medical, financial etc resources could cure diseases, fund education and buy food for starving people so as to help many more persons become more pro-objectivity. It depends on what the optimal pro-objectivity cost-benefit balance would be among such needs and the sexual needs of those male-less females. It is highly unlikely they'd all be homosexual. The pro-objectivity sexual (and other) needs of billions of women would probably require males. Sex can help bond (cohere) pro-objectivity people, making their close-circles even more meaningful and interpersonally engaging in pro-objectivity ways. Here heterosexuality can be important for many females, as can homosexuality for others. Lucinda's and Maggie's cases, discussed in Part II, Section 1.8.1-1.8.1.1, exemplify this, and help show there are functions of sex apart from reproduction, involving various sexual needs, and how these relate to pro-objectivity overall. (Such arguments can be adapted to apply to males' and inter-sex persons' sexual preferences, needs etc.)

Whether a person is homosexual, heterosexual or bisexual can perhaps be a predisposition due to brain events the person has no control over, e.g., via their genes, or at least an interaction between genes and other physiological and/or social etc events the person (e.g., when a child) could not control. If someone's sexual predisposition is hence (probably) unchangeable, it would be anti-objectivity to try to pressure them to change, (e.g., to get all those females to be homosexual,) e.g., due to the frustration and disharmony involved. If there is that unchangeable predisposition,[14] and all-things-considered the preference is overall a-objectivity or at least as pro-objectivity as the alternative(s), there is no objective warrant for people not being free to act on their preferences.

Still, there can be various complications. E.g., if sex with another person is the most pro-objectivity sexual option for heterosexual H, but for a long time the only available and willing person is not of the preferred gender, then an at least temporary change to homosexuality might be H's overall most pro-objectivity option. And vice versa. One pro-objectivity need can outweigh another.

Similarly, if a person will be alone for ages, and the only way to reduce anti-objectivity sexual frustration is by masturbation or some other non-anti-objectivity sex act not involving some other person(s), e.g., involving a sex toy, then, all else equal, the masturbation or whatever is (temporarily) this person's most pro-objectivity option.

Concluding here:- There seems nothing overall-objectively-unwarranted about homosexuality or heterosexuality or hence bi-sexuality as such. Similarly regarding lone sex acts. It is the overall situation which is normatively relevant.

Regarding censorship, there seems to me no warrant for much of the censorship of sex (and nudity) in many present (2010) societies. Much violence and cruelty is not censored, but sex is heavily censored, often at least indirectly due to religious-based normative views, i.e., delusions, i.e., mistakes. I think research suggests the reverse censorship would be most pro-objectivity here. (E.g., for some persons at least, some media violence or cruelty seems to generalise to how they treat various real persons.) An increase in media sex would need to promote only pro- or a-objectivity sex. Points elsewhere in this book suggest that sex on the media (and anywhere) would only be pro-objectivity if within an overall pro-objectivity context, e.g., involving mutual care and respect, and was not the primary aim or interest of the persons and/or media-institution involved. Similarly regarding a-objectivity sex or aspects of sex. Regarding family structures and the number of one's sexual partners, the choice among some alternatives could be a-objectivity. Here, or to choose the most pro-objectivity alternative, the likely long-term outcomes over all involved, especially children, need to be known. And what applies here for some prospective family-makers or sexual partners may not apply to others, or among other differing situations.

Part II, Section 2.5: Revisiting Some Political And Legal Issues

These deserve a final revisiting because it is political institutions, via directly or indirectly[15] making laws, which have the ultimate power in society—and are hence crucial regarding achieving a pro-objectivity society. History shows that political institutions and laws can change greatly, so there is much hope here. It is at least implicit in the above that present (2010) political and legal institutions need fundamental and related changes. Part I implies they are all fundamentally incoherent and far from maximally pro-objectivity. Their at least implicit arguments sometimes conclude that in-effect pro-objectivity prescriptions ought to be law, e.g., non-racism. But there is only the above-criticised conclusion-overlap here: the bases or premises of those arguments are far from entirely pro-objectivity, and so are unreliable overall, namely regarding prescribing pro-objectivity laws in all areas. E.g., Australia's government outlaws sexism only in some areas, not, e.g., in religion and the media.

Another example of fundamental politico-legal problems is that various Western democracies' politico-legal systems have some version(s) of Utilitarianism in their at least implicit foundations or premises. And various countries base many laws simply on whatever community standards (allegedly) predominate at the time, e.g., regarding sex and public nudity, or on some religion's normative pronouncements, or on some tradition defended by an irrational argument such as 'X is right because our culture has traditionally done X', e.g., had a monarchy or practised female circumcision. No such basis is that of an objective normative political, legal etc theory. They all need changing, via education.

CONCLUDING REMARKS

There are plenty of concluding remarks above, the most important and here-relevant being in Part I, Section 1.4 and Part I's conclusion. So there seems no need to say much here, except:-

Something like this book's theory is, I think, the best we can do regarding objective normativity. If there is any (truly or objectively) better theory, I welcome it. If someone can prove, i.e., objectively, via evidence, that this book's theory needs modifications, then those modifications will give us a more objective theory. Philosophy and life are so complex, and humans so fallible, that I probably made at least a few minor mistakes. If so, we can learn from those mistakes and thereby get closer to an objective theory. The critical, rational, evidence-seeking approach I advocated and tried to use in this book needs to be applied to the book, so as to improve the theory.

The book's primary, positive aim is to show there is a normative theory applicable to all areas and able to motivate at least nearly all, a theory at least close to objectivity and as close as is possible for a normative theory. The main negative aim is to show that believing any alternative theory means one believes unobjectively, in a mistake, and that practising it is wrong. If a theory is not objective, what is it? '1+2=7' is not an objective, evidenced theory. What do we think of such theories? What would someone be doing by believing or practising such a theory?, say by lending you $1, then $2, then insisting that therefore you owe them $7.

That positive aim is an attempt to make the world a better place by showing people a way of life they can know is objectively better than the alternatives, giving objective and related optimal subjective meaning to their lives.

Subjectively, emotionally, I hoped to relatedly justify great freedom, certain rights and responsibilities, types of peace, societal harmony, kindness, love, caring, fairness, sharing, enjoyment, flourishing and so on. But I needed to be very careful not to distort the theory, or simply construct a theory, merely in order to achieve those subjective, strongly emotional aims. As far as I know, I've avoided doing that and the mistakes involved therein. If not, I hope the book here at least indirectly suggests how a more objective theory could be developed.

ENDNOTES TO PART II, SECTION 2

1 This, discussed near Part I, Section 2's beginning, is the core *any* society needs to believe and practise if it is to survive, e.g., the value, 'Care for children (if resources permit, etc)'. Beyond that core, a society can use any of various values to cohere itself.

2 Simplistically, or also, it can mean: 'What reward (or punishment) will I get if I do (or do not do) that?' But children tend to grow beyond such simplistic enquiring, to asking at least implicitly normatively important questions.

3 This is because it is impossible to achieve an overall psychological harmony which includes false beliefs or the unobjective. And unverifiable beliefs are either false or are true but, if true, are only believed to be true by chance. So beliefs here are unreliable regarding harmony.

4 The problems were at least implicitly discussed above. One is that virtue-based theories involve rationally insoluble conflicts. E.g., if it is virtuous to be both honest and kind, sometimes is unkind to be honest. E.g., an honest answer to someone asking , "Do you think I'm attractive?", could be unkind (and anti-objectivity). Only a single objective standard/end can solve such conflicts between alleged virtues regarded as ultimate ends.

5 Being cruel, defined here as being cruel for the sake of cruelty or to achieve another anti-objectivity end, is definitely anti-objectivity, as it conflicts with the peacefulness and positive social relationships implied by the (sub-)end-aim here, 'Universal harmony regarding achieving the pro-objectivity end'. However, 'hurt' need not mean cruelty, and regarding hurting there can be hard choices. E.g., it could be pro-objectivity to hurt someone's feelings, e.g., by making honest criticisms of them which seem likely, on all available evidence, to shock them into pro-objectivity self-criticism, thereby becoming more pro-objectivity in the long run—as in appropriately asking, "Why are you so lazy and selfish?". (A thence-qualified version of the saying, 'Sometimes you need to be

cruel to be kind', can apply.) The *overall,* over-time intention or end-aim here is not to be cruel, but to be helpfully pro-objectivity.

6 One aspect of this would be producing meat only in factories, without an animal's brain attached to the meat. This has been done via stem cell technology.

7 But there is more to this issue than that. E.g., errors can result from intended practices virtuous persons would not practise, e.g., selfishly lazily neglecting to learn how to avoid the errors. It is the selfish laziness which is normatively wrong, not the errors.

8 Most types of lying would occur far less often in an achievably ideal pro-objectivity society than in probably all existing societies. E.g., the social harmony would mean far less chance of murder, so far less such exceptional circumstances; and due to the nature of pro-objectivity democracy and economics there would be none of the frequent lies as told by politicians and capitalists to serve their own selfish or groupish interests.

9 Flexibility regarding honesty is also needed regarding a-objectivity ends or situations. Here truthfulness can be either appropriate or, where truth is inapplicable, inappropriate. E.g., fiction inherently requires untruthfulness; sometimes art involves untruthfulness as in purely imaginary, hence unobjective paintings.

Fiction and unobjective art can also be pro-objectivity, and virtuous to write or create. Another pro-objectivity untruthfulness involves pro-objectivity humour which inherently involves untruths (but not normatively-problematic lies). These untruths have their humorous pro-objectivity effect because those involved at least implicitly know that the lack of truth is why the situation is humorous, and pro-objectivity. (Humour can also be a-objectivity—and anti-objectivity, e.g., funny for a cruel joke-teller but, due to the joke's lie, cruel to the hearer.)

10 Australia's ABC Radio National program, "Life Matters", 9th Dec 2003, covered this.

11 This, referred to in Part II, Section 1.6.1.2, can help foster meaningfulness and social engagement within such communities. Pro-objectivity democratic local government would meaningfully engage and directly interpersonally care for each person here.

12 They could make decisions for adults lacking autonomy. E.g., benevolent carers of intellectually-disabled adults should decide to encourage them to have sex in certain (safe etc) circumstances.

13 An exception would be, e.g., an adult for who sex would only cause pro-objectivity-disabling pain due to some unrepairable physical abnormality.

14 A general point:- There is no warrant for acting via a predisposition just because it is a predisposition. E.g., consider a predisposition to violence or selfishness. The above criticisms of simplistic, nature-based moral theories apply here. A predisposition is just an inclination or tendency. It is not a necessity we cannot avoid acting on, as in breathing being survival-necessary and normal conscious humans unavoidably having to breath (except briefly). We can choose to redirect a predisposition, or to not act on it. (This book is in-part a result of me redirecting my (previously often acted-on) predisposition to be violently aggressive, turning the aggression instead towards, positively, trying to make the world better via solving normativity's problems, and, negatively, opposing what seemed objectively unwarranted, ignorant, selfish, cruel, unfair or unjust etc treatment of persons, including by violent aggression.)

15 E.g., in powerfully capitalist societies, capitalists can constitute an informal political institution indirectly influencing formal political law-making. It is pro-objectivity-important to consider such indirect or informal politics.

APPENDIXES

APPENDIXES ORIGINALLY REFERRED TO IN THE BOOK'S INTRODUCTION

Appendix A: Problems And Strategies Regarding Knowledge

To sufficiently understand the book's theory it is not necessary to understand the problems mentioned here. It is only necessary to accept the Introduction's argument that the problems are sufficiently manageable for the book's practical, normative purposes. The problems and strategies mentioned here are only representative, and because they concern knowledge they concern objectivity. The problems, explained in any good philosophy dictionary or encyclopaedia, include those concerning induction,[1] the criterion problem,[2] human limitations and fallibility, the coherentism versus foundationalism etc controversies,[3] and, regarding various issues, 'How much evidence is sufficient to confirm that X is true?'. The problems mean there is sometimes unavoidable significant uncertainty or vagueness regarding knowledge or objectivity.[4]

Apart from that issue, there is some future-avoidable lack of knowledge or evidence meaning significant uncertainty or vagueness regarding some specific practical applications of the book's theory (as opposed to the theory's basic general notions, which the book argues are rationally-unquestionable[5]). So the new theory is inherently somewhat fallibilist and hence self-skeptical.

Here provisional acceptance can be an appropriate strategy. This involves not believing statement X—because one does not (yet?) know X. Here, e.g., when you must act on statement X or an alternative, say either 'Try method M1 of disciplining that child' or 'Do not try M1; it won't help. Try M2', or 'Do nothing to discipline the child', you act on X only because you think X is at least as likely to be correct as the alternative(s), but acting here is to some degree trial-and-error: you believe X might not be correct. Regarding knowing X, you suspend judgement till sufficient evidence is available. (Again, precisely what 'sufficient evidence' is can often be at least somewhat uncertain.)

Similarly:- There can be degrees of probable knowledge. Here one hypothesis seems likely to be true, but a rational strategy is to suspend judgement regarding it being undoubtedly true—until there is sufficient evidence to confirm whether the hypothesis is true. (E.g:- Scientists once had only probable knowledge that smoking can cause lung cancer. Now they (definitely) know it can and often does.) Similarly, there can be approximate knowledge, as in many weather forecasts. Some of the book's theory's suggested applications are probable or approximate knowledge. The at-the-time appropriate strategy here is to act on such knowledge, because there is at least temporarily no better guide.

Appendix B: More On The Applicability Of 'Be Pro-Objectivity'

'Be pro-objectivity' might on-first-view seem too abstract. Yet some popular older normative theories have extremely abstract ends applicable to morality etc, as with Kant's widely-accepted general end, 'Act only on a maxim you can will as a universal law'. (Similarly regarding Rawls.[6]) The book shows that, as with Kant's universalisability end, when 'Be pro-objectivity' is applied to specific moral, social, political etc situations or issues, e.g., selfishness, applicable moral, social, political etc prescriptions can be arrived at. This shows that 'Be pro-objectivity' is not inherently too abstract to be a normative end. Universalisability is far more abstract.[7]

'Be pro-objectivity' might also on-first-view seem a category mistake and hence inapplicable to morality, society, politics etc. E.g., it may seem too cognitive, too cerebral and narrow, or applicable only in areas such as science, not belonging in categories or areas such as morality, society and politics. Arguments below (and in the main body) show this is not so. This is primarily because that end only *involves* objectivity and hence knowledge, just *some* knowledge, and is *not* that knowledge as such, and is *not* objectivity as such. The ultimate end will be shown to be the substantive *practising* of normative moral etc knowledge. Here the theory distinguishes between being *pro*-objectivity and being objective or knowledgeable as such:-

Being *pro*-objectivity overall includes but is not the same as objectivity. Analogously, being pro-jazz is not identical with being jazz. If your normative end is 'Be pro-jazz', achieving this end involves jazz but much more. E.g:- You, your parents/carers and society must also have done much in order for you to be alive, safe and have enough health, money, ability, time, freedom, peace, energy etc to hear/play jazz. Your society needs to not stop jazz playing and jazz musicians training, and preferably promote such things and liberty here. Also, much work, knowledge and technology is needed to produce jazz instruments. Parallel to this, 'Be pro-objectivity' applies to society, politics, education, economics etc.

Relatedly, an important difference between pro-objectivity and objectivity further demonstrates such applicability. This difference is shown analogously by further comparing being pro-jazz with (hearing/playing) jazz. If one's highest-priority end is being pro-X, one will be overall, as far as possible, *maximally* pro-X. But to be maximally pro-jazz *overall*, one cannot spend the maximum time, energy etc only hearing/playing jazz, stopping only to get unavoidable minimal sleep. 'Overall' includes over all humanly-possible time. If we all spend our time etc maximally only hearing/playing jazz, i.e., stopping only unavoidably, we'd soon die. Firstly, no-one would produce, get, prepare and eat food.[8] Even if that was no problem we'd soon lack other survival-necessary resources, e.g., healthy water, hygiene, enough rest for life-preserving immune-system health and, probably thereby, soon probably some life-saving medical treatment needing some of our, doctors' etc time etc. There'd also be no time etc to fulfil other human needs, e.g., socialising, sex and reasonable accommodation, needs we must have fulfilled if we are to optimally enjoy jazz long-term. And if we all spent our time etc maximally thus, soon there'd be no next, cared-for, fed etc generation. Being pro-jazz would soon become *im*practicable—because we focused only on jazz as such, i.e., directly on hearing/playing jazz. (To practicably be pro-objectivity, we must practise much more than being objective.) Here we ignored the many other, *pro*-jazz factors needed to free us (and allow future generations) to be able to spend, over a much longer life-span, only that time, energy etc directly on jazz maximally consistent with spending time etc on those *other, pro*-jazz factors. To achieve the maximum possible quantity/quality of jazz listening/playing over the longest possible term, a *balance* is needed—involving much besides jazz. On-first-view perhaps paradoxically, because 'Be pro-jazz' would be your highest priority, you would *not* spend the highest possible amount of time etc on jazz as such. If you are realistically maximally pro-jazz, you would not maximally spend your time etc on jazz as such.

In various recent sentences, 'objectivity' can meaningfully replace 'jazz'. That is, to be maximally pro-objectivity overall as far as possible, a pro-objectivity-optimal balance is needed. This book will show that this includes making normative choices, all such choices, in all areas. In sum, pro-objectivity is applicable to morality, society, politics and so on—normatively applicable.

Also on-first-view perhaps paradoxically, and relevant regarding applicability, just-mentioned arguments imply that pro-objectivity theory is *not* pro-using-objectivity or pro-acquiring-knowledge within all areas (as opposed to *about* all areas). The explanation is that knowledge in many areas is no help regarding pro-objectivity's needed normative applicability. E.g., if everyone focused entirely on personally counting and hence knowing the world's number of pebbles, this would take so long that all would soon die from not also focusing on other areas. Everyone would lack and/or not apply all the needed survival-necessary knowledge. So pro-objectivity theory is pro-acquiring-knowledge and anti-ignorance in survival-necessary and many other, moral, social etc areas—but pro-objectivity is pro-ignorance regarding knowledge the acquisition of which is anti- our being maximally pro-objectivity over the longest possible term.

The previous paragraph explains another important way in which pro-objectivity is not the same as objectivity or acquiring knowledge as such, and relatedly why 'Be pro-objectivity' does not concern, and hence is not just applicable to, knowledge/objectivity as such. Here, pro-objectivity persons value some knowledge, as this knowledge is *applicable* in *practical* moral, social etc areas, but reject acquiring other knowledge due to its *lack* of that normative applicability. (Pro-objectivity is applicable *concerning* the rejected areas in that here pro-objectivity theory says: 'Do not acquire knowledge *in* these areas'.)

As the previous and other recent paragraphs imply, that which could be artificially isolated as 'purely cognitive' here is, for pro-objectivity theory, inextricable from and concerns practical, substantive issues across life-as-a-whole, and is hence far from narrow and cerebral. E.g., as the book shows, great liberty, enjoyment and diversity would exist in pro-objectivity society primarily because its citizens understand, i.e., cognitively understand, that such liberty, enjoyment and diversity is normatively-objective.

A general argument showing further that 'Be pro-objectivity' is applicable to morality, society etc begins with the fact that, regarding *any* one thing, including any humanly-achievable end, logically *every* other thing *necessarily* has either a positive (e.g., causal or promoting), negative (e.g., destructive or forbidding) or neutral relation to that thing or end. So, from the viewpoint of humanly-achievable end, E, or the associated standard, E, e.g., 'Be pro-jazz', *everything* with a positive relation to E, e.g., here, a society liberally promoting jazz playing, is of positive normative value and so *ought to apply*. Careful investigation will show that 'everything' here covers innumerable moral, social, political etc areas. E.g., any E is applicable to politics; e.g., regarding the pro-jazz example, that society's political institutions did not forbid and successfully banish jazz.

Similarly, from the viewpoint of humanly-achievable end E, anything with a negative relation to E, e.g., regarding 'Be pro-jazz', a morality, society, education, religion or government forbidding jazz, ought not to so forbid, and should be changed. So any E is also widely normatively applicable here.

And, from E's viewpoint, each thing with a neutral relation to E is permissible because such things have no effect on E. There is no reason for E to prescribe that they should not be as they are, or that they should be changed. So here complete liberty is allowed by E. Here E is applicable because in this area it is E which in-effect prescribes or decides that you are free do whatever you like.

Concluding here:- As the book shows, being pro-objectivity is a humanly-achievable end. *Any* humanly-achievable end is applicable in some way to *everything* because, logically, *each* thing necessarily has either a positive, negative or neutral relation to each other thing. So *any* humanly-achievable end is necessarily universally normatively applicable. Part I and, especially, Part II, demonstrate this applicability far beyond reasonable doubt, often in detail.

APPENDIXES ORIGINALLY REFERRED TO IN THE BOOK'S MAIN BODY

APPENDIX 1: More Concerning Coherence

Centuries ago there was ignorance and cognitive incoherence concerning the overall situation regarding gravity. Consider people then aware of events such as water sometimes rising, e.g., as steam and high tides, and sometimes falling, e.g., as rain and low tides, and of events such as the relative positions and movements of the sun, Earth and its moon. Before Newton[9] it seems to have not occurred to such people that all such events were linked, all significantly explainable by knowledge concerning gravity. So the overall situation was not understood. If anyone hypothesised that all such events were linked, or coherent, without an explanation involving gravity, other people would probably have considered the hypothesis incomprehensible. E.g., it would have seemed incoherent to be told that water both rises and falls for the same basic reason that the moon orbits Earth, and so on, without plausibly explaining what the reason is.

But later the here-unifying, cognitive-coherence-creating notion, 'gravity', became significantly understood. Scientists here systematised all such events by knowing they all came under the law of gravity, i.e., by explaining those lower-level events via that higher-level unifying or coherence-giving notion. This resolved apparent inconsistencies, making all risings, fallings, orbitings etc here comprehensible and hence able to become knowledge—unifying or cohering them together systematically, as the knowledge area: 'Gravity's effects'.

Coherence involves consistency but is much more than mere consistency. Coherence also involves a positive, supportive relationship, a system. Consistent notions can be neutrally related, importantly separate, non-supportive, not fitting systematically together. The knowledge-area, 'Gravity's effects', is consistent with but not overall importantly coherent with the knowledge that Mozart was a musician. Parts of a motorbike engine which need to be combined so as to make the engine work are mutually coherent. Remove one part, e.g., pistons, and the engine ceases to work: it lacks the (full) coherence needed. Knowledge and related coherence here involve the pro- relationship, causality. Mere consistency here would involve, e.g., the engine being red:- Redness is consistent with but not coherent with (or causally positive or supportive regarding) the engine working in that the engine could work if it was any other colour. 'X and Y are consistent' merely means X and Y are both the case and can apply or exist together, with no conflict, and they can be importantly irrelevant to each other.

Any normative knowledge would involve those same general qualities involved in any knowledge area, namely unity, support, positivity, systematicity and hence coherence.

APPENDIX 2: Some Other Arguments For The Theory; Unavoidable Circularity

Introductory paragraph:- Because objectivity's central activity is acquiring knowledge, objectivity inherently at least implicitly knows that knowledge is its internal general end. Objectivity can know also that because any discovered objective normative end would thereby become knowledge and hence part of its internal end, objectivity could not coherently doubt or reject that normative end. So inherently *non-incoherent* objectivity could not doubt or reject it, period:-

A discovered objective normative end would become internal to or part of the discoverer's objectivity because the end-principle would, via its discovery, become normative knowledge. For objectivity to doubt or reject that end-principle or any other knowledge, objectivity would have to doubt or reject itself from outside itself—an impossibility. (Only notions *external* to objectivity, and hence unobjective or not able to be knowledge, can doubt or reject objectivity or any part thereof, or anything coherent therewith.) Further explanation here:-

If objectivity has a basis (foundation), then, as suggested in Ancient Greece, if objectivity could refute or prove doubtful its own basis, objectivity would have no basis for that refutation or proof. If the basis is objective, and hence irrefutable, so is the rest of objectivity because it is implied by or involved in that basis—including any objective normative end, an end coherent with that basis via being implied by or involved in that basis.

Regardless of whether epistemic foundationalism applies, in every knowledge area objectivity/knowledge is *coherent* (somewhat via reasonable construction). If knowledge has some foundation(s), the rest of knowledge must be in an important sense be coherent with that foundation-knowledge, and vice versa, in that a foundation cannot imply anything incoherent with or separate from itself and, relatedly, in that a foundation is a premise and a premise at least implicitly *contains* its implications and hence cannot be incoherent with them. If there are no foundations, and coherentism alone applies, any knowledge of an objective normative end would be coherent with the rest of knowledge in some way(s) other than via being implied by some foundation(s). So, via appropriate adaptation, the previous paragraph applies here too regarding refuting or proving doubtful all or any part of objectivity, including any normative knowledge. This refutation or proof would have to show that the objective is unobjective, namely that inherently *coherent* objectivity is *in*coherent. So here such refutation or proof regarding a part would mean refuting or proving doubtful all of objectivity. This is impossible because that could only be done correctly, namely objectively, by inherently coherent objectivity being incoherently both (i) entirely objective and coherent, and (ii) at least somewhat unobjective and incoherent—and via objectivity being external to itself in order to assess itself, indeed attack itself, objectively, analogously to a ball being outside of and hitting itself.

If some adaptation of foundationalism or coherentism applies, or a combination of them applies, perhaps along with some other inherently non-incoherent part-nature of knowledge, a thereto appropriate version of previous paragraphs must also conclude that objectivity cannot refute or prove doubtful any normative knowledge. *Whatever* the overall nature of objectivity/knowledge is, objectivity/knowledge cannot get outside itself to objectively refute or prove doubtful any normative (or other) knowledge.

Objectivity can only prove doubtful, or prove wrong and reject, (self-)coherently—namely things outside objectivity in that they are incoherent with objectivity, e.g., illusions, irrationality, mistaken or doubtful knowledge-claims, and ends apart from non-a-objectivity ends, its own cognitive end and (knowledge of) an objective normative end.

In sum, a correct (i.e., objective) doubt regarding or refutation of objectivity/knowledge is logically impossible. (So only the illogical or irrational (incorrect) could believe it is possible.) Those and other recent points relate to unavoidable circularity, mentioned in Part I, Section 1.2 and elsewhere above:-

Because objectivity or knowledge cannot externally assess itself, there is *unavoidable, holistic, necessary* circularity in some of this book's arguments. This involves objectivity assessing (each part of) itself as objective via its own hence internal (appropriate-to-the-part[10]) standards of assessment, as in Part I's assessing pro-objectivity theory as objective via the standard, 'coherence', and so on. Is this book's unavoidable normative circularity any better, or less rationally-problematic, than circularity involved in other normative theories' arguments, e.g., than 'Maximising happiness is what we should do (e.g., because happiness is naturally desired and hence good); therefore, we should maximise happiness (because happiness is naturally desired and hence good)'? Each such argument has the circular form, 'X, therefore X'.

Inherently, pro-objectivity theory's circularity, because for us the theory is (or can be) knowledge, is not rationally-problematic for us. Necessarily, logically, we cannot know whether what is for us knowledge is not or may not really be knowledge according to a possible super-being unknowable by us, a being who can accurately externally assess that which is knowledge for us, via reading our minds from outside (of our unavoidable circularity), and who has real, absolute knowledge, namely ideas beyond our comprehension—beyond our knowledge and hence outside it and the unavoidable circularity it involves. So, even if that which is knowledge for us is rationally-problematic for such a being, it cannot be rationally-problematic *for us*. We could never *know* of the problematicity.

It is crucially via much inherently holistic-circularity-involving knowledge that we exist, namely survival-necessary knowledge. Everyone whose survival is impossible without such knowledge, which is at least indirectly all of us, (survivally-)necessarily at least implicitly in-effect accepts such circularity as non-problematic. Consider numerous statements here for which rational persons have evidence sufficient to regard the statements as knowledge, e.g., the statement: 'To survive, we must avoid cliff-falls, decapitation, starvation and poison'. Consider someone *acting on* the view that such statements are too problematic and hence not knowledge, and hence deserve to be ignored, because they involve unavoidable circularity. This person's actions here will soon lead to the person's death. In sum, in *practice* we all depend on holistic-circularity-involving survival-necessary knowledge being viewed as knowledge; so we view it and that unavoidable circularity as rationally non-problematic for us.

Concluding here:- That which is knowledge for us involves unavoidable circularity, but is logically and contingently necessarily regarded by us (rational persons) as knowledge. Because objectivity-as-a-whole[11] cannot get outside itself to assess itself, there is that unavoidable, holistic circularity if objectivity argues for its correctness. Yet this is irrelevant regarding a theory which is for us objective. The irrelevance is because external self-assessment is *impossible* for us. It is irrational to be concerned about the impossible here. Relatedly, such circularity is not rationally-problematic (for us). And this circularity is universal among knowledge/objectivity, e.g., it applies to empirical knowledge. So to reject any normative knowledge due to this circularity, consistent and hence here-rational persons must reject all knowledge, (fatally) including their empirical survival-necessary knowledge, and, incoherently, that rationality and their (alleged) *knowledge* that all knowledge must be rejected.

Via one's objectivity, and so via such circularity, it *is* possible to avoid any *rationally-problematic* circularity—the type occurring with unobjective normative theories, and with various other arguments:-

Circularity as such is no problem for objectivity in that all valid (formally-objective) argument-forms and all sound (objective) arguments are circular in that their conclusion is contained in their premise(s). Circular valid arguments are only rationally-problematic when the only alleged evidence or justification for the content of their premise(s) is internal to the argument and questionable or proven wrong via our having an objective standpoint external to the argument as such. (We can objectively assess innumerable arguments from *this* external standpoint because that standpoint can be *within* one's objectivity, within one's mental events, as indicated by the next paragraph.) In 'X, therefore X', non-rationally-problematic content for X is exemplified by the following:-

Area 1 here is where the premise is confirmed as objective by that standpoint, e.g., as with empirical knowledge. An example regarding this and the previous paragraph:- Consider 'All dogs (dog 1, dog 2, . . . dog n) are mammals. Rex (dog 2) is a dog. Therefore, Rex is a mammal.' Because dog 2 is in 'dog 1,dog 2, . . . dog n', the argument is circular and valid: it includes the crucial 'X, therefore X', i.e., 'dog 2 is a mammal, therefore dog 2 is a mammal.' Circularity and validity are also the case with 'All dogs are birds. Rex is a dog. So Rex is a bird'. But this is of course not sound. It is overall unobjective, because its premise is false. Here only that former valid argument is sound and so not problematically circular, because there is available evidence external to the argument, namely empirical observations showing that dog 2 (etc) has (have) characteristics we define as 'mammalian', which exclude birdness. (These are observations one can make, and would hence be within one's objectivity. That is, one uses one's brain to reflect on and assess arguments one's brain is aware of. This involves a higher level of thought reflecting on a lower level, so the higher level, using those observations, is cognitively above and in that sense outside of the argument in the lower level—but both levels are within one's mental events as a whole, within one's brain, within its assessing-for-objectivity parts.)

Note that the empirical argument supporting pro-objectivity theory, first explained in Part I, Section 1.4 (4), comes under Area 1.

Area 2, which covers Area 1's general nature,[12] is where there is that *un*-avoidable holistic circularity, where it is impossible to have an objective standpoint external to the argument. This is the case with pro-objectivity theory's basic overall argument. An abbreviated version of this is:-

Premise(s): 'A theory assessed by objectivity as fitting the appropriate standards among objectivity's own, hence internal standards, is thereby objective. Pro-objectivity theory is objective via objectivity's here-appropriate standards, namely, as argued in Part I, via coherence and so on.'

Conclusion: Therefore the only objective normative theory is pro-objectivity theory (because it is a theory assessed by objectivity as fitting appropriate standards among objectivity's own, hence internal standards).

A subsequent argument's premise(s): 'The only objective normative practices are pro-objectivity.' 'Practices P1, P2, . . . Pn are pro-objectivity.'

Conclusion: 'Therefore P1, P2, . . . Pn are objective normative practices.' Or, say, if the arguer is at the time specifically concerned with P2: 'P2 is an objective normative practice'.

That basic argument is clearly unavoidably holistically circular, as in 'X, therefore X' or 'X because X' . But, as previous parts of this Appendix argue, this is not rationally-problematic for us.

In that subsequent argument, P1, P2, . . . Pn are (implicitly) within the premise's phrase, 'objective normative practices'. In 'X, therefore X', X can specifically be any pro-objectivity practice, say P2. Thence, 'P2 is an objective normative practice, therefore P2 is an objective normative practice' is also an example of the only objective content for the general valid unavoidably-circular form at least implicitly involved in all normative theories, i.e., 'X, therefore X'.

Any other normative content for X in the basic argument, e.g., 'maximise-happiness' content, is hence rationally-problematic, a content we cannot know to be objective. Part I shows that those pro-objectivity basic and subsequent arguments' premises (contents) are sufficiently evidenced, and hence objective, which relates to Areas 1 and 2:- E.g., with that subsequent argument, for any specific pro-objectivity contents for P2, we can have sufficient empirical evidence showing this content for X is coherent with objectivity and the objective normative end—evidence external to the argument's claim that this X (P2) is a normatively objective practice. That is, we can have overall-objective-warrant, i.e., (pro-objectivity) knowledge, e.g., that in situation S this rather than that political system or education is more likely, all else pro-objectivity-relevant equal, to as far as possible maximise pro-objectivity. We cannot have such (or any) evidence that, e.g., happiness-maximising, is normatively-objective.

Concluding here:-

As A.P. Griffiths suggests,[13] the choosable factors needed *for* being normatively objective, namely pro-objectivity practices, are uniquely necessarily immune *from* objective or rational criticism. The objective, being inherently non-incoherent, cannot (self-)coherently criticise or reject the pro-objectivity, or objective, pro-objectivity theory. (Analogously, a ball cannot hit itself.) Relatedly, objectivity cannot (self-)coherently criticise or reject its own universally-applicable, inherently pro-objectivity normative presuppositions, or any normative knowledge.

Within the area, 'Non-pro-objectivity normative theories', there are many, conflicting theories. One major problem here is that there is no way to correctly (objectively) choose among them. From an objective or rational viewpoint, here there is ultimately only (infinite) regression or an arbitrary stopping of regression via in-effect merely asserting that some claim is the correct (objective) fundamental premise—with each theory ultimately only able to argue for its fundamental premise via *avoidable, problematic* circularity. This means permanent, insoluble, unmanageable, fundamental uncertainty.

Pro-objectivity theory's overall degree of uncertainty is manageable. Its circularity means certainty in that, regarding normativity, it alone is objective or sound. Its non-problematic circularity involves that which helps *constitute* objectivity. With this, its circularity is unrejectable and undoubtable via rationality, knowledge or evidence—unlike alternative theories. To rationally or objectively doubt its circularity, or to prove it is problematic, the doubting or proof would have to use and hence accept that the doubting's or proof's circularity is proven non-problematic. But its circularity here would be the same as pro-objectivity theory's. In sum, that doubting or proof is impossible: pro-objectivity theory cannot be rationally rejected.

All alternative theories at least implicitly reject pro-objectivity theory. To doubt or reject the objective is to be overall-objectively-unwarranted, i.e., objectively wrong. And it is absurd that such rejection is ultimately done on the basis of problematic circularity and hence no evidence. Evidence is objective.

APPENDIX 3: The 'Necessary Presupposition/Foundation' Argument

Every normative theory suggests it should be *believed*—or explicitly says it should simply be practised, hence implying that people should believe it should be practised, and hence in-effect *believe* the theory. Regarding acted-on normative theories provisionally-accepted or similar, there is a believed at least implicit higher-level normative theory here claiming we should believe it is normatively correct that one provisionally accepts and acts on that acted-on theory. Similarly, someone could say they believe no normative theory, or believe that two or more are equally most believable. As, when conscious, they must choose what to do, they in-effect or in-practice at least implicitly choose a theory. Suppose they choose via chance, e.g., coin-tossing. They still believe it is correct to practise the in-effect normative theory here, the higher-level theory prescribing, 'Here choice via chance is normatively correct' or similar. In all such cases there is still an at least implicitly *believed*, higher-level normative theory.

Similarly regarding other theories, in all areas, e.g., scientific, meta-ethical and skeptical theories:- If one's here-higher-level theory states that here-lower-level theory T is true, false, doubtful, partly true or neither true nor false, or provisionally acceptable, then one *believes* the higher-level theory stating that about T. And so on.

In sum:- In every area one is aware of, one either (i) believes the theory one acts on, namely a theory in the area, or (ii) one believes a higher-level theory concerning the theory or theories one acts on in the area. Every choice or intention involves belief. Hence every intended practice, every practised normative theory, involves *belief* (at some level).

'Believed' means 'believed to be *true*'. E.g., if one believes that theory T is false, one believes it is *true* that T is false. *'It is true (objective) that' is unavoidably, necessarily, part of the at least implicit foundation of any belief.* In a way this truth- or objectivity-presupposition involvement in all theories is trivial, but there are also important normative implications:-

Because 'believed' means 'believed to be true', and 'true' means 'objective', and knowledge involves true belief, all theories involve a claim concerning objectivity, a knowledge-claim. This has important implications regarding an objective normative theory or normative knowledge:-

As suggested in the book's main body and recent paragraphs, all normative theories at least implicitly ultimately involve a general claim something like: 'X is the correct end'. As with 'belief', the 'is' in the claim, 'X is the correct end', also implies truth: 'is' means 'is truly' or 'is objectively'. To verify that claim and implication regarding any specific theory, sufficient evidence is needed. This would give 'X is the correct end' objective warrant. Yet 'is' here defines that claim as true and hence as *already verified.* If it is verified, the verifier has sufficient evidence for it. This means the verifier *knows* it, so it is objective. So, regardless of whether belief here is knowledge, here there is necessarily a *claim* that one knows, i.e., a knowledge-claim or objectivity-claim. Relatedly, every belief's fundamental truth-presuppositional 'It is true that' also implies objective-warrant or knowledge.[14]

Via some such objectivity/knowledge-claim, all normative theories are unavoidably, necessarily, fundamentally at least minimally *pro-objectivity.* Many normative theories explicitly aim and claim to be objective/knowledge, so here they are even more intentionally pro-objectivity, explicitly positively so. Even 'I hate (am anti-) knowing statement Z' involves pro-objectivity in that this 'I' is pro- the knowledge that 'I wish I did not know Z'. Here, most minimally, 'pro' only means 'am agreeing that, i.e., believing, there is'. Further, the preface 'It is true that' to 'I hate (am anti-) knowing Z' includes the 'is' which, as the previous paragraph suggests, involves a more positive pro-objectivity.

In sum:- All believers, and all normative theories, necessarily involve being at least minimally intentionally pro-objectivity.

Regarding theory-believing as such, minimal fundamental pro-objectivity obviously only exists theoretically or mentally, via one *believing*, as part of one's theory's in-effect foundation or presuppositions, that one's theory is true and knowledge. That is, the pro-objectivity here is not practised or substantive, in the world outside believers' minds. Of course, as is typical with normative theories, believed theories are often not true and hence not knowable; there is often no evidence, or only evidence disproving the theory. Regarding that important issue, necessary pro-objectivity is trivial, insignificant. But the next few points lead up to showing that necessary pro-objectivity has other, important substantive practical implications for normative theories. This is partly because, regarding *practising* one's believed normative theory, the here-necessary pro-objectivity is not just theoretical or mental. Apart from the just-mentioned unavoidably pro-objectivity part of one's theory's in-effect foundation, the other part is the substantive, practised, normatively important part, and this part is from on-average to maximally normatively either pro- or anti-objectivity—and (in)coherence and hence normative (in)correctness issues arise here:-

Those who use knowledge in anti-objectivity ways are substantively or *in-practice minimally* pro-objectivity. E.g:- To be highly *anti-objectivity*, say, via murdering highly pro-objectivity persons, the murderer must be instrumentally minimally substantively *pro-objectivity.* This (Type-A) pro-objectivity then is used in a normatively anti-objectivity way. The murderer has to know, e.g., how to commit the murders. To knowingly achieve any end, including anti-objectivity ends, one must first in-*practice* be at least minimally pro-objectivity, namely in order to know oneself exists, is conscious and what one's end is, and via acquiring and using (practising) the necessary means-to-the-end knowledge.

Because, as with the recently-discussed theoretical 'prefacing pro-objectivity', here one must *first* be pro-objectivity, pro-objectivity is *substantively fundamental* regarding practising any normative theory. This means unavoidable practical pro-objectivity.

An important implication here:- Full coherence with that necessary theoretical and practical pro-objectivity requires one to regard the pro-objectivity *end* as one's only ultimate normative aim. Otherwise one's beliefs overall here are incoherent, i.e., *wrong*. Relatedly, one cannot in-practice be fully coherent with any *anti-objectivity* aspect(s) of one's theory—because that would mean one would in-practice be anti- *all* knowledge, rejecting all knowledge, and hence not know of or how to achieve any end. A totally anti-objectivity, anti-knowledge or unobjective viewpoint or theory is impossible. One would not know oneself exists. One would soon die: one would lack the required survival-necessary knowledge. Paradoxically, one could not even know how to be coherent with those anti-objectivity aspect(s), or how to reject all knowledge, or what 'knowledge' and 'anti-objectivity' mean. So practising and hence believing in a non-pro-objectivity theory means non-total but still major fundamental incoherence or mistakes. This non-total coherence means one('s theory) is incoherent via being self-contradictory: one('s theory) implies that one('s theory) is wrong. Part of what one accepts, say the fundamental pro-objectivity part, disagrees with the other, here the anti-objectivity part, i.e., the former part implies the latter part is wrong, *and vice versa*. That is, at least implicitly, one disagrees with oneself or views oneself as wrong—everywhere within one's theory. Relatedly, because here one practises and hence believes an overall (on-average) non-pro-objectivity normative theory, which is hence overall objectively wrong, one's incoherence and theory-belief here are substantively objectively normatively wrong. These are important substantive issue regarding normative theories.

This means that, from an overall (here 'sufficiently fully-informed'[15]), objective viewpoint, *any* anti-objectivity, namely any rejection or fundamental doubting of pro-objectivity theory, involves self-contradiction or incoherence, and is mistaken. All alternatives to pro-objectivity theory at least implicitly reject it. So they are all at least significantly anti-objectivity overall. All fundamental doubting of pro-objectivity theory implies that the doubter doubts the fundamental pro-objectivity of the doubter's own, alternative theory, and hence here one incoherently fundamentally doubts one's own (believed to be believed and hence undoubted) theory. This is also anti-objectivity.

Concluding here:- The only normative theory coherent with that objectivity-presupposition and necessary theoretical and practical fundamental pro-objectivity is pro-objectivity theory. All alternatives are at least significantly anti-objectivity, and hence wrong, including via lack of evidence. That coherence involves pro-objectivity theory being the only normative theory able, via arguments concerning coherence and related empirical observations mentioned in this book, to supply sufficient evidence for its objectivity. Evidence crucially involves coherence. Appendix 4 suggests more here.

Related points:-

We are also often pro-objectivity because in-practice we survival-necessarily believe and practise the objective in that we have no alternative objectivity or knowledge. E.g., regarding 'To survive, avoid cliff-falls, starvation etc', the alternative is 'To survive, fall over cliffs, starve etc'. That is, there is no alternative we can survivably practise and (coherently) call knowledge. (Similarly regarding there being no objective alternative to an objective normative theory.) Coherence requires that all our beliefs and hence chosen practices cohere with that which we in-practice, in order to survive, necessarily hold—namely that which reliably works here, because it is objective/knowledge. This means overall coherence with survival-necessary pro-objectivity, i.e., being normatively maximally pro-objectivity. Or, if one is not yet aware of sufficient evidence regarding the survival-necessary, one's beliefs here which reliably work are true, and potential knowledge. Being in-effect pro- using potential knowledge, i.e., the believed to be true or objective, is still a type of pro-objectivity. Survival-necessary actual/potential knowledge and related pro-objectivity is another, substantive, contingently necessary and fundamental issue for normative theories: to believe and practise any theory, we must first be alive. What comes first is in an important practical sense fundamental.

In sum, coherence with survival-necessary actual/potential knowledge/objectivity requires our believing pro-objectivity theory. Any incoherence here also means one is necessarily self-contradictory within the whole constituted by every statement one believes. That is, here oneself, like and via one's normative theory, is incoherent, mistaken. Appendix 4 suggests more here.

APPENDIX 4: Only One Overall, Coherent Mental System Is Possible

Appendixes 1-6, especially 4, are largely interpretable as epistemology. 4 concerns overall (total possible) mental coherence, achievable only by being maximally pro-objectivity (as far as possible etc). Objectivity has an overall view: the only fully normatively-objective conscious life is one which, as far as possible, involves overall (total) (orthogonally-systematic) coherence—which must involve coherence with one's necessary knowledge and thereto-related and other necessary fundamental pro-objectivity as discussed in Appendix 3:-

Various interrelated issues are discussed below. They all primarily concern two related notions. One is that an incoherent normative theory is highly rationally-problematic. The other is that, to achieve overall coherence either *absolutely* regarding beliefs as such, or *relative* to or regarding objective beliefs, i.e., knowledge, means the *same* thing. It means: (1) coherence among one's beliefs-as-a-whole, achievable only via them all being objective; and (2) coherence concerning one's intended, practised life-as-a-whole, achievable only via all practices here coming under objectivity/knowledge in that it is *objective/knowledge* that they are either warranted (pro-objectivity) or permitted, i.e., neither warranted nor unwarranted (a-objectivity).

Intentions in (2) are intentions to practise one's normative beliefs. Because intended practices are *belief*-based practices, (2) comes under (1). So discussing (1)'s beliefs covers (2)'s intended, normative practices. The beliefs in (1) include the values practised in (2). So this Appendix's focus on a psychological or mental system, one involving the cognitive and non-cognitive, primarily concerns the cognitive, i.e., an overall, theoretical-practical belief-system.

Firstly here, an issue arising from Appendix 5:-

Near its end, the involvement of pro-objectivity values (oughts) in acquiring facts (objective is-statements) as knowledge is discussed. Throughout history, pro-objectivity here has typically been limited. As shown in Appendix 3, all conscious persons are necessarily fundamentally at least minimally pro-objectivity. Beyond that, as argued there and in Part I, Section 1.2, people are typically only pro-objectivity partly—to the limited degree they need knowledge to reliably achieve *anti*-objectivity ends.[16] Achievements here are typically only Type-A.

Because being partly pro-objectivity is not maximal Type-B pro-objectivity, being partly pro-objectivity involves some anti-objectivity values or aims. Being *partly* pro-objectivity means one's values-as-a-whole are not fully coherent with or are not aspects of objectivity. So one's values are not fully coherent with the practices and associated values involved in one discovering facts. So here, from an overall view, there is only a tenuous or rationally-problematic, limited link between facts and values. With this, one's beliefs-as-a-whole are incoherent, because values claiming rightness or wrongness are beliefs.

It is obviously possible to be partly pro-objectivity and hence partly anti-objectivity. It is also possible to be as maximally pro-objectivity as possible (for the individual in the situation in question). Importantly, as Appendix 3 shows, it is *impossible* to be fully anti-objectivity and hence have coherent beliefs-as-a-whole here, or to have any beliefs, and not only because here one must soon die (unless others preserve one). Relatedly it is also survival-impossible to be as maximally anti-objectivity as possible (for the individual in the situation in question) because it is possible for the individual here to reject all survival-necessary knowledge, meaning one would soon die here too. So it is also impossible, except very briefly, to achieve the maximum possible regarding anti-objectivity. Maximal possible anti-objectivity would mean a quick end to the minimal mental coherence here, leaving none.

Some general conclusions here:- As suggested elsewhere in this book, its knowledge-involving normative theory, and only this normative theory, is rationally unquestionably fully coherent with humanly-*necessary* knowledge and associated and other *necessary* pro-objectivity (involving the at least implicit belief and at least potential knowledge that being pro-objectivity is valuable). No other theory has such coherence in its basis. Full coherence among beliefs is only possible if all beliefs cohere with any *necessary* knowledge, via all non-necessary normative etc beliefs also being knowledge/objective. (And one's non-necessary values or normative beliefs need to cohere with that necessary at least implicit normative belief, i.e., the at least potential knowledge that pro-objectivity is valuable, this coherence only being achievable via the former values or beliefs being pro-objectivity.) Similarly, as one necessarily at least implicitly prefaces all one's beliefs with the belief that 'It is objective (true) that', to achieve coherence with that necessity, all one's beliefs need to be objective. One can only know this if they are knowledge. As Appendix 3 shows, that preface-belief also involves a necessary minimal pro-objectivity belief. So, again, to achieve coherent beliefs-as-a-whole, one needs to maximally explicitly believe a pro-objectivity theory. This belief can and should be normative knowledge.

A conclusion here regarding Appendix 5's is-ought topic:- Limited or part pro-objectivity involves one's 'oughts' being importantly incoherent with the objective, with what 'is'. Here there is a gap between one's values and facts, or between one's is-statements (knowledge) and one's oughts or normative theory. Only via being as pro-objectivity as possible is the is-ought link as firm or total as possible. Indeed, being maximally pro-objectivity means that one's values and knowledge, involving 'is' and 'ought' beliefs/statements, are inextricably linked. Here alone they can be and are coherent with each other.

Partly via such coherence the maximum at-the-time achievable coherence is achieved among one's beliefs. Maximum possible psychological coherence for persons at any one time, given that persons cannot know and control everything, involves four practices (see also Part II, Section 1.3 (i)-(vii)):- (a) having pro-objectivity knowledge; (b) suspending belief, i.e., having *no* beliefs, in areas where they know they cannot know or do not yet have specific pro-objectivity knowledge, including suspending belief where they know they must act without sufficient knowledge and hence act via provisionally accepting some prescription. (Here they still have knowledge—that meta-knowledge about lacking knowledge in those areas. Knowledge at least *about* all areas is possible); (c) as far as pro-objectivity-possible using their present knowledge to acquire more pro-objectivity knowledge, and (d) practising their pro-objectivity knowledge everywhere else too—including regarding practising pro-objectivity emotions, thereby achieving an overall coherent, cognitive plus non-cognitive, mental-system. This would involve controlling one's emotions, involving overruling any anti-objectivity emotion as far as possible.

A-objectivity is no problem regarding belief-coherence here. A-objectivity values can of course be inconsistent, but as Part II, Section 1.7 suggests, this does not mean incoherence within one's beliefs or knowledge overall. The objective belief (knowledge) here is that a-objectivity preferences or values are neither right nor wrong, only subjective and emotional, not cognitive, hence not beliefs: here there are no values claiming rightness or wrongness; here belief is suspended due to being objectively inapplicable. The only beliefs or knowledge pro-objectivity persons have regarding a-objectivity are such *pro-objectivity* pieces of meta-knowledge about the a-objectivity dimension, or, within the dimension, the instrumental knowledge needed to have and achieve one's a-objectivity ends and to treat the a-objectivity as a-objectivity. As instrumental knowledge is knowledge, there is no belief-incoherence issue here.

In sum, a-objectivity related beliefs come under (a)-(d), hence allowing maximum belief-coherence. (However, one could have conflicting non-cognitive values here, as in equally most liking both strawberry and chocolate ice-cream and hence being unable to choose between them, namely via one's emotional preferences as opposed to beliefs. So such conflict is no problem regarding belief-coherence, which is what matters regarding objectivity. And such conflicts would probably be rare and brief, and they come under the *knowledge* that they are *irrelevant* regarding normative etc knowledge and hence belief-coherence—and are easily resolvable. And where such conflicts can be resolved by taking turns, this would over time mean coherence with each conflicting preference. Anyway, maximally pro-objectivity persons would have and practise the belief that there's no point in emotional conflict here. Finally here:- If conflicts here are unavoidable, the maximum *possible* coherence is still achievable. If they are avoidable, we can avoid them.)

The maximum possible coherence via (a)-(d) means being as pro-objectivity as possible in life as-a-whole:-

That coherence involves us investigating as many things as possible, in life as-a-whole, to see in which situation(s) a thing has a positive, neutral or negative relation to objectivity—and then promoting the positive, permitting the neutral and avoiding the negative. Thence, for us somewhat ignorant and fallible humans probably unable to achieve full coherence, over time the scope and degree of one's mental coherence can increase. That investigation and promotion involves an ongoing self-causing or self-developing interrelationship. The notion, 'As far as possible . . . , the pro-objectivity end is presently and cumulatively achievable', applies here. (That cumulative achievement involves the only normatively-objectively progressing and self-improving (self-harmonising), hence flourishing, emotion-thought system and therein-involved belief-system.)

Other related normative issues:-

A coherent belief-system has no conflicts partly because it involves coherence between its believed arguments' forms and contents:- As shown above, pro-objectivity theory's content is objective and hence the only normative content coherent with the objective (valid) forms of argument all normative (and other) theories necessarily use to validly argue for their content, and with the same valid (objective) forms necessary for us to have the objective content, 'survival-necessary knowledge', i.e., content necessary for us to exist. Again, coherence with the necessary requires maximal pro-objectivity.

And via any theorist or theory-believer using the necessary objective forms to argue for their (scientific or whatever) theory means they are pro-objectivity here. Coherence with that pro-objectivity also requires maximal pro-objectivity in the *contents* of their *normative* theory/arguments. To knowingly soundly argue regarding anything, the normative or other content of the necessarily valid (objective) form here must be knowledge/objective. Otherwise there is incoherence in the arguer's mental-system—between their use of valid and hence *objective forms* of argument, and their use of *unobjective* argument *content*.

In sum:- Form-content coherence, involving evidence presented in a valid argument form, is necessary for a coherent mental system—and pro-objectivity theory is the only normative theory with form-content coherence.

Similarly, pro-objectivity theory's orthogonal form involves no form(al) incoherence, and there can be no incoherence among that form's belief-contents.

Concluding this Appendix:-

The only reliable way to as far as possible achieve overall peace within and among persons is via them achieving the maximum possible overall coherence discussed here. Coherence means harmony, peace, a lack of conflict. Apparent types of peace are achievable via other means, e.g., a totalitarian religion and its normative beliefs, but those other means involve only the tenuous, vulnerable, rationally-problematic, limited coherence discussed above, and are merely apparent, not reliable long-term.

To be maximally pro-objectivity involves the maximum achievable overall coherence within persons' conscious lives-as-a-whole. This includes coherence among argument form and content, among facts and the practices required for discovering them, as in inherently impartial (non-sexist, etc) objectivity. These practices involve values (e.g., non-sexism). Practices, knowledge (of facts) and values also involve the non-cognitive, here emotions and feelings—and certain emotions and feelings are also important aspects of that overall psychological coherence. Only via all such aspects harmonising can we have an overall coherent mental-system—a system involving facts and the values and associated feelings and emotions (pro-objectivity motivation) necessarily involved in acquiring knowledge of facts. (The overall maximal coherence here, involving practising pro-objectivity knowledge, is the only correct aim for psychotherapy, education, politics and so on.)

Finally here, this Appendix implies that, as far as possible, pro-objectivity theory alone can solve the 'fact-value' or 'is-ought' problem. E.g., a coherent belief-system means all 'is' and 'ought' beliefs therein are not problematically separated. This implication adds further strength to Appendix 5's arguments:-

APPENDIX 5: The 'Is-Ought' And 'Why Be Moral(Ly Correct)?' Issues

The 'fact-value' or 'is-ought' problem concerns the belief that, regardless of what facts there are, the issue of values is quite separate, i.e., that no fact implies or is a value. In other words, the belief is that whatever 'is' the case, this has nothing to do with what normatively 'ought' to be the case: there is an apparently unbridgeable gap between what (objectively) is and what normatively (objectively) ought to be. If the gap can be objectively sufficiently filled, this would produce coherence where there appeared to be an unbridgeable gap or no coherence. And certain values or oughts would be facts, i.e., objective:-

Appendix 4 argued that only pro-objectivity theory has coherence between its arguments' forms and contents. This is some help regarding solving that problem in that a valid form is an objective 'is', and the normatively objective contents crucially involve an 'ought'. In that there is no objective gap between *objective* form and *objective* content, there is no is-ought gap here. But more than that form-content coherence is needed to adequately solve the is-ought problem. It primarily concerns content-content coherence, namely whether any is-content is coherent with any ought-content:-

Appendix 2's discussion of the circularity in all valid deductive arguments points out that the circularity is rationally non-problematic only when the contents are objective. With objective normative contents, for the 'subsequent argument' discussed in Appendix 2 the circularity involves something like: 'Practice P is objective; therefore Practice P is objective'. That discussion, and of its 'basic argument', and Part I, Section 1.4 (5), imply that the only objective definition of 'P ought to be practised' is 'Practice P is objective'—and vice versa. Here the ought-content in 'P ought to be practised' and the is-content in 'Practice P is objective' are *equivalent* or the *same*. If there is any gap between the 'ought' and 'is' here, it is not the objectively-problematic gap in the is-ought claims of other normative theories. There can be no gap between equivalent or the same contents, as with the analogous 'half' and 'two-quarters'.

Relatedly, any pro-objectivity 'is' and 'ought' can be connected via appropriately examining Appendix 2's 'subsequent argument':

Premise(s): 'The only objective normative practices are pro-objectivity.' 'Practices P1, P2, . . . Pn are pro-objectivity.'

Conclusion: 'Therefore P1, P2, . . . Pn are objective normative practices.'

An appropriate examination thereof:-

That conclusion-sentence can be restated as 'P1, P2, . . . Pn is the set of objective normative practices'. This is equivalent to 'It is normatively-objective that P1, P2, . . . Pn are practised', which is equivalent to 'It is normatively-objective that we ought to practise P1, P2, . . . Pn'—because the normatively-objective *is* that which we (objectively) *ought* to do, and vice versa. The book has argued that those three equivalent sentences are true.[17] True sentences are facts or objective 'is' statements. Each of those sentences has a crucial 'is' near its beginning. If those three sentences are true, they'd be unique true is-statements—unique via containing an (implicit or explicit) objective 'ought'. If true, within each such is-statements there'd inherently be no lack of truth—so no lack of a true connection between any 'is' and 'ought' (at least implicitly) in a sentence here. Such sentences would be equivalent to: 'It is true that we ought to practise P (where P represents any pro-objectivity practice(s))'. If that equivalence is the case, only irrational or uninformed people here could disagree with or doubt such sentences and the recent discussions of them. (Non-pro-objectivity theories at least implicitly disagree with such sentences etc.)

Further, referring to Appendix 2, such and any related, objective normative sentence could be the content of X in a rationally non-problematic circular 'X; therefore X' argument—so any such 'is' and 'ought' in such arguments would be truly or rationally non-problematically connected. Relatedly, circularity is not a gap, and non-problematic circularity is not a problematic gap.

Similarly:- 'P1, P2, . . . Pn are objective normative practices' can be restated as the conclusion: 'The set, P1 to Pn, is objective'. This conclusion is contained in the 'is' (or 'are') statement which is the conclusion's premise(s). Here an 'is' ('are') inherently *implies* an 'is', and the latter, 'conclusion-is', is *equivalent* to an 'ought'. Relatedly, and equivalently, those premises, which are explicitly is-statements, implicitly (circularly) *contain* and hence *imply* the (explicit) ought-conclusion: 'It is objective . . . that we ought to practise set P1 to Pn'. Here, an objective 'is' *contains* an objective 'ought'. Containment is not a gap. Implication is not a gap.

Another way of stating recent points:- The book's arguments confirm that the pro-objectivity end/standard is the only (objectively) intrinsically-valuable end/standard. This means the theory's fundamental 'is' and its 'ought' statements are intrinsically-valuable. Because *both* also *constitute* the associated intrinsically-valuable objective normative theory, there cannot be any objectively- or truly-problematic gap between them.

In sum:- As far as seems possible, recent points give us the previously-mentioned needed content-content coherence. Overall-objective-warrantedness arguably bridges the is-ought gap as far as possible, arguably completely, but at least sufficiently regarding practical normativity. As suggested in Appendixes 2-4, for pro-objectivity theory the is-ought gap is rationally believably bridged, at least compared with other theories—which, lacking objectivity, have no possibility of bridging it: their value-claims are not facts (objective).

A criticism of that suggested solution is that, beyond the pro-objectivity 'ought' discussed so far here, there is another, problematic implicit 'ought' in any version of the pro-objectivity premise(s)—so all the alleged solution does and can do is derive an ought from an ought, because no 'is' implies an 'ought':-

Consider again the premise: 'The only objective normative end . . .'. Clearly, 'end' can be interpreted to mean 'ultimate *ought*'. And the explicit is-conclusion therefrom, 'Therefore, set P1 to Pn is objective', can be interpreted as: 'Therefore, (it is objective . . . that) we *ought* to practise set P1 to Pn'. Under such interpretations, an 'ought' is derived from an 'ought'.

But, from an overall view, such interpretations can be interpreted as involving the recently-mentioned *equivalence* between objective 'ought-' and 'is-' statements, and involved in the argument implying there is no rationally-problematic 'ought' in any pro-objectivity premise. An 'is' implying an 'ought' is one among equivalent argument contents here. Critics of pro-objectivity theory here need to prove (objectively) that there is nothing like such equivalence, or no objective close connection, between the 'ought' and/or 'is' statements involved, under any reasonable interpretation of those statements. They need to prove (objectively) that that implicit premise-ought is rationally problematic, importantly-separate-from and not including a normative equivalent to the conclusion, '(Therefore,) it is objective . . . that we ought to practice set P1 to Pn'. That is, they need to prove that this conclusion is not logically implied by that premise, and that, even if it is, the premise is not objective or not knowledge (or not as close or closely-connected to objectivity/knowledge as possible). (The 'X; therefore X' non-problematic circularity here is discussed in Appendix 2.)

Anyway, the crucial overall point is that, if this book is correct, the (at least implicit) 'oughts' in pro-objectivity premises are not rationally-problematic—so the is-ought problem, or any 'ought derived from an ought', is rationally not a substantive, important or even relevant normative issue here. The overall, *in-practice* most important, fundamental issue is something like: 'Is any normative theory objective?', 'Is any end or practice normatively-objective?' or 'How should one live?'. If the book solves that issue as far as possible, it suggests that any uncertainty regarding its normative theory's is-ought issue is manageable, and in-practice irrelevant to that issue's solution in that all capable of choice must practice via some standard they choose—and, as the book suggests, all capable of choice, including normative skeptics and nihilists, necessarily at least implicitly ask something like: 'Is any normative theory objective?' and so on. And, the book argues, if they use their rationality to genuinely seek an answer thereto, they can discover a normative theory at least close to objectivity, one as close as possible for a normative theory.

Further here:- As Appendix 4 implies, if such skeptics or nihilists aim for coherence (as opposed to being incoherent and hence confused and mistaken), the book suggests that, for pro-objectivity theory alone, any is-ought gap is filled *via coherence.* The 'is' and the 'ought' here cohere or are cohesive (as opposed to being separate and in that sense incoherent (non-cohesive)):- This involves coherence between (potential) pro-objectivity knowledge and pro-objectivity or normatively-objective practising (of that knowledge). This coherence or cohesion between the 'is' which is that knowledge, and the 'oughts' prescribing those practices, is that which (objectively) joins (coheres) what such skeptics or nihilists suggest is a gap between that 'is' and those 'oughts'. The prescriptive oughts here, because the prescriptions are normative *knowledge*, are also an 'is'. This means an inherently cohesive objective is-is, not a gap.

There is also a related necessary cohering here via inherently objective causal-connections. Causal-connections mean more than cohesion; they mean adhesion, which clearly joins any gap here:- There are necessary causal-connections between intended, hence oughts-involving practices needed for the existence (acquiring) of pro-objectivity knowledge and the 'is' which is that thereby acquired (caused) knowledge. Here, pro-objectivity persons know they ought to acquire more of the 'is' which is pro-objectivity knowledge, and implement the ought(s) here needed to do so. (E.g., as in 'I need (ought) to get sufficient sleep so tomorrow I can accurately do the measurements needed to acquire pro-objectivity knowledge concerning Q'.) And as it *is* knowledge that the *oughts* here are objective or normative knowledge and hence an 'is', any alleged is-ought gap here is interpretable as an inherently cohered objective is-is. Similarly, pro-objectivity causal-connections here can be rationally interpreted as both an 'is' and 'oughts'. So there is no unavoidable is-ought gap here.

If there is a general pro-objectivity is-ought gap, it is also one even normative skeptics and nihilists necessarily fill in that it is survival-necessary to in-practice treat it as filled:- Appendix 3's and other arguments above suggest we survival-necessarily assume it *is* objective (true) that we *ought* to be pro-objectivity at least via acquiring and using knowledge to help us survive. All who survive here via their knowledge-informed choices to avoid cliff-falls etc in-practice universally survival-necessarily accept there is no is-ought problem here for us humans. Skeptics and nihilists here do not practice their theory that there is *such* a problematic gap here that there is no point in practising any intention, including an intention to live, i.e., the ought, 'Live' or 'I ought to survive'. In practice they fill or cohere what they (incoherently) believe is a gap. Maximum possible coherence requires maximal normative pro-objectivity.

Those skeptics and nihilists also necessarily accept there is no is-ought problem regarding numerous instrumental pro-objectivity oughts when they at least implicitly accept objectivity in non-survival-necessary areas, e.g., say, regarding how to open a normal hinged door via using (inherently) objective scientific knowledge concerning hinges, levers, muscles etc, as opposed to unobjectively trying to open it, via, say, singing. The general point here applies regarding *everything* one achieves directly via one's intentions, including, as Appendix 3 implies, being skeptical or nihilistic. Here, universally, unavoidably, there is an 'achievement-necessary' instrumental is-ought connection involving knowledge and being at least minimally pro-objectivity. Consistency with one's in-practice accepting the pro-objectivity is-ought connection one necessarily accepts in order to achieve anything intentionally, demands that one accepts a pro-objectivity is-ought connection wherever it exists (and demands relatedly that one accepts the pro-objectivity normative end.)

Concluding comments here:-

The book's main body suggests many specific moral, political etc oughts (or normatively objective is-notions) which are or can be involved in this Appendix's general points. E.g., valuing evidence and, in mixed gender situations, non-sexism, are shown above to be necessary oughts involved in acquiring true is-statements as knowledge. If there was an is-ought gap here, the ought, 'Be non-sexist', would *not* be objectively causally-connected (adhered) with the 'is', objectivity. Here sexism, rather than evidence, could lead us to objectivity, making, e.g., 'singing opens doors' and '1+2=4' true simply because someone of a certain *gender* believes so, even an infant. The fact that, regarding such and much other knowledge, sexists (incoherently) tend to not practise sexism, shows they in-practice accept there is no pro-objectivity is-ought gap—and that there are oughts involved in objectivity, namely objective oughts, including 'Be non-sexist', i.e., that often there is an 'is' which is an (objective) 'ought'. (The same of course applies regarding (non-)racism and so on.)

Just as '1+2=3' is of objective value, and '1+2=4' is not, so too the non-sexist and many other pro-objectivity values involved in acquiring facts are of objective value: without the non-existence or bridging of any alleged is-ought gap here we cannot be objective or have knowledge—and, hence via lacking survival-necessary knowledge, even life.

All those 'going from pro-objectivity oughts to knowledge' bridgings or moves are motivated: 'motivated' means 'moved'. Regarding emotion and pro-objectivity practices such as that non-sexism, pro-objectivity motivation is crucially involved in the causal connections moving across (to adhere) any is-ought gap here before the pro-objectivity practice. So pro-objectivity theory is the only normative theory where there is no objectively-problematic attempt at bridging an is-ought gap via crucially involving *emotion*. Regarding pro-objectivity, the emotion here crucially involves the pro-objectivity (version of) rightness-motivation, motivation moving one from the knowledge that the theory is correct, to practising the theory's oughts, namely from Type-A pro-objectivity to B.

The above-suggested manageability of the is-ought issue relates to a suggested solution to a related issue, which no other normative theory can coherently answer. This issue is sometimes stated as: 'Why be moral?' or 'Why do what is right?'. This assumes normative objectivity, so means 'Why be normatively correct (objective)?'. Consider a skeptic who says, "Yes, granted, practice P is normatively objective, but why should I practice the normatively objective?". This skeptic wonders if there is a rationally unbridgeable gap between the objective and what one ought to do. Yet, as Appendix 3 argues, 'Why should I?' at least implicitly means 'Why is it true or objective that I?'. That shows that this skeptic implicitly asks, "Why is it objective that I practise the objective?". This question *presupposes* that it *is* objective to practise the objective.

Relatedly, that question is restatable as 'Why should I do what I should do?', implying or presupposing the answer: 'Because it is what I should do'. In-effect the question merely asks: 'Is what I (objectively) should do what I (objectively) should do?' Of course it is. How could it not be? A parallel to that skeptical, irrational, in-effect pointless question is: 'Is Z Z?' Of course Z is Z.

Concluding here:- That skeptic's question is ultimately the is-ought question, 'Why is it objective that I ought to do the objective?'. The book and recent paragraphs suggest this skeptic implicitly asks: 'Is there a connection or equivalence between what I should do and what I should do, or between what is objective and what is objective?'. Recent points show that here too there is that presupposed agreement with that which is being questioned.

APPENDIX 6: Emotion And Objectivity

The following in-part concerns Hume's suggestion that objectivity (or reason) alone cannot seek or discover an objective end, nor provide the drive we need to achieve one or any end, because objectivity is the slave of the (drive-providing, i.e., motivating,) emotions,[18] and these inherently drive us only towards *emotionally*-desired, hence subjective or intersubjective ends—and that relatedly, certainly regarding discoverability and achievability, for humans there is no objective end, ultimately only subjective or intersubjective, naturally normally emotionally-desired ends, e.g., one successfully caring for one's children, one's group's next-generation gene-bearers, plus the happiness (approval) naturally (evolutionarily-adaptively) resulting from that success, rewarding one for that successful achievement, motivating more of them. (There are various versions here, but that is beside the points this Appendix is concerned with.)

I accept that human objectivity can do nothing without emotion, i.e., without being motivated, and hence that to discover or know of and achieve any end we must be motivated to do so. But that natural emotion must be naturally associated with thought, at least that thought or knowledge of what the end is, plus, regarding any aimed-at end considered ultimate, the at least implicit thought that the end deserves approval, i.e., *is worth aiming at*, and hence *right*. (Otherwise no such end would be intentionally aimed at, or not willingly or determinedly enough for it to be achievable here.) Just-mentioned points imply that that thought must be naturally associated with (the previously-discussed) *rightness-motivation*, a motivation to do what is (at least believed to be) right. So this is one emotion crucially causally-associated with (achieving) any end considered worth achieving (right). That (motivated) thought can develop into an attempt to discover any truly right end, i.e., objective end, an end one can *know* is right, along with and/or via the thought (knowledge) that other ends are rationally-problematic. Here one's rightness-motivation naturally desires to remove subjectively-painful, emotionally-undesirable, cognitive dissonance or doubt.

That is, though our objectivity is directed by emotion-thought combinations to acquire (and supply) knowledge instrumental for achieving ends those combinations value, there can be a natural combination which values the end, '*Discover and achieve an objective end*'—and directs objectivity to acquire knowledge instrumental concerning achieving that end. Or, if that end is or can only be 'Achieve an objective end', then, because, to achieve that objective end, first one must know what it is, the acquiring must include seeking evidence or knowledge about what the end is. That is, either way, necessarily, one needs to first discover the end or learn what it is. Such knowledge (evidence) is in that necessary sense (indirectly) instrumental regarding achieving an emotion-thought valued end.

Other emotion-thought combinations can of course inhibit objectivity being used to do that. Those combinations aim at 'primarily-emotional ends', as opposed to an objective ('primarily knowledge-involving') end. E.g., greed at the thought of profit, or fear at the thought of losing one's comforting religious faith, can mean one thinks of and aims at ends other than an objective end, namely primarily-emotional ends. However, uncompromised by emotion, objectivity can be successfully driven to discover that end, and we can aim at and achieve it:-

Emotion is still crucially involved here. The natural emotional set here is *pro-objectivity*. It involves emotion causally-necessary for objectivity/knowledge. This directly pro-objectivity emotion involves our curiosity instinct—naturally needed for actual/potential survival-necessary knowledge, but naturally motivating many to know much beyond that. There is arguably also an emotion-involving experience something like Kant's 'respect for reason',[19] and an associated desire to do the normatively or morally etc right thing. Or, of those two, at least there is the latter desire. This is that rightness-motivation. That emotional set is combined with the thought that one needs *knowledge* of what the right thing is, i.e., evidence here.

That emotion-thought combination can overrule other emotions pressuring us to act in anti-objectivity ways, e.g., greedily, or fearfully regarding losing one's comforting faith. That is, we need not aim only at primarily-emotional ends. (Indirectly pro-objectivity emotion, which can include types of happiness, can help with such overruling, and be associated with achieving an objective end, making that end even more motivating (desirable).)

Concluding here:- Human objectivity needs human subjectivity in that objectivity needs motivating and hence human emotion, and vice versa—and they can harmonise best and fully only via one's ultimate end being objective and pro-objectivity, and one's motivation being pro-objectivity. For humans, being pro- involves emotion or motivation.

ENDNOTES TO ALL APPENDIXES

1 Induction involves various possible uncertainties. E.g., if all the crows you have ever seen have been black, it is problematic to induce from those observations that you know that all crows were, are and always will be black. There could be a non-black crow no-one has seen. In future there may be non-black crows: (knowledge regarding) the past and/or present, which is what induction must rely totally on as the temporal source of evidence, is not necessarily a reliable guide to the future.

2 It is in a sense problematic to know whether you know. To (i) know if you have knowledge, (ii) you must know the criterion for knowledge, i.e., the definition via which knowledge is recognisable and separated from non-knowledge, e.g., ignorance or mere belief. But (ii) depends on (i) in that, to know the criterion, you must know that you have knowledge of the criterion. That is, there appears to be circularity, with (i) depending on (ii), which depends on (i), and so on. (See Appendix 2.)

3 Foundationalism argues that all knowledge rests on some foundation(s), so knowledge has a structure like buildings built on firm foundations. Coherentism argues that all pieces of knowledge cohere together, with no foundation, so knowledge has a structure like an orbiting satellite. There are other views here, e.g., pragmatism.

4 Over millennia, many of the world's best minds have tried unsuccessfully to solve various epistemic, i.e., knowledge-related, problems. Various experts here hold conflicting at least plausible views regarding some issues and regarding some other issues there is virtually universal, well-evidenced agreement (knowledge) that there can be no definitive precise answer. Such issues are illustrated by comparing the epistemologies of, e.g., Aristotle, Kant, Descartes, J.S. Mill, Hegel, Russell, C.I. Lewis, Roderick Chisholm, Quine, Sheffler, Goldman, Harvey Siegel, Bosanquet and Wilfrid Sellars, and by problems they and others such as Gettier raise.

5 A distinction is needed between (a) the theory's general, abstract guidelines and (b) specific practical applications of those guidelines. The guidelines are at a different, conceptually higher level or meta-level in relation to the specifics, and their confirmability is hence different. (Much the same distinction applies in rationally careful, sophisticated science. The book's theory's evidence-types and specifics involve science.)

6 Consider Rawls's general end(s) describable as: 'Achieve reflective equilibrium' in relation to 'Act only on prescriptions hypothetically acceptable among rational egoists behind a veil of ignorance'. Rawls (1999).

7 Unlike Kant's too-abstract 'universalisability', 'Be pro-objectivity' will relatedly be shown to not imply problematically conflicting prescriptions. ('Be pro-objectivity' will also be suggested to solve problems Rawls cannot solve.)

8 'Only hearing/playing jazz' includes individuals here not allowing anyone to feed the individuals via a drip. And so on.

9 Newton's science here has been somewhat superseded, but that does not matter regarding the general point here.

10 E.g., a standard involving observation is appropriate for empirical-knowledge-parts, but not for pure-mathematical-parts.

11 One's at-the-moment objectivity-as-a-whole is often expandable over time, e.g., via improved research tools and increased observations, and can in that sense get outside (beyond) a previous whole, but never at-the-moment outside one's at-the-moment whole, or any greatest-possible whole.

12 That is, it covers the unavoidable holistic circularity involved in empirical objectivity generally, and hence the empirical standpoint external to Area 1's arguments.

13 Griffiths (1957-8) pp 103-124.

14 Suppose a theorist claims she/he merely believes a theory—without and not needing evidence to confirm its claimed objectivity. She/he has the higher-level belief that it is objective (true) and evidenced (knowledge) that such lower-level belief is correct. Other just-mentioned points further imply she/he is irrational. And she/he implies that anyone believing an alternative theory without evidence has equally (un)acceptable grounds for believing that or any such alternative, an alternative conflicting with her/his theory—also showing she/he is irrational. This in-effect applies regarding all believed normative theories, as opposed to one which is knowledge.

15 Part I, Section 1.2 explains this and other uses of 'overall'.

16 Various points above show that achieving a-objectivity ends via being pro-objectivity concerning the means to those ends cannot be incoherent (conflict) with those ends or with achieving the pro-objectivity normative end. The former pro-objectivity is Type-A, the latter is Type-B. And the irrelevant or orthogonal to X cannot contradict X. The 'neither warranted nor unwarranted' cannot conflict with the warranted, or vice versa.

17 If such sentences are close or closely-connected to truth (as opposed to being true), i.e., where they are as objective as possible for a normative theory, and highly so, the arguments here can be adapted to apply meaningfully thereto.

18 Hume [2000] E.g., Book 2, Part 3, Section 3, paragraphs 3-7, and Book 3, Part 1, Section 1, paragraphs 9-10.

19 Kant [1949] Royal Prussian Academy page 400

References and Bibliography

Brackets of the [ ] type around a date indicate a posthumous edition of a work, not the work's original date.

Couvalis, George (1997) *The Philosophy of Science: Science and Objectivity*. Sage Publications.

Fodor, J (1983) *The Modularity of Mind.* Cambridge MA. MIT Press.

Foucault, M. (1982) "The Subject And Power" in Dreyfus, H, and Rabinow, P, (eds) *Michel Foucault: Beyond Structuralism and Hermeneutics.* Harvester Press.

Gaudry, E and Spielberger, C.D (1971) *Anxiety And Educational Achievement.* Sydney. John Wiley & Sons.

Griffiths, A.P (1969) "Transcendental Arguments". *Proc. Arist Soc.* Supp. Vol 43. 1969

Griffiths, A.P (1957-8) "Justifying Moral Standards". *Proc Arist. Soc.* New Series. Vol 58. pp 103-124.

Holt, John (1969) *How Children Fail.* Penguin.

Holt, John (1970) *How Children Learn.* Penguin.

Hume, David (1751) *Hume's Enquiries.* Edited by L.A. Selby-Bigge. Oxford. Clarendon Press. 1902

Hume, David in [1968] *Hume's Moral And Political Philosophy.* Edited by Aiken, H.D. New York. Hafner.

Hume, David [2000] *A Treatise of Human Nature*, D. F Norton and M. J. Norton (eds.), Oxford, Clarendon Press.

Kant, Immanuel [1949] *Groundwork Of The Metaphysics Of Morals*, transl by Paton as *The Moral Law*. London.

Kornblith, Hilary (1994) (ed) *Naturalizing Epistemology*, 2nd edition. Massachusetts: Bradford Book, MIT Press.

MacIntyre, Alisdair (1985) *After Virtue: A Study in Moral Theory*. London. Duckworth.

Mackie, John (1977) *Ethics: Inventing Right and Wrong*. Penguin.

Maslow, Abraham (1962) *Toward a Psychology of Being,* New York. Van Nostrand,

Mill, J.S (1859) in *Collected Works Of John Stuart Mill.* Edited by J. Robson. Toronto: University of Toronto Press. (1963ff.) V18, pp 213-310

Moore, G.E (1903) *Principia Ethica.* Cambridge University Press.

Naylor, F.D (1972) *Personality And Educational Achievement.* Sydney. John Wiley & Sons.

Popper, K (1966) *The Open Society And Its Enemies.* (5th ed) Vol 2. London. Routledge.

Putnam, H (1993) "Objectivity And The Science-Ethics Distinction" in *The Quality Of Life,* edited by Nussbaum, M and Sen, A. Oxford. Clarendon Press.

Quine, W.V. & Ullian, J.S. (1978) *The Web Of Belief.* (2nd ed) New York. Random House.

Rachels, James (1999) *The Elements Of Moral Philosophy.* 3rd edition. McGraw-Hill.

Rawls, J (1999) *A Theory of Justice.* Oxford University Press. Revised edition.

Searle, J.R (1964) "How to Derive "Ought" from "Is"" *Phil. Review.* 73

Simons, M, (1976) "Transcendental Deductions Revised" *Educ Phil & Theory* Vol 8. pp 59-67.

Whewell, William [1968] in *William Whewell's Theory of Scientific Method*, Butts, R (ed). Pittsburgh. University of Pittsburgh Press.

Whewell, William (1858-60) *The Philosophy of the Inductive Sciences*, London. Cass 1967

Williams, Bernard (1993) *Ethics and the Limits of Philosophy* London. Fontana.

INDEX

About The Author.

Frederick Farrand is a retired Australian philosopher and psychologist, previously having researched and/or taught psychology and moral, social and political philosophy and some epistemology. He retired mainly to have time and energy to write books such as this. He lives with his partner Mary and dog Buster, their children having grown up and left home.

www.ingramcontent.com/pod-product-compliance
Lightning Source LLC
LaVergne TN
LVHW101613210926
848480LV00008B/374

* 9 7 8 0 7 6 1 8 5 2 8 6 5 *